ANCIENT HUNTERS OF THE FAR WEST

Richard F. Pourade

ANCIENT HUNTERS

Sponsore

Edite

Produced in cooperation with

Publishe

OF THE FAR WEST

A COPLEY BOOK

JAMES S. COPLEY CHAIRMAN OF THE CORPORATION THE COPLEY PRESS INC.

RICHARD F. POURADE EDITOR EMERITUS THE SAN DIEGO UNION

SAN DIEGO MUSEUM OF MAN

THE UNION-TRIBUNE PUBLISHING COMPANY

By MALCOLM J. ROGERS
Former Director,
San Diego Museum of Man

Contributors

H. M. WORMINGTON
Curator of Archaeology,
Denver Museum of Natural History

E. L. DAVIS
University of California
Archaeological Survey

CLARK W. BROTT
Curator of Collections,
San Diego Museum of Man

PREVIOUS BOOKS ON CALIFORNIA AND THE WEST COMMISSIONED BY JAMES S. COPLEY AND WRITTEN BY RICHARD F. POURADE: THE EXPLORERS, 1960; TIME OF THE BELLS, 1961; THE SILVER DONS, 1963; THE GLORY YEARS, 1964; GOLD IN THE SUN, 1965

CONTENTS

DEDICATION

All things must have a prologue to deeper understanding. And so it is with man's achievements in the making of history.

To understand and appreciate Southwestern United States of America, no better prologue can be written than that which relates to prehistoric man in this area.

Ancient Hunters is a prologue to all that we have read in the history of the Southwest, to all that is to come in the years ahead and to any epilogue that may be fancied.

James S. Copley

PART I FOREWORD
...A JOURNEY INTO MAN'S PAST

RICHARD F. POURADE

PART I

DISCOVERING THE SAN DIEGUITO PEOPLE

When the Spaniards first reached the New World they were at a loss to account for the presence of a branch of mankind of which nothing had been known. For a time some even questioned whether the Indians of the American continent were truly men, that is, men with souls, since they had not been specifically mentioned among those whom the Lord had created.

True men they were, and they had been on the continent for a long time. It wasn't until well into the 20th Century, however, that anthropologists began to appreciate the real antiquity of man in North America.

Spanish land expeditions up into what is now Western United States began as early as 1539. When Juan Rodríguez Cabrillo made the first Spanish sea explorations of what is now the West Coast of the United States in 1542, he found a country thickly settled by people described as comely, large and well built and some of them were in possession of ocean-going canoes in which they crossed from the mainland to the Channel Islands off California. They were fully aware of Spanish land expeditions which had ventured up into the interior from northern Mexico or along the Colorado River.

On a second Spanish sea expedition a

In a three-hour walk along the rocky terraces of the California desert in 1924, an archaeologist counted 364 small cleared circular spaces, some of them rimmed with boulders.

In his mind he was beginning to put together what he considered to be their meaning, that they were the open sleeping places of a people long vanished from the scene.

The archaeologist was Malcolm J. Rogers and the site of the circles was the Borrego-Anza Desert in Southern California.

The three shown here are on a gravel terrace just off Highway 78 in San Diego County, seven miles from Borrego Springs and just west of Ocotillo Wells.

He speculated that the site, which he designated C-122, was first camped on by people he named the San Dieguitoans, and probably over a very long time in order to account for so many cleared areas.

This is the greatest concentration of circles in the domain which Rogers described as that of a people who, it is now known, lived in the Far West at least as long as 10,000 years ago.

Rogers concluded that after another long interval the region was visited by the much later Yuman people following the trail from Harper's Well in the low desert through the narrows and up into the San Diego County mountains.

3

number of years later, a priest, Fr. Antonio de la Ascensión, noted that the islands off California were inhabited by many friendly Indians who had commerce with those on the mainland and was impressed by a generous though obviously unacceptable offer:

...there are many people in this land, so many that a petty king, seeing there were no women on the ships, offered by signs to give every one ten women apiece if they would all go to his land, which shows how thickly populated it is.

Further conquests by land in the New World, however, were suspended after 1550 while a debate proceeded as to what was an Indian. The clergy insisted that they had determined the Indian of the Americas was a human being who did possess an immortal soul and was capable of enjoying freedom and being educated. In the view of the landholders of the New World, however, the Indian was a "natural slave" set aside by nature to serve his enlightened betters. By 1573 new regulations formally conceded the Indian a measure of humanity.

There were a number of expeditions into the central interior of the United States soon afterward. Of one of them into New Mexico, the relation of Pedro de Bustamante reads:

...they passed on up the same river, and found many pueblos along the road they travelled, as well as others off to the sides, which were to be seen from the road; and they came to another nation of Indians of different tongue and dress, where they were also received peacefully and gladly by the Indians, who kissed the hands of the religious. These Indians are also clothed and have three-story houses, whitewashed and painted inside; and they plant many fields of maize, beans, and gourds, and raise many chickens.

From there they passed on to another nation, dwelling farther up the same river. These were the finest people of all they had met, possessing better pueblos and houses, and were the ones who treated them best, *giving them the most generously of whatever they had. They have well-built houses of four and five stories, with corridors and rooms twenty-four feet long and thirteen feet wide, whitewashed and painted. They have very good plazas, and leading from one to the other there are streets along which they pass in good order...They dress in cotton.*

Though Spanish land expeditions reached as far as Kansas and Nebraska, and they became familiar with the buffalo hunting Indians of the Great Plains, they found no hoards of gold and gems, and the distances were vast and beset with difficulties. The past and future of the Indians, despite the best intentions of the crown and the clergy, was not of great concern to those who actually settled the New World.

For more than a century, though, the land on the farthermost rim of the Spanish empire largely lay neglected, until about the time of Fr. Junípero Serra and the Royal expedition led by Capt. Don Gaspar de Portolá which had instructions to establish presidios and a chain of Franciscan Missions in California.

In 1769 on his way up the peninsula of Baja California, in the country between the present bay of Ensenada and Upper California, Fr. Serra noted in his diary:

There is an immense number of pagans, and all those of this coastal land of the South Sea along the way we have traveled from the Bay of Todos Santos — as it is called on the maps and charts — live prosperously and supplied with the various seeds and the fish they catch...They are most affable people. All the males, adults and youths, go about naked. The women and young girls, even female children at the breast, are decently clothed. In this manner they approached us along the road as well as at the places we tarried. They dealt with us as confidently and in as peaceful a manner as if they had known us all their lives.

References to the density of population probably reflected the continuing Spanish surprise at finding any people at all. The Indians living north of Mexico were not numerous if viewed against the vastness of the territory. It has been estimated that in the limits of what is now the United States there were no more than about 850,000, but that California was relatively densely populated, with estimates varying between 130,000 and 150,000.

Agriculture had spread only into limited areas, in the Southwest and on the Eastern seaboard, and most of the Indians lived as had their prehistoric ancestors, as hunters and gatherers of food. In Southern California the matter of existence did not seem to demand more than an easy acceptance of an abundant land and sea and a mild climate which favored a close affinity with nature.

The missionaries soon learned, as had the explorers, that all Indians of the West Coast and the interior desert areas were not alike and not always peacefully inclined. Their places of abode varied in size and quality and their crafts showed differences in skill and artistic expression. They were divided into great linguistic families, and in California there was a bewildering number of dialects.

The stronger and more independent resisted change and were willing to fight for the territory they occupied as their own, though they could not know that it had not always been theirs or that the Old People long before them had been wanderers, by choice or by necessity, in a strange land. Here and there in their songs and stories were hints of racial memories of a great flood that had washed the earth long ago.

That the Indians along the coast had shown they were aware of early Spanish expeditions in the interior indicated well-established exchanges of information and goods along accepted trails connecting great areas of Western United States and Mexico. Many of the early exploring parties received directions from Indians and assistance in drawing maps and generally followed pathways obviously used by In-

dians for generations and many of which in time became the routes of modern travel by train and auto. Just how old some of these routes were was not even dimly realized until the 20th Century.

It was in a backwash of Indian development, however, from which came the first but at the time little-appreciated indications of the long history of man on the continent.

Long before the Franciscans had reached California, the Jesuits had built a chain of missions in Baja California. One of their missions, San Luis Gonzaga, on the Pacific side of the peninsula, served the primitive Guaicura Indians. South of this were the still more primitive Pericu. Padre Lambert Hostell, a German, who served at the mission first in 1737 and again beginning in 1740, wrote:

These barbarians lived in their paganism without any beliefs, without shelter, without authority, without knowledge of their origin, with neither village nor houses, in the mountains or in the open country ...each one obeying the impulses of his degeneracy and his sensual nature.

A successor to Fr. Hostell at San Luis Gonzaga was Johann Jakob Baegert. He served seventeen years and then returned to Germany and wrote of his experiences. Though he did not precisely distinguish between the Guaicura and the Pericu, he reported that skin color of the isolated Indians of southern Baja California shaded from dark chestnut to almost black. The details he furnished of their daily lives hinted of racial remnants of a people from out of a distant past who perhaps had survived from an age of different climate or had retreated before waves of later men to the dead end of a barren region of a remote and inhospitable peninsula.

They had no camps of a permanent nature and seldom slept in the same place for more than three consecutive nights. For protection from the wind they lay together in "sleeping circles" behind low and hastily improvised walls. Each morning the man and the woman went their

separate ways in search of the sustenance each were trained to hunt and prepare. Their only receptacles were turtle shells and a simple type of crude basket made from palm bark. While the bow and arrow had been introduced, at the time of the appearance of the first White Men they also were still using the more ancient dart thrower.

The languages spoken by the Pericu and the Guaicura did not seem to have any relationship to those of other North American Indian linguistic groups. They had no word for marriage nor for son and daughter, nor for old and young. The Pericu could comprehend amounts only up to six. Brought reluctantly, and sometimes violently, under mission influence, they struggled to learn the words necessary to a new way of life thousands of years removed from their experiences. They applied the first words they learned to anything new. To them a door was a mouth, bread was light and iron was heavy.

The men were beardless and their eyes were almond-shaped. They visited no other tribes and none visited them. Jealousy was unknown, and according to Fr. Sigis-

Malcolm Rogers spent more than forty years following the trail of Ancient Man in Southern California, northern Baja California and in the American Desert.

In earlier days he often slept in the open, long before deserts became playgrounds, and he walked alone through the silence of the centuries.

In later years there were four-wheel drive vehicles and financial help.

He gave the name La Jolla to the people who lived along the Southern California and Baja California coast for thousands of years before the coming of the Yumans, who were encountered by Spanish explorers.

He gave the name Amargosa to another culture, roughly contemporary, which had existed in the Colorado Desert.

And he gave the name of San Dieguito to those who had arrived before either of them.

mundo Taravel, another Jesuit missionary who also served among them, they ran together like sheep. In his translation of a Latin quotation, he described the Pericu as a "four-fold people; the first division composed of women, the second of animals, the third of thieves, the fourth of men."

How much of their way of life represented cultural heritages from remote ancestors, or age-old adaptions to an isolated environment, is not known. Teaching Christianity and religious ritual to people with very limited vocabularies exasperated Fr. Baegert. In his general references to the natives of that part of Baja California he said they often put sandals on the feet of the dead, as if to prepare them for a journey, but professed not to know why they did it. So, he left them as he found them, with, he sadly commented, no conception of God and Soul. Nevertheless, he concluded, "they are true human beings, true children of Adam, as we are." But the Pericu already had been marked for extinction.

The survival of remnants of prehistoric cultures also was noted by the great naturalist Charles Darwin on his famous voyage around the world on the *H.M.S. Beagle* in the 1830's. Of the Indians on isolated islands and along the coastal inlets of southern Chile he wrote:

At night five or six human beings, naked and scarcely protected from the wind and rain of this tempestuous climate, sleep on the wet ground, coiled up like animals...one can hardly make oneself believe they are fellow creatures, and inhabitants of the same world.

In the late 1800's and early 1900's anthropologists began to lift the curtain on some of the mystery of the past of the Indians of North America. The task was made more difficult because of the swift rate at which the American Indians had been killed off or had succumbed to the White Man's indifference and to his diseases, before even their customs and traditions had been fully recorded or appreciated.

In 1885 Dr. H. Ten Kate of Paris visited Baja California in search of any remnants of the Pericu. He was accompanied by one L. Belding who reported on the expedition in *The West-American Scientist,* a little magazine published in San Diego by one of California's first scientists, C. R. Orcutt. They found what they believed may have been one of the last of the Pericu, a very aged woman of dark coloring and of good stature, differing widely in appearance from the more familiar Indians of the north. She refused to be photographed. Her cranium, Belding reported, was similar to the skulls which Dr. Ten Kate also found in dry caves in the same area, and all of which were of the same general pyramidal form: high, long and narrow, with wide, prominent cheek bones.

In later years other skulls were found, and they are perhaps the narrowest of any human population known. The Pericu themselves had disappeared from man's horizon.

But other dedicated archaeologists elsewhere were turning up weapons and utensils retrogressively cruder, and skeletal remains indicating the differences in types and development, often in larger patterns of time and area. Determining ages and unraveling the cross threads of their movements over vast areas, were not easy matters.

It became known, for example, that the Yuman people who were present in Southern California at the time of the arrival of the Spaniards had spread from the Colorado River Desert into the coastal area about 1400 A.D., with the drying up of Lake LeConte, also known as Blake Sea and Lake Cahuilla, which once covered much of Imperial Valley.

But even the knowledge of the physical characteristics of the Indians who lived in Southern California in pre-Spanish times is limited because of widespread practices of cremating the dead.

A century and a half after Fr. Baegert had written of the strange people in Baja California, a mining geologist turned archaeologist, was slowly putting together a pattern of life as it existed in the Southwest long before the missionaries or anyone else in Europe had ever even heard of California. He was Malcolm J. Rogers, on the staff of the San Diego Museum of Man and later to become its director.

He realized that many centuries, perhaps thousands of years before the arrival of the Yumans, a different people who buried their dead had occupied San Diego County and northern Baja California. He called them the La Jollans. While burial conditions in many places along the coast were not conducive to preservation, and the rise of the sea covered many of their coastal camps and burial sites and others were eroded away, skulls and bones were found. They were seed grinders and seafood gatherers, more than hunters, a rather small people, the men about five feet, four inches tall and the women, four feet, eleven inches, and had large heads.

Their characteristics suggest some racial affiliation with Indian stocks of the San Francisco Bay region, the Sacramento Valley and the Great Basin rather than with the more recent Yuman people of Southern California or the Chumash of Santa Barbara and the Channel Islands. In the view of Dr. Spencer Rogers, Chairman of the Department of Anthropology at San Diego State College and present scientific director of the San Diego Museum of Man, and no relation of Malcolm Rogers, there is an impressive similarity in many physical characteristics between the La Jollans and a prehistoric population of the Island of Kyushu, Japan.

"This suggests," Dr. Rogers has written, "that the peopling of the coast of North America from Asia involved the movement of population groups which retained their ancestral hereditary structural characteristics for a considerable time after their arrival in the Southern California coastal region."

Though early missionaries had despaired of alerting the later though very primitive Indians of Baja California to the concept of a soul, there was enough standardized practice in burial to indicate the La Jollans were well-developed in their thinking about an after-life and that they preserved their traditions carefully from generation to generation.

There is evidence that as a result of the melting of the Polar Ice Caps toward the close of the last Ice Age, beginning about 18,000 years ago, the level of the ocean rose sufficiently to cause a flooding of the canyons and valleys of the coast, forming deep bays and lagoons which, besides the rocky reefs along the shore, provided an abundant supply of seafood for the La Jollans.

In 1966, an accumulation of driftwood was recovered by Dr. Robert F. Dill, marine biologist of the Naval Electronics Laboratory at San Diego, from an ancient beach deposit exposed in the wall of a submarine canyon off La Jolla, California, at a depth of 125 feet. This wood, and hence the ancient sea level, has been dated as 13,200 years before the present. In shallow water in this same area have been recovered about 2000 stone bowls, believed used by the La Jollans.

Radiocarbon dating was not available when Rogers began his work and he had no precise way of determining the passage of time, but over the years he did find evidence that there had been several phases of the La Jolla people.

One of the intriguing mysteries of these Early Men is that from all archaeological evidence their economic culture never greatly changed, despite the circumstances that they gradually drifted down the Pacific Coast over thousands of years and that they probably introduced the metate into California. They stood still in time, and how and when their culture came to an end has not as yet been determined.

In 1919 Rogers was searching for Indian artifacts on a sandy loam ridge along a river in San Diego County. It was on Christmas Day and the site was in the San Dieguito area north of the city of San Diego and near the town of Escondido. On the ground in the open he found pieces of stone that were to open a historic door to the past and embark him on his life's major work. Later he told his own story:

Since I was well aware of the kind of tools left behind by historical Indians and the people of the La Jolla Culture before them, I knew immediately that these tools were of a still earlier period.

When you compared them with the Old World tools, they were parallel to the Aurignacian cave people in France who lived before the last Ice Age. On that hill we found twelve tools intact and a number of others, including some of the largest, broken. They must have been broken deliberately, probably in some sort of rite connected with death.

Although he recognized these tools as quite primitive, he was to come to look upon them as fairly sophisticated. For he had discovered a prehistoric people at an advanced stage of their culture. When he followed their trail backward, he found much cruder tools than the stone scrapers and points found near Escondido, and some of them were almost indistinguishable from ones found in Asia; others reflected relationship to European and South American cultures.

The mountains and deserts of Southern California began to give up the secrets which had been waiting for thousands of years for someone to find, probe and decipher.

Slowly over the next years the trail back into time led Rogers through the Laguna Mountains and into the Borrego Desert and the Imperial Valley, up the valley and around the east flank of the San Bernardino Mountains into the Mojave Desert. Here, in the open desolation, nothing had been disturbed since nature's climatic revolutions. It took him up along U.S. Highway 395, east of the Sierra Nevada, to the Oregon line. While the tools in some locations became more crude, in others they became even more sophisticated than those found near the San Dieguito River.

Thousands of artifacts were found over

wide areas of Nevada and southern Arizona, in Imperial Valley and in Baja California, and even on the Mexican mainland. Separating and defining them into different phases was a complex and at times frustrating task. In the desert area he ranged the sandy washes and rocky terraces in his beaten vintage auto, before four-wheel drives and the big-tired "dune buggies," and at night he lay down on the desert floor in the open and using his bedroll only as a pillow. Sometimes he had the assistance of his father or of Donal Hord, his friend and noted sculptor, or of

No skeletal remains of the San Dieguito Man have been found, and his physical appearance remains a mystery.

Not so with the La Jolla Man. The La Jollans buried their dead and enough skeletons have been found to give a reliable idea of what they looked like.

This reconstruction was made by the young sculptor, Francis Chenelle, under the direction of Dr. Spencer Rogers of San Diego State College.

The skull used for the model came from Lower California, Mexico, and is believed to be one of the oldest yet found.

According to Dr. Rogers there is an impressive similarity between their physical measurements and those of a prehistoric population of the Island of Kyushu, Japan.

This suggests that the peopling of the coast of North America from Asia involved the movement of population groups which retained their ancestral hereditary structural characteristics for a considerable time after their arrival on the southern coast.

The La Jollans were a rather small people with large and somewhat wide heads, and there was a definite variance in size between men and women. They differed considerably from the Yumans and Shoshoneans who later occupied much of the same region.

Dr. Carl L. Hubbs has recently suggested that the La Jolla culture may have emerged perhaps 9000 years ago, and remained in the area 7000 years.

the Museum staff. In these lonely and parched desert areas he found he was dealing not with one people but several. One of these Old People he named the Amargosans. They were, he thought, perhaps roughly contemporary with the La Jolla people living on the coast. He wrote sometime later:

The scant evidence with which we have to work suggests southern Utah as their departure point and that the migration pushed through southern Nevada and hence into California and the Mojave Desert. At this point, the Amargosans fanned out to the west as far as the Owens Valley. Despite this marginal movement, the main trend of colonization was ever to the south, but in a curvilinear direction which eventually caused them to cross the Colorado River valley into western and southern Arizona. A further southern trend led them into Sonora, in, as yet, an unknown distance. For some inexplicable reason the Amargosans in their wanderings failed to cross the mountain ranges of Southern California into the Pacific slope terrain.

Besides the Amargosans and the La Jollans, there were other people whose artifacts Rogers had found on the mesa near Escondido in San Diego County. In 1925 and 1926 Rogers had extended his domain of these older people into Arizona and the Mojave Desert and in 1927 into Nevada. Principally camping around the shores of lakes and streams long extinct, in what is now the desert or semi-desert, these ancient people enjoyed a hunting and food-gathering economy that was to be the basis for all the aboriginal cultures of the Far West. It seemed to him that when they had wandered or retreated to the south, and one branch had turned into southern Arizona and Sonora, the Amargosans had dogged their footsteps.

It was not until about the 1930's that other institutions became interested in the problem of the Far West's early inhabitants, and because of Rogers' work the San Diego Museum of Man remained the major source of research materials, even

if largely neglected by his fellow archae-ologists.

Bones and relics being found in the dry caves of the West also were brought un-der scrutiny, and M. R. Harrington hurried to examine charcoal beds in Pleistocene deposits that had been exposed on the banks of a wash near Las Vegas, Nevada.

These beds yielded bones, some of them scraped or split and others burned, which were identified as belonging to the large American camel, or *camelops hesternus,* and to a huge species of bison, both now extinct. Other pieces looked like those of the American horse. There also was an elephant molar. To Harrington the beds represented an ancient camel-hunter's camp, and, as had Rogers, he asked himself:

What kind of dart points did our Nevada camel-hunters use — the old boys who knew the mammoth? Were they like those at Gyp-sum Cave, not forty miles away? Did they

Hundreds of years ago in the Borrego-Anza Desert the climate was different from that of today.

The edge of the Fish Creek Mountains was a rim of the sea which covered much of Imperial Valley long before the Salton Sea was formed.

Today the Carrizo Wash swings by there on its course into the deep desert.

Along the banks of the wash and follow-ing the edge of the Fish Creek Mountains are dim trails.

Malcolm Rogers found the lower trail loaded with artifacts which probably were those of the Yuman culture. Yuman camp sites have been found along the old shore line.

The higher trail, however, is less distinct and may have been associated with the sleeping circles and stone age tools of a much older people, the San Dieguitoans, who Rogers believed camped on the nearby terrace at site C-129B.

In the foreground are rocks dark with the desert varnish of age.

This picture looks south toward the Coy-ote Mountains and Mexico.

bury their dead in their camp grounds? Did they belong to our own species, or to some forgotten bestial type...?

A number of years later, Rogers noticed that a flood had exposed a midden in the bed of the San Dieguito River below Hodges dam and not far from where he had first found the very early artifacts on a nearby mesa. He interpreted it as being an ancient tool factory which had been used for many generations of men and covered for thousands of years by silt of successive flooding of the river.

With the aid of funds from the Carnegie Institution, he began digging of the first buried San Dieguito site yet discovered up to that time. He had long suspected that two phase patterns were involved. Now, the discovery of a complete lithic pattern, which he postulated as that of a closing phase of a prehistoric people, in a geologi-cal position indicating that it was preced-ed by an earlier pattern, helped him to conclude finally that there had been at least three phases of San Dieguito culture and thus probably three distinct waves of the same Early Man.

He named and classified these people as San Dieguito I, II and III, and also listed four zones of concentration in the Far West which he identified for convenience as the Central, Western, Southeastern and South-western Aspects. He thought their flow had been from north to south through the Great Basin. The San Dieguito men them-selves avoided the higher mountains and only in a few places near the coast left their artifacts, which always have been found in subordinate positions to those of the La Jollans. He wrote:

During the many years of field research, marginal sallies were made in all direc-tions of the compass in an attempt to dis-cover the migration corridor of the San Dieguitoans into the Great Basin. For a time it was thought that their ingress might have been from Wyoming through the low pass in the Continental Divide, leading down into the Great Salt Lake Basin...it was found that an unbroken line of archae-

ological sites extended north up through western Nevada to the Oregon State line... This condition suggests that the corridor lies down through central Washington and eastern Oregon.

In order to support a hunting population the now arid West had to be a different land then, with water and game, and not as we know it today.

For all anyone knows, the early hunters abandoned their dead to the elements and the vultures, or placed the bodies on a platform in trees, perhaps to assist them on their way, as no human bones have been found. Really nothing but rock tools and weapons of a Stone Age. They were wanderers, with no permanent attachments, following game and gathering food as they went. The seasonal wanderings of ancient peoples perhaps was not haphazard but based on the life cycles of various animals and insects as well as plant life. What wood they might have used, or baskets they might have made, have long since been reduced to dust.

But there remain in the desert many sleeping circles, which Rogers thought had been made by early hunters. Some are merely simple clearings and others are rimmed with rocks, similar to those reported for the Pericu; again thousands of them. Evidently brush was built up around the circle, or against the rocks, to provide protection from the prevailing wind. In Rogers' view these people were more primitive than the Patagonians:

All over the country we found these rough circles, made of stones on top of mesas. They were from five to twelve feet in diameter...Apparently they wore no clothes. The only way they had to keep warm at night was to get into these circles and lie like sardines in a can. There is no evidence of their putting any kind of a roof over the circles.

Rogers found many dim trails beaten into the desert pavement, which, through the strange processes of nature, time and the elements had not been able to erase. Often closely paralleling these ancient trails were similar ones of the later Yu-

mans, who, Rogers thought, evidently preferred not to walk in the path of the dead. Where the two trails might cross, Rogers found a line of boulders laid across a more ancient trail, as if to stop the spirits of the dead from going any farther.

Sometimes these older trails converged and became one on one side of a mountain pass. Rogers found that on the other side they divided again and lead in diverse directions, but not to any modern source of water, nor to anywhere in particular, as far as anyone today could discern.

Their principal places of camping seemed to be on the low and rocky desert terraces from which they could see for great distances. Some of these mesas Rogers identified as ceremonial ones on which the San Dieguitoans laid rocks in long lines, sometimes straight, sometimes curving, and sometimes connecting circles which may have been cairns or hearths, but all with no discernible pattern or meaning, and which remain today to puzzle the most astute of anthropologists.

At the camp sites attributed by Rogers to the Amargosans and the La Jollans were broken heaps of milling stones and metates. He concluded that these implements had been "sacrificed" in some ceremony, perhaps in the vaguest sense of religion, or at death, or perhaps merely in an act of departure.

The discovery of Ventana Cave in Arizona was taken by Rogers as proving out his thesis. In this dry cavern with its age-old spring, through which animals and men had wandered for thousands of years, were found stratified artifacts of three phases of what Rogers identified as Amargosa culture and below them cruder artifacts which he classified as those of the first wave of the still earlier people who had disappeared before the tides of Amargosans. However, all indications pointed to a much greater age for these "First Men" than Rogers had conceived.

It was only in the last years of his life that Rogers began to fully realize the real antiquity of the Early Men to whom he had given the name of San Dieguito. At the time of his first discoveries near Escondido he thought the scrapers and points must surely be of an extremely ancient time. Later, however, with the finding of more tools and weapons along the shorelines of long-vanished lakes in the Mojave Desert, he speculated that the San Dieguito Man might have appeared only at the beginning of the Little Pluvial period, about 4000 years ago.

While Rogers' work primarily was in the open country, where artifacts were found on the surface, other archaeologists were excavating buried sites in New Mexico, Texas, Nebraska, and, as time went on, in more and more states. The evidence they yielded was profoundly changing the accepted concepts of man's occupancy of the United States.

Excavations in New Mexico and up into Colorado from 1926 to 1938 yielded the bones of fossilized camels and bison, a few of them with crude carving and stone implements which led to an identification of an ancient "Folsom Man." In eastern New Mexico near the Texas border came evidence of another Early Man who was called the "Clovis Man." Projectile points were uncovered in unmistakable association with the bones of the mammoth.

In southern and central Arizona came other artifacts, again in general association with the bones of long extinct animals, and the tentative identification of the "Cochise Man." Rogers examined these finds, and while he was convinced that the Cochise Man and the San Dieguito Man probably were one and the same, he did not believe that the evidence of association with animals extinct so many thousands of years was at all conclusive.

Radiocarbon dating subsequently pushed the La Jollans far back into time. The La Jolla skeletal remains found buried along the coast apparently were from a period approximately 5000 to 7000 years ago. Dr. Carl L. Hubbs has recently suggested they may have emerged perhaps 9000 years ago.

As the refuse of the La Jollans had been found above that of the San Dieguitoans, the latter certainly would seem to have been a still older people. Radiocarbon dating of organic material in newer sites indicated that the first of the San Dieguito Men probably were in the Great Basin at least as long as 10,000 years ago. In the story of mankind this would have been 4000 years before the first walls of an organized community were being raised around an oasis in Jericho.

Perhaps, Rogers began to speculate, the San Dieguitoans were not Indians as most people think of Indians, but darker and with thicker frontal bones, and not much different in appearance from the aborigines of Australia, to whom all but the present was a "dream time," and who in their own isolation persisted into modern times, even as perhaps had the Pericu, and an ocean removed from the middens, or historic rubbish heaps, of the American West. But the skulls of other early men on the continent, subsequently found in Texas and Mexico, and the characteristics of the La Jolla Man, indicated no affinity with Australian types.

The first people to arrive evidently left Asia, or their former lands, through Siberia, long before the bow and arrow had come into use, and certainly before the last of the ice had retreated from the Great Lakes, and presumably crossed a land bridge in the Bering Sea now lying below the ocean level, and drifted south through Alaska.

Though still primitive, they were far advanced in time and presumably in appearance from the earliest forms of men that have been uncovered by archaeologists in other parts of the world. They and their successors flowed in waves down the Great Basin, between the Rocky Mountains and the Sierra Nevada, thousands of years apart and amid great geological and climatic changes.

The Pluvial period which ended 10,000 years ago was followed in historical time by what Rogers has described as the Long

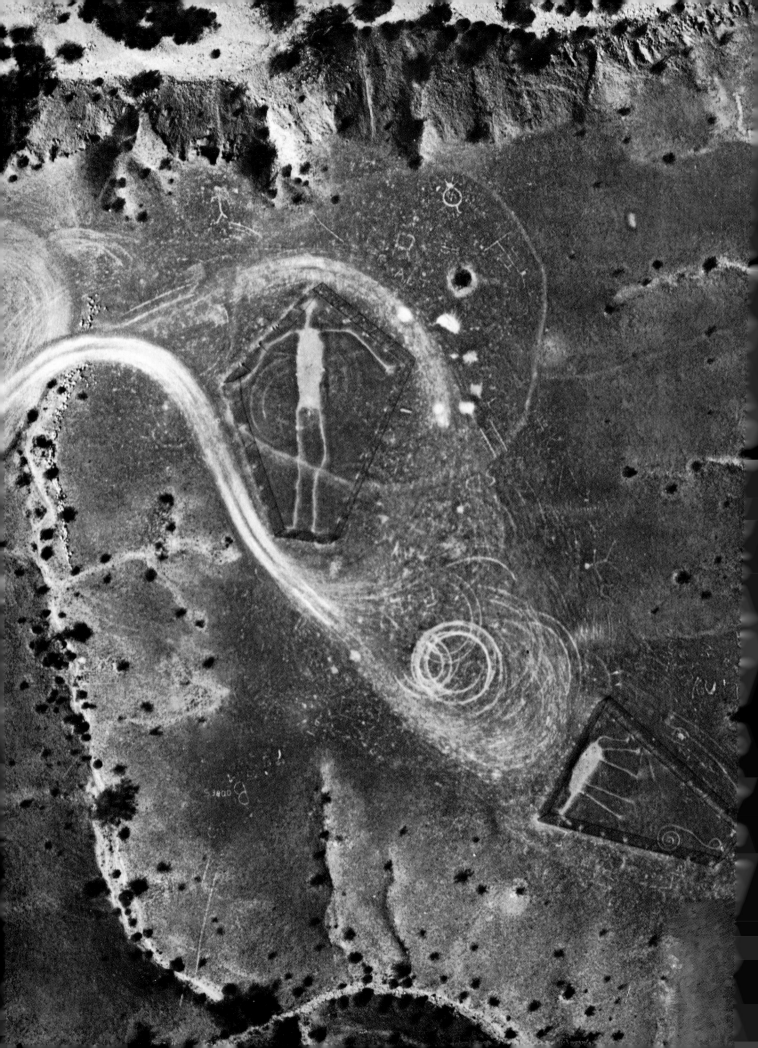

Drought, which lasted for about 3000 years, from 5000 B.C. to 2000 B.C. This in turn was followed, he thought, by a wet period of 1500 years, from 2000 B.C. to 500 B.C., one of sufficient precipitation to again produce permanent streams and lakes in the California Desert; followed by still another, but shorter, drought of 1000 years, between 500 B.C. and 500 A.D.

The movements of prehistoric people were no doubt affected by such climatic changes, and the racial memory of them may have persisted with later Indians into modern times. The flood of the Old Testament is akin to references to high water flooding the land, which are found in the stories and songs of historic Indians.

Many thousands of years of Indian advancement are represented in two aerial photographs, one on the adjoining page and the other on the following page.

In the desert near Blythe, California, are raked gravel "pictographs" of the Mojave Indians, shown at left.

One of them is a crude representation of a man; the other of a horse.

The horse clearly places these gravel arrangements in the historic Indian period, as the original Western horse vanished from the continent many thousands of years ago and only was reintroduced by the Spaniards arriving from Europe.

These pictographs are protected by fences.

On the next page is an aerial photograph of a mesa on the edge of the Panamint Mountains which separate Panamint Valley from Death Valley.

The photograph reveals the dim outlines of carefully-placed lines of rocks stretching for hundreds of feet.

This was probably a "ceremonial mesa" of an ancient people. How ancient may be a matter of dispute. Malcolm Rogers associated such alignments with the San Dieguito people.

What the figure, or figures, represent, no one knows. In the rocky alignments of Ancient Man there are no discernible patterns nor meanings that have been interpreted.

The migrations of Early Man into the New World have raised natural questions for anthropologists:

Why was it that bands of hunters left their old land and traversed great distances over unattractive territory to reach the New World, and in the course of a few thousand years spread down as far as the tip of South America?

The San Dieguito Man was first of all a hunter. The earliest of them may have killed their game with pointed sticks hardened in fire, even as some of the most aboriginal people have done even into modern times. The hunters of the second phase, or San Dieguito II, had developed to where they employed darts tipped with flaked stone points and propelled by wooden throwers called atlatls. How much time elapsed between the use of the wooden points and the stone-tipped dart is not known. It may have encompassed several thousand years.

The variety of prehistoric animals whose fossilized remains have been found in the dry caves of the Southwest testify to an abundance of life in a country that may have been richer in grass and marshes. Ventana Cave in Arizona and the Gypsum Cave in San Bernardino County have yielded the fossilized bones of the bison, dire wolf, tapir, horse, giant sloth and the jaguar. Rogers, too, found lying in the open in San Dieguito Indian country fossilized bones which he was certain were those of a prehistoric camel or a large Western horse which had become extinct on the continent long before the arrival of the Spaniards. Their exact time relation with the early peoples has not been clearly established as yet.

Radiocarbon dating of remnants of organic material found in the famed La Brea tar pits in Los Angeles indicates that the greatest accumulation of the bones of prehistoric animals occurred about 14,500 years ago. Inexplicably many of the animals seem to have become extinct at about the same time.

Was it the pressure of other peoples be-

hind that caused Early Man to make such a long migration to a New World, or was it just his pursuit of game?

And why, after arriving in a new and favorable land, did he experience such variations in development?

Despite a continent rich in food and metals, in many phases he lagged behind other men in the invention and perfection of the material manifestations of civilization. Yet, there were instances of high artistic development, and, from central Mexico to northern South America, high scientific and intellectual accomplishments.

The search of man's indistinct past is an endless one and an endless fascination. For Rogers it had been a life's work. Trained in the exact and natural sciences at Syracuse University, he had worked as a mining geologist and served in the Marine Corps before joining the Museum of Man at San Diego and becoming its curator in 1928 and director in 1943.

There never was enough money to do all that should have been done and over the years expanding populations erased much of the record. Farming operations buried vast areas of archaeological interest. Road and then superhighway construction bulldozed sites. Towns and subdivisions of new migrations rose over the graves and middens of peoples who had preceded them into the favored coastal areas. Now the desert vehicles of modern man and the amateur hunters are tearing up much of what has been lying on desert surfaces for hundreds of generations.

Though Rogers did not rush into print, nor join in the professional controversies of the day, he would willingly discuss his work with anyone who would listen, and with casual newspaper reporters seeking interviews on an unfamiliar subject, he was patient and thorough. He had an exciting way of describing his findings and graphically relating them to the whole story of ancient man, all the time smoking, one after another, cigarettes made from tobacco he himself had carefully sun-dried.

To him, crude man-worked rocks were Rosetta Stones which, if read properly, could tell of humanity's early struggles in the conquest of environment.

Occasionally Rogers secured small grants from institutions, or gifts from anonymous patrons. On the other hand, there were the persistent demands of routine museum responsibilities. He left the museum during World War II, when its facilities were taken over for defense purposes, and he worked as a free agent generally for thirteen years. But, as he wrote, "the time came when I could go no further without access to my life's work on deposit in the San Diego Museum of Man." He returned and at last received from a new administration the support he had always hoped for, and began the final work on the first overall synthesis devoted to solving the problems of prehistory in the Far West, only to be struck down and killed by an auto in 1960.

He had gathered specimens from 6000 sites and left twenty volumes of notes, along with maps, charts and photographs, and the first draft of a manuscript in which he had hoped to present his great synthesis on the San Dieguito Complex.

Anthropology is a fast-moving science, and Clark C. Evernham, managing director of the San Diego Museum of Man, knew it was necessary to edit and bring Rogers' work up to date for purposes of publication. His latest conclusions were incorporated, and obsolete references and some unimportant material deleted. Deletions are indicated by asterisks (***). This was done under the direction of the museum's scientific director, Dr. Spencer Rogers.

This book for the first time presents the story of the San Dieguito Man of which anthropologists generally have known very little, and Rogers' vast collection of artifacts, of which almost nothing has been known. There are some in his field who do not agree entirely with all details of his findings and his conclusions, as is natural in such a new and developing science, particularly as to the age of the sleeping circles and desert trails. Many archaeologists will argue that they surely must belong to a much later time. However, he had done far more than any other man in advancing our knowledge of Early Man in the Far West.

Other archaeologists are taking up where he left off, and are relating what he learned with their findings on the Ancient Hunters, and relating all of it to the larger story of man in North America and to the New World as a whole. Radiocarbon dating has indicated that it was the last phase of the San Dieguito people who reached San Diego County 10,000 years ago. When did the first actually arrive in the Great Basin? At any time the edge of knowledge may be moved back another block of thousands of years.

George F. Carter, formerly of the Museum of Man and now a professor of geography at Johns Hopkins University, has published the results of extensive investigations he has made of formations in San Diego County, and from evidence obtained at a cliff site west of Texas Street on the south side of Mission Valley he has at least convinced himself that Man was in the area perhaps 40,000 years ago. But the majority of archaeologists do not believe he has proved his case.

This book primarily takes us back along the paths charted by Rogers, finding and sorting the evidence of the existence of the oldest man so far as we know now, though, as with Rogers, we will not meet up with him or ever know what he looked like, or learn what really happened to him.

PART II   THE ANCIENT HUNTERS ...WHO WERE THEY?

MALCOLM J. ROGERS

PART II

THE SAN DIEGUITO COMPLEX — HISTORY, BOUNDARIES, AND TERMINOLOGY

This report is a summation and digest of data which have been gathered over a period of forty-one years. It is natural, since the first evidence of the San Dieguito culture was found in San Diego County, California, in 1919, that theories and contentions have had to be revised several times, with the accumulation of additional data. Through the years, as archaeological surveys were made in an ever-widening sphere from the original focus into Baja California, the California Desert, Arizona, and Nevada, the San Dieguito boundaries were extended and other phase patterns established. For a long time it was not realized that the culture had passed through three developmental phases, for vertical stratigraphic deposits had not been found and the horizontal stratigraphic technique had not been applied.

In 1929 and 1930, with the aid of subsidies from the Smithsonian Institution, excavations were conducted in all the larger shell middens of San Diego County and in western Baja California as far south as San Quentín. This work established the San Dieguito culture in a basal position to the La Jolla and Diegueño horizons, but did not determine which San Dieguito phase pattern was the oldest.

It had long been suspected that two local phase patterns of the San Dieguito culture were involved, because of the different degrees of patina exhibited on two different assemblages of artifacts, but excavations did not provide the stratigraphic evidence. Then, in 1938, through financial aid from the Carnegie Institution in Washington,

From Interstate Highway 8, about fourteen miles west of Yuma in the Colorado Desert, a road runs north to a now-vanished mining settlement of Ogilby and here it swings up into a desert mesa variously called Pilot Knob or Black Mesa.

After about ten miles a secondary road turns northeast toward Indian Pass, with the red buttes of the Colorado River in the distance.

Here are numerous gravel terraces, camping grounds of the ancients. A silent area,

it speaks only to archaeologists.

This photograph is of a trail on one of the higher elevations, at site C-45, which is a very large terrace, well-traveled thousands of years ago by feet which wore a path in the desert pavement.

The trail disappears to the north into a canyon below the Chocolate Mountains.

The ground along the trail is littered with the artifacts which Malcolm Rogers classified as those of the earliest of the San Dieguito people.

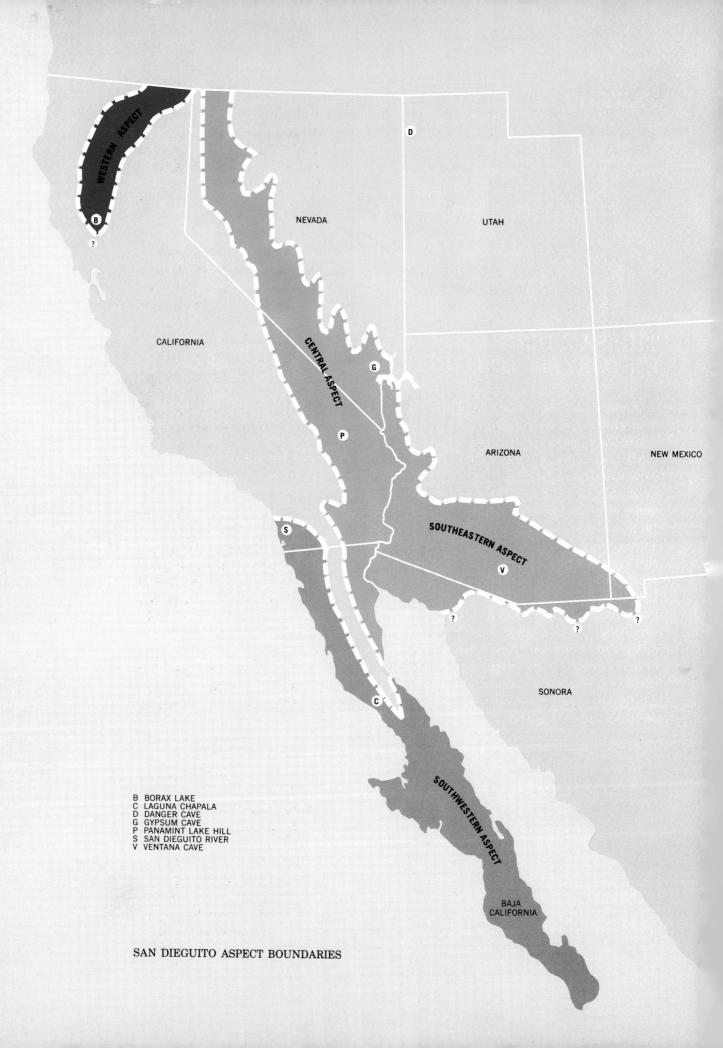

SAN DIEGUITO ASPECT BOUNDARIES

B BORAX LAKE
C LAGUNA CHAPALA
D DANGER CAVE
G GYPSUM CAVE
P PANAMINT LAKE HILL
S SAN DIEGUITO RIVER
V VENTANA CAVE

the excavation of a fossil stream channel in the San Dieguito River valley was made possible (Rogers, 1938 [*and Warren, 1966 — ed.*]). This work yielded a complete lithic pattern of what was postulated as the third San Dieguito phase, in a geological situation which set it chronologically above the earlier pattern.

BOUNDARIES

Between 1925 and 1940 there was never a year that San Diego Museum of Man field parties did not explore new areas of the Far West in search of new San Dieguito sites and new boundaries, until by 1940 the extremities of the domain were set.

The term *Far West,* as used in this report, embraces all the territory lying west of the Continental Divide [*and south of 42° north latitude. — ed.*]

In his long explorations of the Far West Malcolm Rogers recognized four major areas of archaeological concentration.

These areas are outlined in this map.

His work began in San Diego County but it soon was extended into the northern part of Lower California in the western areas and into the California Desert, and then into Arizona and Nevada.

A few of the artifacts he identified as resembling those of the San Dieguito people also were found in the drier regions of eastern Oregon and Washington.

He called these areas "Aspects" and within them he established to his own satisfaction that the culture endured long enough to permit cultural evolution.

His classification of cultural patterns was based upon what probably were regional variations of one broad pattern.

He defined the "Far West" as embracing all territory west of the Continental Divide and south of the 42° north latitude, which is roughly parallel to the northern borders of California, Nevada and western Utah.

In all of this Great Basin country was evidence of vanished lakes and streams which could have helped support a fairly large aboriginal population.

Further explorations by myself in the 1950's enabled me to extend the first phase of the complex a short distance into Sonora and Chihuahua. At the same time, evidence was being sought for determining the oldest center of occupancy, the relationship of one geographical concentration to another, and the direction of initial ingress.

Everything pointed to the probability that the ancient corridor was from the north into the Great Basin, but the actual region of the north to south longitudinal line was difficult to place.*** A line of sites were located in western Nevada as far north as the northwestern part of the state and contiguous to the Oregon state line. Sporadic finds of some San Dieguito-like artifacts in the arid parts of Oregon and Washington also lent clues to the direction of ingress.

TERMINOLOGY

Complex

In the past and at present, the term *complex* has had several different meanings. Perhaps the most common one is used to designate an admixture of two or more culture patterns. I do not use it as such, but rather to indicate the widespread range of the culture and the variations within this range.

Phases

As early as 1940 I had recognized four major areas of archaeological concentration, with a thinning out in the peripheral country lying between the four. Within these zones, the culture endured long enough to permit cultural evolution, and there were three rather distinct subpatterns which I have termed *phases*. Wherever the three were found, the basic pattern was the same. They deviated in only a few local elements, something to be expected because of their geographical separation. With time, each phase pattern became slightly enriched. It was also observed that the percentage relationships of specific elements varied from zone to zone. Pressure flaking technique during the third phase period brought about the most conspicuous change in the overall pattern.

Aspects

The four major zones of concentration are designated as *aspects,* and specifically identified as the Central, Western, Southeastern, and Southwestern aspects. Together they form the San Dieguito Complex. Regional naming was adopted to gain elasticity, as future exploration may establish new centers of the culture. The "aspect" concept has a static sense, while the "phase" concept is more mobile, in that after each phase developed it was diffused either through migration or marginal acculturation. Until some more absolute system of dating is devised, migrational time-lag, however logical it may seem, cannot be proved. Meanwhile, I remain skeptical whether identical phases occurred at the same time in different aspects, because of the climate variation evidenced in the several aspect areas.

All three phases are represented in but one area, the Central Aspect. The Southeastern Aspect has produced first and second phase patterns, but not the third, while in the Southwestern Aspect the first phase is missing and the second and third are present. Because of my incomplete knowledge of the Western Aspect, I am certain only that the third phase is strongly in evidence.***

[*The author's reference to horizontal stratigraphy perhaps requires some preliminary explanation.*

The customarily recognized condition of vertical stratigraphy, where one level of characteristic artifacts lies over another as a result of successive cultural deposits at the same site, is occasionally found in the San Dieguito Complex. However, some sites were not occupied by a series of peoples who produced artifacts of a different cultural character. In other examples, sparse deposits of cultural materials are sometimes found in lower strata, as a result of erosion which carried away soil materials containing the artifacts, allowing them to become mixed with those of the lower level.

A horizontal stratigraphy, in the author's usage, is derived by studying artifact assemblages from separate terraces of a lake which receded in stages during a period of increasing aridity. In such a study, the archaeologist can expect to find the younger deposits on the lower terraces of the lake. Caution must be taken, however, since a renewal of the lake at a later date, accompanied by human occupation, may upset the expected stratigraphic sequence. When artifacts are gathered from different terrace levels, kept separate, and analyzed with reference to the establishment of patterns, a succession may appear representing a series in time and tool types analogous to the serriation demonstrated in vertical stratigraphy.—ed.]

CHAPTER II

GENERAL DISCUSSION: CULTURE AND CHRONOLOGY

CLEARING THE PICTURE

In 1941, the late Dr. Edgar B. Howard discussed with me the confusing picture concerning Early Man in the Far West, brought about by conflicting reports in the archaeological literature. I felt this resulted mostly from two factors: the use of single elements as indicators of diverse cultural patterns when often only one pattern was involved, and the custom of naming individually each deviation in the form of a projectile point. After several conferences relative to the problem, which included trips in the field together, he urged me to write an article devoted primarily to the number of culture patterns involved, their nature and geographical distribution, both in space and time. Time relationships did not intrigue me then, nor do they now, in comparison with the more important issue of culture definition, a study which still today is in great need of development. Without this we cannot know how many patterns are to be reckoned with nor how to fit sporadic finds over a great territory into their proper niches.

I do not mean to disparage the importance of the time element nor the need for a time frame. However, I wish to point out that time epochs, climatic distinctions, and geological strata interpretations from Pluvial to recent times are not yet established with sufficient finality to serve as a firm structure for pigeonholing our archaeological discoveries.

Confusing Terms

Two terms which I proposed in 1939 were the dual names, San Dieguito-Playa Complex and Pinto-Gypsum Complex. These were not well chosen even though my information at the time was sufficient to avoid such vagaries. In the former, I already was convinced that I was dealing merely with different geographical aspects of the San Dieguito culture in the Basin and Range area of Nevada, California, and Arizona. I should have presented them as such. One choice on the basis of previously established terms would have been San Dieguito-Lake Mojave Complex, but that would have been inconsistent as the first term had an areal significance and the other had been applied to a single archaeological site in an ever greater area; also the word Mojave was already preempted in both an archaeological and ethnological sense. It is almost as unfortunate a term as Yuma Point culture.

The other compromise was the term Pinto-Gypsum Complex. Each of the originators of the two culture terms was convinced that he was dealing with a distinct culture. I felt we were faced with regional variations of the second phase of a three phase complex, which I had named Amargosa.

Soon after this, the discovery of the splendid stratigraphy in Ventana Cave in Arizona (Haury, 1950) gave rather conclusive proof that my interpretation of the first two Amargosa phases was correct. In this marginal position a certain amount of acculturation was in evidence at the beginning of the second phase. In Arizona the most significant addition to the pattern was the metate.

Then in 1957, Newberry Cave (Smith, et al, 1957) in the Mojave Desert provided us with the lithic implements of the second and third phases and, of even more importance, a host of perishable items which could be correlated with similar artifacts from Gypsum Cave in Nevada. Unfortunately, adequate cultural levels were

either absent or not recognized.

The Harris Site

Another deficiency of my 1939 report, pointed out at the time, was the absence of a detailed publication on the 1938 excavations in a fossil river channel of the San Dieguito River valley in San Diego County, California, which disclosed a local culture sequence with San Dieguito in a basal position. Although the same culture sequence has not been duplicated in the California Desert, it does lend support to the San Dieguito-Amargosa sequence concept, because of the considerable antiquity of the former in contiguous territory. This work and the records of other stratified sites on the Pacific slope, should have preceded the 1939 report.***

[*A full report on this important and classic site was assembled and edited from M. J. Rogers' notes. See San Diego Museum of Man Paper, No. 5 (Warren, Claude N., 1966).—ed.*]

This curving line of rocks is laid on a low gravel terrace in the Mojave Desert south of the Mesquite Hills in central San Bernardino County.

This is an area south of Baker and north of Ludlow, at site M-40.

There are a series of such rock alignments on this terrace, as well as seven cobble structures resembling hearths, and one cleared circle.

The terrace is encrusted with deeply varnished "desert pavement" which includes a quantity of patinated and wind-scoured flaked rock.

Malcolm Rogers first visited here in 1928 or 1929.

It is possible that the San Dieguito I people camped here when the adjoining dry lake was filled with water, laying out rock alignments and hearths.

Much later, perhaps when the lake was filled once again, a second culture took over, designated by Malcolm Rogers as the Amargosans. Still later, with the complete drying of the lake, a third prehistoric people camped in the dunes on the lake bottom.

Ventana Cave

Soon after this, sufficient evidence had been accumulated to indicate that the basal lithic industry of the Basin and Range province, originally termed the Malpais Culture, was an initial phase of the San Dieguito Complex, and the term San Dieguito I phase was substituted for the old designation. The change, however, did not appear in print until 1950 in Haury's Ventana Cave report. Here it was used both in the text and in the schematic charts (Haury, 1950, pp. 533-535, Figures 115, 116 and 117). The new terminology and the correlation of San Dieguito I with the basal stratum and two subsequent culture horizons with Amargosa I and Amargosa II were the result of work done by Haury and myself together in the field, in the laboratory, and in conference in the year 1943.***

[*The editors would like to correct a long-standing error that has been perpetuated in the literature of Southwestern archaeology. The error is that the basal stratum of Ventana Cave (volcanic debris layer) is considered culturally comparable to the classic assemblage of San Dieguito III material from the Harris site (Southwestern Aspect).*

1. Malcolm Rogers specifies clearly, "the culture of the basal horizon in Ventana Cave is pure San Dieguito I." The culture found at the Harris site, SDM-W-198, is San Dieguito III.

2. The error probably occurred when Haury, wishing to describe the salient features of San Dieguito culture in general, mistakenly selected traits descriptive of the San Dieguito III phase (Haury, 1950, p. 193). Haury's error no doubt resulted from Rogers' early, confusing terminology (1939), wherein he called San Dieguito I the Malpais Culture.—ed.]

GEOLOGICAL CONSIDERATIONS

From the time of my earliest geographical distribution studies of San Dieguito archaeology, I observed that its topographical zoning was at variance with other regional cultural zoning, and that the camps were not located close to modern water sources (Rogers, 1929). This was true, whether the site were in Baja California or in the Basin and Range province. In the latter area the sites were, with few exceptions, near extinct stream channels and lakes.***

Danger Cave
In approaching the problem of when man first arrived in the Basin and Range province, and whether his occupancy was of a permanent or intermittent nature, the archaeology of Danger Cave in Utah (Jennings, 1957) is of greater importance than any other stratified site found to this time. I say this because of the volume and depth of the deposits, the wealth of both nonlithic and lithic artifacts, the long chronological attendant series of Carbon 14 dates, and Jennings' diagnosis of the combined data. But when all this is set in juxtaposition to the combined data gathered by other students of the problem, some disharmony becomes apparent. This may be due in great part to the inadequacies of the tools with which we work; however, as incompatibilities do exist, they should be discussed.

The archaeology of Danger Cave is relevant to the present problem in two respects: is a San Dieguito culture pattern represented, and at what level; and, has the younger culture, the Amargosa, been properly placed in prehistory with regard to its inception date and duration? In answer to the first question, it may be affirmed that a few Danger Cave elements could be duplicated in a San Dieguito III phase pattern. Because they were not confined to any special cultural level, it is more probable that they are regional variations added to an otherwise pure Amargosa-like culture. The known eastern boundary of San Dieguito III lies some 240 miles southwest of the cave, with much high mountain country intervening, a country particularly poor in archaeological evidence of any aboriginal group.

An exhaustive discussion of Jennings' interpretations would take me far beyond the restricted scope of this report. Consequently, I shall cite only his major premises. He has pointed out the uniformity and the persistent nature of the cave culture from level to level throughout a great period of time, and has deduced that it was devised to cope with a desert climate more arid than that of today, hence his designation, the Desert Culture. Its duration and place in time, derived from an imposing array of Carbon 14 dates, is 7000 B.C. to 3000 B.C. No known climate meets the requirements except the Altithermal.

My first criticism is that both the basal date and the durational length assigned to the Long Drought appear considerably exaggerated. The duration time is at least 1000 years, and possibly even 1500 years too long. I refer the reader to recent revised estimates made by geological and climatological authorities of the Basin and Range country. I realize that this assumption challenges the validity of the local Carbon 14 dates, and that I have nothing to offer in rebuttal, except that there must be a "fly in the ointment" somewhere. Jennings recognizes in post-3000 B.C. times on up to the protohistoric period an accretion of new elements, as an applique upon a surviving basal pattern, but still geared to desert existence. If one considers the elapsed time between 3000 B.C. and the protohistoric, at least 4500 more years must be added to this picture of a frozen economy, a concept which to me is inacceptable. Somewhere in Danger Cave history the moist Medithermal climate should have reflected its influence through an increase of mammalian bone and vegetal debris, even to species not available in the immediate vicinity of the cave during the Long Drought.

I think Jennings' thesis that a people coming into a new ecological zone would be compelled to fashion a way of life to meet the situation is correct, but I cannot agree with the concept of an almost complete cultural stasis of even 4000 years' duration during which only a few technical improvements were introduced. To believe that this one occupation center existed in complete isolation and immunity to acculturation for many millenia seems extremely unlikely.***

Further, his contention that the cave culture was essentially a seed-gathering vegetal-foraging economy is inconsistent with the wealth of projectile points and specialized scraping tools (3000 items) characteristic of a hunting people. If I am correct in interpreting the small thin slabs of relatively soft stone not as conventional metates, but functionally diversified artifacts employed in grinding pigments and immature seeds and in the maceration of edible vegetal items, then the hunting interpretation becomes even more strengthened.

The Amargosa Culture

San Dieguito and Amargosa histories are so closely associated in time that the chronological positioning of either one affects the positioning of the other.*** Danger Cave has provided us with the most complete Amargosa pattern yet to be found. Both the Amargosa II and III phases are in strength, although the presence of Amargosa I is most dubious. Three characteristic points of the first phase are the small leaf-shaped point, the shouldered broad-stemmed point, and the oblate concave-base point; only the last two types (Jennings' types W-12 and W-13) were represented, meagerly and not in a basal position. The perishable elements of the Amargosa I phase are not known, but they must have been similar to those of the subsequent phases.

Among the other cave deposits having a direct bearing on the Amargosa problem, only Ventana Cave has yielded an Amargosa I horizon. Although a partial lithic pattern was present, perishable material was unfortunately absent. Here, the basal-notched point was again missing. I do not attribute significance to this, since the site is geographically remote from the Central Aspect. The popularity of the type might not have spread that far. As a matter of fact it may never have crossed the Colorado River valley, for it has not been found in the chain of sites extending across southern Arizona from the river to Ventana and beyond, nor is it present in Sonora. Gypsum Cave produced a partial pattern of Amargosa II elements, and Newberry Cave a richer cross-section of the second and third phase patterns.

My concern from the first has been with culture pattern building, and I have been anxious to avoid making any one element indicative of a pattern entity. I have deplored the common practice of using a projectile point type which could be found in a dozen different places in the United States as the hallmark of any particular culture. Great Basin sites formerly offered splendid examples of the limited distribution of distinctive dart point types, wherein one type was almost completely confined to one intermontane drainage basin, while in an adjoining basin an entirely different type of point could be found associated with the same lithic pattern found in the first. In the archaeology of Early Man this situation has often been used as a basis for the formulation of distinctive cultures. If the same analytic technique were applied to a local bow and arrow people, such as some Yuman group, who made three different types of arrow points, it would be obligatory to assume that three different cultures were involved and that each was of a non-Yuman facies.

PATINA AND ANTIQUITY
Since the word *patina,* when applied to lithic artifacts, has often been used as a catchall, it is necessary to define its nature and meaning as used in this report, and to define as well other postfabrication features. Here, patina applies only to chemical alteration of mineral constituents, and might better be termed *oxidation. Ground-patina* signifies a coating of a different nature and origin. Although two different processes may be involved in the formation of ground-patina, the end product is chemically much the same. In one process, the

chemical alteration results in a porosity, which will with time absorb iron and manganese salts if these are present in the soil. This phenomenon has been sometimes referred to as *soil-stain*. The second type does not necessitate the presence of an initial chemical alteration, and will form on the under side of an artifact fashioned from even glassy materials which have rested for a long time in a static position. The deposition is the result of capillary action, but its formation is entirely dependent upon the presence of a ferruginous soil, and therefore its distribution is limited.

Patina

When using patina as a basis for determining the relative age of similar artifacts, the artifacts compared must be fashioned from the same lithic material, as different media do not decompose at the same rate. Stones and minerals of a highly silicious nature, such as chalcedony, jasper, and obsidian, are particularly resistant to chemical alteration. San Dieguito artifacts made from such materials generally display no patina, and in those which do have a patina, it is of an incipient nature. These are invariably associated with soils containing a very high percentage of alkali salts. Some chalcedony implements occasionally possess an imposing depth of patina, because they have been subjected to a high degree of heat. These can be identified by their crackled surfaces.

The parent rocks from which artifacts are made often have a very deep and ancient patina. If this was not completely removed in making the tool, the examiner may believe that he is studying a postfabrication patina. Therefore, in measuring depth one should select a section through a facet showing the least altered thickness of all, and even then one cannot always be certain that he is not viewing some portion of the original cortex. Regardless of the material used, I have never found a San Dieguito implement to have a patina in excess of two millimeters in thickness, and in such cases they were all, with one exception, of the first phase. The exception is in the Southwestern Aspect, where artifacts of the second phase, when made of a local felsite, sometimes have a patina of equal depth.

Sandblasting

The effects of subaerial erosion are often found on the most ancient tools in the sandy regions of the American Desert. This applies both to San Dieguito and, to a lesser degree, to Amargosa artifacts. Cultural material of later cultures is exempt, except for the gathering of a slight sheen. This phenomenon, which is caused by sandblasting, sometimes is advanced to a stage where all evidence of faceting is obliterated, and formerly sharp margins are rounded until a biface or projectile point can only be distinguished as such by its profile shape. The scouring action naturally removes all patina. If, however, the artifact has become firmly lodged in a desert pavement, the patina and faceting of

This ceremonial mesa, with its strange series of circular cairns, is in southeast Inyo County, California.

It is in the desert region east of the southern end of Death Valley, south of Shoshone and near State Highway 178.

Nearby is the Amargosa River, with its intermittent flow of alkaline water.

It is from this river and its dry valley that Malcolm Rogers drew the name of Amargosa for the people who he believed followed the San Dieguitoans into the lower basin.

He concluded that this very large gravel pictograph, a series of twenty-eight cairns, was of Amargosa I age because the enclosed worked flakes were too fresh to be of the San Dieguito period.

When the Amargosans occupied this mesa, the river probably had a much heavier flow.

As so often is the case, some artifacts of the San Dieguito I people were found in this same area, at site M-118, though only a few cleared sleeping circles were present.

33

its under side will be preserved.

Desert Varnish

The lustrous brown to black veneer known as *desert varnish,* which is found on both desert stones and artifacts, is also of some dating value, but to what degree is as yet uncertain. The coating, which is due to the deposition of iron and manganese salts, is a world wide phenomenon, and is found at all elevations from sea level up into very high mountain altitudes, but its origin is not always the same. When its derivation is from the decomposition of ferric minerals, no particular altitude or climate is involved. In the American Desert, the type with which we are concerned is confined to low altitudes and is seldom to be

The various kinds of surface alteration found on Far Western Early Man stone tools are of some aid in determining their relative age.

Malcolm Rogers used tool typology, settlement pattern distribution, and geology in conjunction with patina to develop the phases and aspects of the San Dieguito Complex.

Many of his conclusions, drawn from surface site evidence, have been substantiated through the excavation of buried, stratified sites.

In the first column, top to bottom, are three Central Aspect San Dieguito I specimens exhibiting a dark desert varnish.

The middle column shows a San Dieguito II-III chopping tool from W-81-B, reworked by La Jolla people; a San Dieguito I chopping tool from C-43-A, reworked by later Indians; and a San Dieguito II-III end scraper from W-167, reworked by La Jollans.

In the right column are three San Dieguito II-III artifacts from the Central Aspect. The top two are a Lake Mojave knife and crescentic stone, both badly eroded by sandblasting. On the bottom is a small domed discoidal scraper from C-127-A, which shows no patina nor sandblasting. (Scale in inches).

found above the 1000-foot contour. Its presence has been demonstrated by Laudermilk (1931) as originating from the decomposition of a local species of lichen and its spores, both of which have a high content of iron and manganese salts. Subsequent to decomposition, the salts become oxidized through long exposure to intense sunlight. Afterward, the veneer gains high luster through the action of wind-driven silts and fine particles of sand. It is evident that porous stone was not essential to the formation of desert varnish, as it is commonly found upon such glassy material as chalcedony and jasper. In the Colorado Desert, San Dieguito I artifacts often exhibit a dual veneer layer of postfabrication age, a patina overlaid by desert varnish, while San Dieguito II artifacts show only incipient stages of the two. Neither Amargosa nor Yuman lithic work possesses either patina or desert varnish, and some of the Yuman artifacts are at least 1000 years old.

There are many unknown factors which need to be understood before desert varnish can be of chronological value. First, it is not known if the lichen involved is still an active element, nor if this organism thrives in cycles with intermittent periods of near extinction and subsequent recolonization. Nothing is known about the time required for the formation of desert varnish (except for what can be gained from a study of undated cultural material) nor the length of time it will persist after the formative period. It has been observed, however, that in sandy regions which are subjected to periodic winds of high velocity, the veneer has been scoured from the upper surfaces, and although this appears to be a quite recent phenomenon, it could have been duplicated in past eras of extreme aridity.

Despite the unsatisfactory evidence of postfabrication alterations when applied as chronological indicators in surface archaeology, their use along with other data has been of considerable importance in establishing distinct lithic patterns.

35

CHAPTER III

SAN DIEGUITO I IN THE CENTRAL ASPECT

A FEW COMPARISONS

It has been some thirty years now since a widespread lithic industry, thought then to be peculiar to the Colorado Desert, was formally presented under the name of Malpais Culture. With the artifacts, certain associated architectural elements were incorporated to complete a pattern. Varied interpretations and commentary followed, but this long period of speculation was ended in 1950, with the publication of the cultural stratigraphy of Ventana Cave by Haury (Haury et al., 1950). Here, in a basal position, was found the complete San Dieguito I phase pattern in association with an extinct fauna. Although there

On a low terrace at the southeast foot of the Fish Creek Mountains in Imperial County, in the Borrego-Anza Desert, at site C-129-B, there is a little circle of rocks held fast in desert pavement.

It is classified as a "sleeping circle" of a primitive people who sought shelter at night behind rocks or rock-supported brush and grass.

The people referred to as San Dieguito-ans preferred the terraces of the desert region above lakes and streams now long extinct, and perhaps from which they could watch for game or their enemies.

In the reckoning of nature's time, this particular terrace is swiftly being reduced to sand by aridity.

There is evidence that over the centuries the Colorado Desert became progressively though slowly drier, reaching its present state less than 100 years ago. Even today, as at the time the Spaniards crossed the hot land with great hardship, to those who know its secrets the desert can yield sufficient plant and animal life to support an aboriginal existence.

was some disagreement among the authorities who studied the exact time implications, there was among them unanimity as to the geological period with which the San Dieguito I horizon was associated and that was the Last Pluvial.

In 1958 (Rogers, 1958) I presented the alternative that perhaps the Little Pluvial was the one represented. I am, however, agreeable to accepting Carbon 14 dates.

Crude and Scarce

The lack of pattern, crudity of workmanship, and the apparent meager amount of worked stone left in this area by these early Paleo-Indians seems to bother some critics. However, the paucity of San Dieguito I worked stone results from the diffuse nature of the occupation. The situation here is quite different from those involving settled encampments or those of an intermittent nature, where a high yield develops from deposits left through reoccupation over a considerable period of time. If an area of twenty square miles is explored, the resulting yield is disappointing unless practically every part of it is crisscrossed on foot. Furthermore, a few short field excursions to an even greater area will yield no greater results, unless the examination is of the same intensive nature. There are few small rich areas in the entire San Dieguito I domain.

San Dieguito II Comparisons

When comparing the relative amounts of San Dieguito I and San Dieguito II worked stone collected from one area, the yields may equate, while in other areas one phase yield will exceed the other, or both be unrepresented. The situation is due to a change in the method of living at the inception of the second phase. For some unknown reason the people of the second phase preferred to camp in certain selected spots, even if intermittently. As a result of this manner of living, the archaeological debris of this period is found to be concentrated in a few places, and the numerical importance of the artifacts becomes a study of diffusion versus concentration, rather than a study of quantitative importance.

Pericu Comparisons

In presenting the everyday life of the Pericu of Baja California, Baegert (1772) provided a cultural parallelism representative of the San Dieguito I way of life. The Pericu had no camps of a permanent nature, and seldom slept in the same place for over three consecutive nights. Each morning the man and woman went their separate ways in search of the sustenance which each were trained to hunt and prepare. Because of the separation, each individual must have fashioned his or her individual tools, a situation leading to an archaeological distribution of a diffused nature, as well as to duplication. This would upset any modern study of the relative numerical importance of specific elements in the complete pattern, unless the sex-tool relationship is kept in mind. As it is a known ethnological fact that there was a sex-origin deviation in the nature of certain lithic tools, it stimulates and challenges the archaeological mind to speculate, but probably to no avail.

La Jolla Comparisons

A similarity to the San Dieguito I lithic pattern, with all its crudities and an even lesser variety of artifacts, is met with in the San Dieguito confines of the Pacific Coast, where it is found in the La Jolla culture.

As San Dieguito archaeology is intimately associated with La Jolla archaeology in the Southwestern Aspect, one cannot be studied to advantage without a knowledge of both. Unfortunately, I have never published either a final report or a partial resumé of La Jolla culture. It is hoped that this brief note will indicate to some extent the nature of the relationship in the absence of a more complete discussion.

La Jolla economy was dependent upon seafood, almost exclusively of a shellfish nature. The diet was supplemented to a great degree with edible seeds, a conclusion derived from the large number of metates present in the middens. The material culture was an impoverished one with a flaked stone tool assemblage so restricted in distinct types of artifacts and primitive in form fashioning, that one would have to turn to some Lower Paleolithic pattern of the Old World to find a comparison. Although I had worked on the La Jolla problem many years previous to 1929, it was in that year that investigations on a large scale were first made possible through a grant-in-aid from the Smithsonian Institution. All the large middens of San Diego County and those of Baja California, as far south as San Quentín were test-trenched.

The work indicated the presence of two major developmental phases and I recorded them as La Jolla I and La Jolla II.

The differentiation was established through stratigraphic studies and settlement-pattern distribution, in conjunction with the land forms involved, and recorded changes in sea level.

The La Jolla I artifact pattern is unbelievably simple and the artifacts few. Ninety percent of the worked stone is confined to simple primary flakes. The La Jolla II phase carries over old forms, and adds some new ones, showing considerable increase in the number of tools and improvement in flaking technique, but all together it provided a poor kit of tools for performing the acts necessary to survival; yet for the La Jollans it sufficed. The investigations also proved that the San Dieguito culture occupied a basal position to the La Jolla horizon.

If the entire assemblage from the La Jolla shell middens were to be scattered over any equal area of the San Dieguito I terrain, it is doubtful that more than a fraction of it would ever be found, or recognized as tools if found. The artifacts of the first La Jolla period are mostly of one nature, namely, primary flakes. Not until the second phase, La Jolla II, were flaked implements of the nature and technical quality of San Dieguito I artifacts produced. In fact, a chief difference between the contrasted patterns lies in the absence of the metate in the San Dieguito I pattern and its presence in the La Jolla I pattern.

DISTRIBUTION AND AGE OF SAN DIEGUITO I

With the years, and a broadened program of exploration, the distribution of San Dieguito I sites was expanded to a much wider area than was originally supposed. It involves sections of four American and three Mexican states, and wherever it is found, it retains its individuality. It crosses all known cultural boundaries, and yet remains unacculturated. Other peculiarities lie in its distribution. Fully seventy percent of its sites have been found below an elevation of 1000 feet. These in turn are not adjacent to modern water resources, except in two instances, the terraces of the Colorado and lower Gila rivers. The major distribution is marginal to the minor dry wash channels of the American Desert where it is found on upper terraces, adjacent mesas, and broad expanses of desert pavement.

Conditions necessary to maintain life in the San Dieguito I environment require a climate which has not been obtained since the Last Pluvial, or at least the Little Pluvial. Either one might have provided sufficient precipitation for man to exist anywhere in the Basin and Range province. If either of these periods of excessive precipitation were coeval with the San Dieguito I occupation, we should expect to find the archaeological remains distributed over the strands of fossil lakes of one of these periods, but such is not the case. The San Dieguito I cultural features are marginal to fossil stream channels and seldom near lakes.

This is a challenge to engage in climatological restoration, and although I have pored over the problem for several decades, I can find no sound basis for a plausible explanation. There is a possibility however, that many San Dieguito II elements are but refinements of their San Dieguito I equivalents. Therefore, in surface archaeology, the older elements could become lost in the general melange or be judged San Dieguito II rejects. The weak point of this theory is that the cruder specimens found on San Dieguito II sites have no greater depth of patina or sandblasting than do their refined counterparts.

Some of the reasons for assigning great antiquity to San Dieguito I, aside from the necessity of a universal water supply, are these: The artifacts display a greater depth of alteration than that found on implements of subsequent cultures, even those of the following San Dieguito II phase. San Dieguito I artifacts are not found associated with later cultural material, except in rare instances. Furthermore, all of the elements are essential links leading to the fuller pattern and refinements of the San Dieguito II phase. Some geological evidence indicates that the artifacts, sleeping circles, ceremonial figures, trail shrines, and even trails antedate the formation of the desert pavement phenomenon.

DESERT PAVEMENT

Desert pavements are residual features resulting from surface degradation of large expanses of mildly inclined alluvial material. Their surface gradients are so slight that precipitation runoff may be excluded as an explanation of their origin. It would seem that wind-scour was the chief degrading agent. The major effect of thunderstorms, accompanied by heavy and sudden precipitation is to produce surface sheet-flooding, which results only in the sanding in of shallow pavement depressions. The inception of this cyclonic type of climate in the American Desert is recent, and seems to have begun not more than a hundred years ago; at least it has reached its climax during that short period of time.

Those who have been able to observe the topographical alterations of even the last forty or fifty years in the Far West have witnessed the sudden rejuvenation of a land form that was stable for perhaps several millenia. There is no geological evidence to indicate that, previous to this most recent climatic change, desert pavement was not primarily brought about through aeolian erosion.

As the alluvial material concerned is preponderantly composed of sand, silt, and a minor percentage of stones, accumulated to considerable depth, much fine material had to be carried away in order to produce the end product—a tight mosaic of small pebbles and some coarser cobble elements. Experiments have been conducted to de-

The scene at the top has not been disturbed for many thousands of years.

It shows what has been described as a large sleeping circle, or shelter, perhaps just as it was when a group of primitive people may have lain down behind its black volcanic rocks and huddled together for warmth and protection.

Much of the area around it has changed. Gone are the waters which once enriched the desert floor. The summers then were not as hot nor the nights perhaps as cold as now.

This circular clearing is on an exceptionally high terrace on Pilot Knob, or Black Mesa, at site C-45, west of the Colorado River in an area criss-crossed by remnants of many prehistoric trails.

It was on this mesa that Malcolm Rogers said he first recognized what he described as a sleeping circle.

The picture below is of Silver Dry Lake, a remnant of ancient Lake Mojave, in central San Bernardino County. The old shore line can be seen etched against the hill in the distance.

In the view of Malcolm Rogers the San Dieguitoans lived here long enough to follow a shrinkage of Lake Mojave down to newly exposed features such as sand spits and bay bars.

termine how much of a vertical section must be winnowed away in order to produce the same number of pebbles which went into the composition of the final capping pavement.

Among the several tests which have been made in order to determine the amount of alluvium which was removed during the development of a desert pavement, the following one has been singled out, as it served a twofold purpose, having both a geological and an archaeological value. The site lies on a pavement one mile back of the west shore line of the Blake Sea, in Imperial County, California, specifically T-17-S, R-12-E, Section 25. Here a San Dieguito I pick and a Yuman II pick were found in close proximity on a desert pavement.

The square yard of pavement was measured, cut, and all the pebbles from the surface to a depth of three inches were removed and counted. Beneath this level, the alluvium was screened and the pebbles and larger cobbles saved, until their count equaled the number found in the capping three inches. Then the depth of the excavation was measured, the result being a rough estimate of how many inches the original surface might have stood above the present pavement. I removed 178 stones from the pavement and 178 from the excavation, at which point the excavation reached a depth of eighteen inches. This was considered to approximate the prepavement elevation.

These artifacts [*now in the possession of Mr. Julian Hayden of Tucson, Arizona —ed.*] are almost twins, in that both are fashioned from elongated chalcedony cobbles of the same size, color and magmatic origin. The San Dieguito I pick was sandblasted and slightly altered, and sat well down in the pavement mosaic. The Yuman II pick was neither altered nor eroded, and rested on the surface of the pavement, surrounded by spawls which had been struck from the parent cobble during the process of manufacture. It can be argued, it is true, that the San Dieguito I pick did not pre-

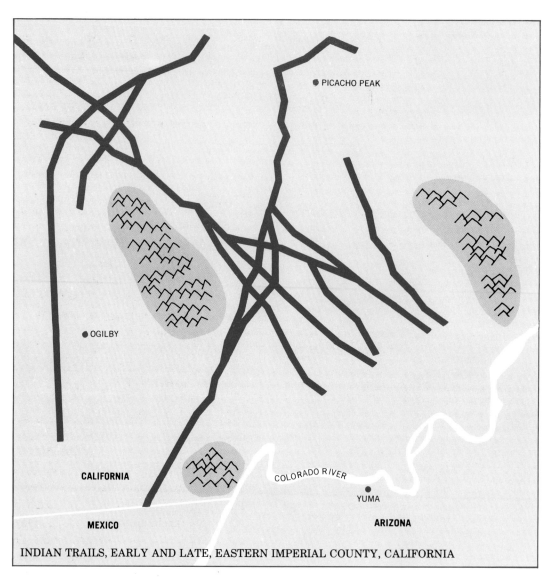

INDIAN TRAILS, EARLY AND LATE, EASTERN IMPERIAL COUNTY, CALIFORNIA

CHARTS SHOWING GENESIS OF DESERT PAVEMENT

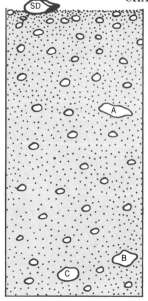 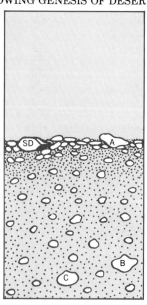 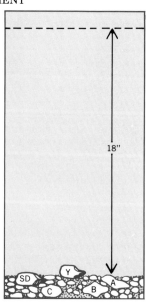

date the beginning of the pavement evolution and that it was deposited on the surface during a transitional stage, but it still demands a certain antiquity far in excess of the deposition of the Yuman pick.

Like experiments have been conducted on marginal lacustrine features of several fossil lakes of the Basin and Range province. When strands, bay-bars, and spits composed of fine sediments were tested, a maximal elevation reduction from the original amounted to as much as thirty

The Colorado River's desert country is crisscrossed with old foot trails.

Not all of them are ancient, in terms of man's existence in that region, though some of them were used perhaps as long as 10,000 years ago.

These, mapped by Malcolm Rogers are in eastern Imperial County, California.

Some of them were distinctly early trails, others late ones, and some have been used by all Indian peoples. Not all can be traced to any destination.

Generally they connected what Rogers thought were camping or ceremonial sites. Others perhaps were war trails.

Rogers had a theory that the desert surface on which the oldest trails and artifacts were found by him and others was exactly the same as when they were laid down perhaps a hundred centuries ago.

In a test which he conducted, and for which the lower sketches were made, he demonstrated to his own satisfaction that desert pavements were residual features, "fossilized" as it were, and resulting from surface degradation probably brought about by wind scouring.

In his test he marked a pebble as a San Dieguito I artifact and gauged its descent to finally mix with other pebbles and cobblestones (A, B, and C) in the formation of a tight mosaic in the final capping pavement. At this stage the Yumans left their artifacts (Y) with those of a long vanished people.

The original surface impression would be imbedded permanently.

inches. While this is not impressive in itself, it is important in estimating the ancient volume of impounded water and the relationship of one shore feature to another as well as to the overflow level, when there was one. The factor of post-lake depression of shore features has an archaeological significance, in that it may explain why surface artifacts of the same age vary in the degree of alteration and sandblast erosion displayed. It is quite possible that the fresher appearing implements originally occupied a subsurface position for a greater length of time than did the greatly altered ones.

The studies of degradation of such land forms have no significant time value until the associated archaeology is dated; then the elapsed time will permit correlation with the degree of degradation. This is but one of many ways in which archaeological time can be of aid to geological time interpretation.

In order to visualize what has happened since the San Dieguito I period, it seems necessary to assume that the artifacts, cleared circles, intaglio ceremonials, cairn structures, and trails were created while most of the alluvial surfaces were more or less soil-like, and that present features are not pictures of the near recent, but fossils of the past. The non-boulder-rimmed sleeping circles, trails, and some ceremonials are so much a part of present land forms that many are observable only under the most favorable lighting, a crosslight just after dawn or just before sunset. There are hundreds of apparent circles and ceremonial lines of such an indefinite nature that it is impossible to determine whether they are man-made or due to natural erosion. An untold number too, have been destroyed by the meandering of drainage channels. It is common to find, on the beveled margins of terraces and mesas, only halves and portions of sleeping circles left intact, as well as abrupt trail endings.

Further evidence pertinent to terrain conditions in the San Dieguito I period is the location of artifacts and worked stone.

43

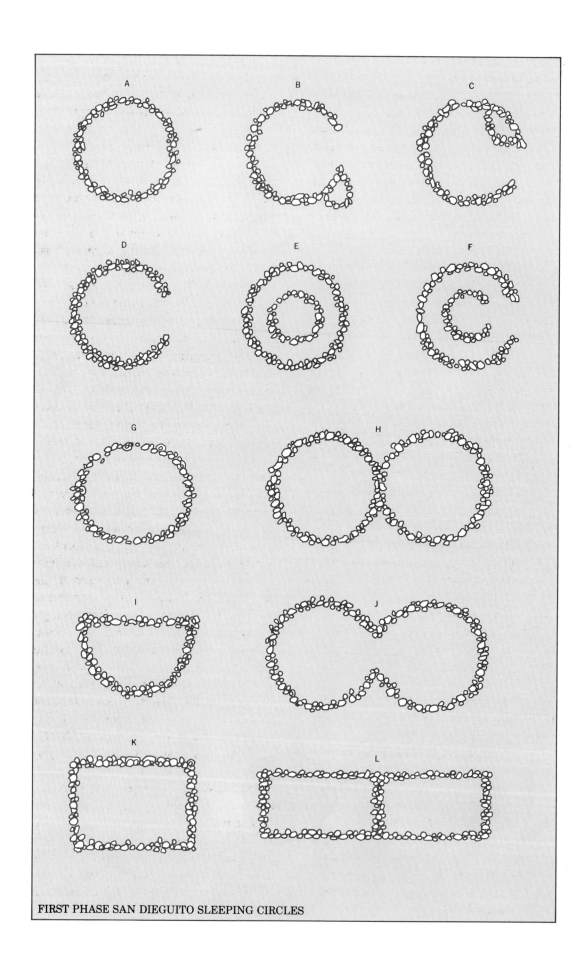

FIRST PHASE SAN DIEGUITO SLEEPING CIRCLES

Because of their position on the talus slopes of terraces and mesas, we can postulate that the latter were so covered with soil that flakable lithic material could be found only on the exposed talus slopes. The condition is universal in the entire San Dieguito area. Artifacts are seldom found in or around the sleeping circles. Further, marginal recession would tend to produce concentrations of artifacts on the talus slopes.

Sleeping Circles

The boulder-rimmed type of sleeping circle was made at the same time as the type without boulders. The construction and distribution of the two forms are governed entirely by the nature of the terrain upon which they are found. They appear on rocky land forms where coarse stones and even small boulders had to be removed from the surface in order to produce the

The rock formations which Malcolm Rogers identified as the "sleeping circles" of prehistoric man were not always circular.

In all, he counted more than 8000 of them in his forty years of archaeological investigations in the desert and semi-arid regions of the Far West.

This chart was drawn under his supervision and it records the many strange shapes that he found, from tight circles to double oblong shapes.

The most usual common types were A, D, G, H and J.

The rarer types were B, C, E, F, I, K and L.

The ones shown here he considered as belonging to the first phase, or the oldest, San Dieguito people.

Why some were circular and others square, no one knows.

Rogers once described the prehistoric people as lying down together in these enclosed rock formations "like sardines in a can."

The people of recent prehistoric and historic cultures also left stone-rimmed circles, but these always had a space for a doorway and served as the foundation for a thatched wickiup, or hut.

circular clearings. The stones were then used to build the confining rims, or windbreaks. Today the rims, when found intact, are never more than two tiers high, with a maximum height of fourteen inches. Rim rocks above the ground level are of the same color and possess on all sides the same depth of chemical alteration, while the members of the lowest tier which set into the ground carry a coating of caliche on the under sides. Even the boulder-tiered circles have no apertures suggesting a doorway.

The discernible sleeping circle seems to have gone out of vogue with the beginning of the second phase. If any were constructed during this period, none which can be positively identified are extant. Several sites which appear to be transitional have been found. A typical site of this nature is on Chemehuevi Wash, San Bernardino County (SDM-M-67), where rimmed circles and both San Dieguito I and San Dieguito II artifacts were found in conjunction.

The nature of sleeping circles, their distribution, and their restriction to a particular type of terrain has been described several times before. As this is not a study of a particular section but an overall report for the first time, some addenda may be of value. Fully ninety percent of the clearings are circular; the other ten percent, with the exception of a few rectangular ones, are oval in outline. They often occur in group combinations up to the number of nine. When this is the case, they are in close juxtaposition, some clearings being only three feet apart, and the perimeters of two often merging. These groups could have been constructed by the members of a single family, sleeping in the area for a few nights only, a custom often followed by wandering hunting bands. As sleeping circles occur in such great numbers and over such a vast area, it must have taken a population of nomadic hunters, thin in numbers, several thousand years to produce so many.

There are, marginal to the Central Aspect and in scattered loci within the gen-

eral field, boulder-rimmed clearings built by later peoples, such as Yumans, Papagos, Shoshoneans and Paiutes. They cannot be confused with the San Dieguito structures, as either in them or in close proximity is found characteristic cultural debris of those who built them. Also, their topographical positioning is different from that of the ancient ones, since they are close to present or recently available water resources. Furthermore, they are not to be found on desert pavement, nor on the terraces of fossil streams. Unlike San Dieguito clearings, they are frequently found at high elevations, near mountain springs and water holes. The problem of cultural allocation has also been simplified through studying style structures within understood archaeological and ethnological

This line of rocks 129 feet long, at site C-70, is laid across an ancient trail in the Colorado Desert in eastern Imperial County north of the Carga Mucacha Mountains.

In the opinion of Malcolm Rogers, the rocks may have been laid by the San Dieguito I people as part of a ceremonial alignment.

Or, they might have been laid by subsequent Yuman people to effect a superstitious blocking of the spirits of the departed San Dieguito men which might still be using the trail out of habit.

This is in a very large area he classified as San Dieguito I, with numerous boulder-rimmed circular sleeping clearings, or "houses," a few of them ranging to sixteen and eighteen feet in diameter.

In later years, early Yuman Indians blazed a trail across this area, from the Colorado River to the lower delta region.

During the Yuman period, according to Rogers, a war trail from the Mojave country to Yuma was laid over it and used until the early 1800's.

The Yuman men passing over these trails seemed to have frequently stopped off to work the gravels. For an average distance of 100 feet on either side may be found unoxidized flakes and cores.

areas. Late desert peoples always left a door aperture in the enclosing boulder rims, oriented either to the east or south.

Ancient Trails

One impressive phenomenon left by the San Dieguito ancients is the great number of trails, and the fact that so many of them survived, even in a fragmented condition. They are best preserved on the extensive flat desert pavements of the American Desert in its southernmost parts. Any unnatural alteration of a pavement surface seems to become an imperishable record, no matter how much time has intervened; the record simply becomes more blurred with elapsed time. Regardless of how ancient the disturbance was, a discerning eye can detect some vestige.

Desert trails, because of their number, diverse origins, and wide dispersion in the arid regions of the Far West, warrant a separate report. Therefore a restricted area has been chosen for consideration at this time because it embraces all aspects of the problem. On both banks of the Colorado and Gila rivers are innumerable trails leading into the interior regions. Those which have potsherds on their margins are not difficult to assign culturally, because of the characteristic Yuman ceramic types present. This does not preclude the possibility, however, that the Yumans in some instances used the trails of more ancient peoples. An observer who has had a fairly broad and lengthy experience with desert trails cannot help noticing that nonceramic trails have certain distinctions which set them apart. Their pathways are not trenched, but are in the same plane with the surrounding surfaces; hence the degree of alteration on the stones which lie in them is the same as that found on the stones of the surrounding surface. For these reasons they are difficult to discern. Furthermore, when found, they can be traced but short distances, and only on very flat terrain, so many millenia of erosion have passed since they were made. Exceptions to this are paths crossing broad expanses of desert pavement, where a trail

may be traced for a mile or two before it becomes lost in post-trail erosion features. If one keeps to their courses they can often be picked up again on the next area of desert pavement. Another peculiarity of the older trails is that several will converge at a low mountainous pass until they all become one. Then on the opposite side of the pass, the single trail will divide directions and lead to no modern sources of water, nor to anywhere in particular, as far as anyone today can discern.

Trail Shrines

Along these trails and in their vicinities are found artifacts, sleeping circles, cobble trail shrines, and boulder-outlined ceremonial configurations. The early shrines are barren of offertory material, except for an occasional man-made flake. The shrines unfortunately contain no identifiable intermediate cultural deposits, such

Trail shrines of ancient people were made up of simple offerings, generally rocks, presumably in the belief they would prevent fatigue, sickness or injury while traveling.

One ancient Indian trail can be followed for sixteen miles through the Picacho Hills on the Colorado River in the country north of Yuma but on the California side of the river.

It is mostly a migration and trade trail of many prehistoric and historic peoples.

In Picacho Pass, at the half-way point, is a large trail shrine at site C-80, one of three, and its base and most of the bulk is thought to be of San Dieguito I origin.

The top half, according to Malcolm Rogers, is of Yuman origin capped with Mexican and American deposits.

This trail forms a short cut around the big east bend in the Colorado River for travelers going north and south and as it approaches the Yuma Vally it has several branches leading to different parts of the valley.

Besides the numerous gravel pictographs, in the south section are many petroglyphs, probably of Yuman origin, carved on small boulders along the course of the trail.

as Amargosa artifacts, lying between the San Dieguito and Yuman periods. If any intermediate people indulged in the practice, they merely added more stones to the cairns. Those which are adjacent to Yuman trails contain a capping of material characteristic of the period. The San Dieguito I type of shrine is most often found on the summit of a divide or in a mountain pass, as are the later Yuman shrines. There are, however, sporadic occurrences of this type which are not on summits and have no discernible trails leading to them or near them. A common variety has a large boulder as a nucleus, around and over which the cobbles were deposited. A good example of the type is to be found in eastern Imperial County, California. It is located in Section 30, T-14-S: R-22-E, east of the outer Picacho trail (SDM-C-86). It lies on a detached mesa 300 feet from the nearest San Dieguito I trail, from which it is separated by a deep arroyo.

The Sacrificial Shrine

With the beginning of the Yuman period, wayfarers turned to a sacrificial debauch of personal property. Men deposited their tobacco pipes and women deliberately smashed whole ceramic vessels on the shrines. Shell jewelry and food offerings were also made. The trait continued throughout the Yuman period down into historic times, until even the American prospector, perhaps in a facetious mood, added contributions to the cairn in the way of a mule shoe or a whiskey bottle.

At the end of the Yuman I period (Rogers, 1945), travelers ceased to deposit and destroy intact property and became content to pick up a trail sherd or a stone while en route, for deposition in the nearest shrine. This change, in conjunction with the disappearance of many other traits of the first period, emphasizes the difference between Yuman I and later Yuman culture phases. In southern Arizona there are some comparable conditions, but shrines outside the Yuman sphere contain only a few potsherds representative of local ceramic horizons.

49

Some of the large shrines were vandalized as early as ninety years ago, in the belief that they covered buried Spanish treasure. The diggers, after trenching through them, often dug pits down three feet into the cemented underlying rocks because of their misplaced faith. Those which had but a single trench through them have been of some archaeological value, but it was the few intact ones which provided the developmental history and invaluable cultural sequences.

Another type of Yuman shrine, which is usually barren of potsherds, is to be found on men's trails. These were long trails blazed out by Yumans for either trade purposes or the movement of war parties. Some of these shrines are so large that their beginnings must have predated the Yuman period, providing each traveler deposited but a single stone, which was the historic practice of the Yumans. The largest one I have ever seen is on the Yuma-Mojave war trail at the apex of the Mopi Pass in the Turtle Mountains of San

This is an ancient "ceremonial" site in the Mojave Desert.

Its location is on a long spur of the Cady mesa running out into the Crucero Basin, north of Ludlow and just east of the Cady Mountains in central San Bernardino County, California.

Malcolm Rogers classified it as M-56, and almost strictly a San Dieguito I ceremonial site, with many boulder alignments composed of snake-like patterns and simpler forms based on circles and connecting lines.

The largest alignment is a double line more than 400 feet long. This picture was taken looking westward up the spur along one of the snake-like alignments.

They have been disturbed only by erosion and growth of creosote bushes. What they represented to the Ancient Hunters of the Far West is not known.

Thousands of years later the Yumans used the site as a quarry, as they so often did in the passing of time.

Bernardino County, California (SDM-M-125). Here three identical cairns grew so large that they eventually coalesced to become one. The total weight of the stones in this shrine must approximate three tons.

There is no mystery regarding the purpose of the trail shrine, as the thought behind the offering is similar the world over, whether the shrine is in California or Mongolia. The wayfarer believed that this offering, even though it was but a simple stone, would prohibit his becoming fatigued, sick, or injured through falling while in transit. From what is known of the primitive mind, it is safe to conclude that the controlling concept had to do with appeasement of an evil spirit which caused misfortune and was a resident of the region. There is some material evidence to substantiate the assumption. It has been quite often found that where San Dieguito peoples, and, later on, Yumans, were traveling in the same direction, the latter made a new parallel trail some feet away from the more ancient trail rather than walk in a trail of the dead. The two will converge into one where they pass through a narrow defile, but will immediately diverge on the other side. A few instances have been found of a Yuman trail crossing a San Dieguito trail at right angles, or nearly so, where the Yumans had arranged lines of boulders across the more ancient trail, as if to stop the spirits of the dead from walking the trail.

The accompanying cultural debris along the trails of the American Desert has provided a horizontal cultural stratigraphy of considerable value, even though certain horizons are missing. For instance, typical San Dieguito II and San Dieguito III artifacts are almost never met with on the ancient trails. It is therefore adjudged that the intricate and widespread system of trails was laid down during the first phase period. This theory, however, leaves us with an inexplicable dilemma. The people of the second and third phase periods, during their migrational movements and especially on hunting excursions to and from their home grounds, either had to travel older trails or make new ones for themselves. An even more baffling situation exists, in that San Dieguito II and San Dieguito III inhabited both sides of the Colorado and Gila river valleys, but left no trace of occupancy on the immediate terraces of either river, while San Dieguito I artifacts are strongly represented on both. Then, to further perplex the prehistorian of the region, one finds the same situation repeated again by the immediate inheritors of the general area, the Amargosans —no Amargosa artifacts on the trails, some in trail shrines, and none on the terraces of the two major rivers of the territory. The sole exception is the finding of late Amargosa culture (basic Basketmaker, my interpretation) in a basal position at Willow Beach on the Colorado River (Harrington, 1937).

Aligned Rock Ceremonials

The creation of cultural features by the alteration of natural surfaces is widespread in the territory concerned, and takes many forms. Because of certain structural characteristics they all fall naturally into three categories: the intaglio or surface-depressed configuration, the boulder-outlined figure, and the grouped cobble-cairn figure. The first named type is to be found only on pavements which consist of small pebbles and some cobbles. It seems plausible to believe that their patterns were produced by the concerted effort of a group of dancers moving in more or less controlled directions, as in the main they take a circular or oval form. Van der Post (1958, p. 266) witnessed the Bushmen of the Kalihari Desert dancing in a circle hour after hour until they had worn a groove up to their calves. Much more has been witnessed and recorded about the Australian aborigines' ceremonial dances wherein the participants moved in more or less restricted lanes. The American patterns have become so much a part of the desert pavement that it is seldom possible to trace the complete circumference of a dance circle, if such they were.

Cultural Association of Rock Alignments

The entire subject of ceremonial ground figures is extremely complicated in terms of cultural origins, and their numbers and distribution are so great that the topic warrants a study in itself, far beyond the scope of the present report. The subject was discussed at some length in an earlier publication (Rogers, 1939). The fact that various aborigines, even down to historic time, made arrangements of natural surfaces, and often more than once on the same surface, makes it frequently impossible to do more than assign the work to two classes, the older and the younger. Superposition, when found, proves the greatest aid in establishing relative antiquity. Variability in art form, studied in conjunction with weathering, is also of importance. Only types which are considered to be of sufficient antiquity for a San Dieguito age will be discussed at this time.

The most ancient figures might be termed gravel or boulder alignments since not one of them delineates even an impressionistic reproduction of a faunal or floral form. During the Yuman period, however, realistic figures of a recognizable nature were constructed. As these and Yuman sherd trails are sometimes found imposed on the older figures, vertical cultural stratigraphy is provided. We still have no clue to the exact period when the pre-Yuman ones were created, except that only artifacts of the San Dieguito I period are found with them and in their vicinities. This seems to indicate that the custom was not carried on during the second and third phases. The Amargosans, the immediate inheritors of the old San Dieguito territory, left no evidence of having built such structures; they seemed to attain an artistic escape through making petroglyphs and a few cave paintings (Smith, 1957). The motifs used in both forms of petrography are reproduced in the Basketmaker culture, and also appear in the petrographic work of later peoples of the Basin and Range province.

Boulder-outlined ceremonials are almost absent from the terraces of the Colorado and Gila rivers, perhaps because of the lack of large boulders in the river gravels. This type is invariably found on the mesa lands of the American Desert, whose surface ingredients are of a coarse, rocky nature. They take the form of long alignments of irregularly spaced boulders; these usually set well into the underlying surface. Their bases are caliche-encrusted to the same thickness as that found on subsurface boulders. At some sites only a single line is present, but usually the ceremonial is composed of two parallel alignments. There is no constant spacing to be found anywhere. Sometimes there are short ancillary lines present which join the main lines at various angles, and cleared pathways paralleling the long lines. In rare instances there are a few cobble cairns found scattered about the figures, spaced with no discernible plan. Occasionally a line ends at a cairn. I have never seen any two that faintly resemble each other, except for the single and double alignment types, and even these are seldom oriented in the same general direction. The lines vary in length from forty to 500 feet at various sites. Except for a few deviates, they were all built on flat terrain. The few that have been found on gently to fairly steep gradients all show the effect of subsequent erosion, and the boulders are mostly out of line.

The Construction of Alignments

The size of the boulders used is in direct relation to immediate availability, with no attempt made during construction to bring to the site boulders of a larger size than those close at hand. Hence there is considerable disparity from site to site in the size of the boulders used. In one site they may average only twelve pounds in weight, and on another some may weigh up to one hundred pounds. As with other San Dieguito I architectural features, foreign cultural material has seldom been found in or near them.

The grouped cairn structure is as important, numerically, as the boulder align-ment ceremonial. Most, because of their nature and cultural isolation, offer no problem as to their cultural affinity. There are some, however, in the Mojave Desert, especially at quarry sites, which involve non-San Dieguito elements and seem to have resulted from the efforts of more than one people. The quarry material left reflects the same situation.

Although Yuman ideographic thought is relatively understood, the question is, is it valid to project it back for thousands of years into the past as an unmodified abstraction, and to equate it with foreign thought? I do not think so, except in the case of the trail shrines. In the main, San Dieguito cairns lie in complete archaeological isolation, without trails leading to them. Although they possibly were made as appeasement to evil spirits, it is just as probable that they mark taboo areas or initiation sites.

In the cairn groups no purposeful arrangement is apparent except in the longitudinal alignment which is sometimes present for short distances. If they were built as material adjuncts of some cult under shamanistic supervision, one would expect them to be placed in conspicuous positions, but such is seldom the case. Perhaps the best example of such an inexplicable location is a site SDM-LC-55 (Rogers, 1932) in northeastern Baja California on a rugged lava plateau lying between the Sierra Juarez and the Sierra de las Tinajas. Here on the broken undulating surface of a basalt overflow the aborigines gathered large blocks into many cairns over a great area. The plateau is broken by steep-sided canyons and could not be fully explored at the time of discovery. In an area of three acres, sixty-three cairns were located. They blend so completely into the natural buckled and fractured surface of the flow that not more than three can be seen at one time from any vantage point. At two places they are roughly aligned in east to west directions. All are barren of any cultural material. Below the plateau on the gravel terrace of Palmitas Wash,

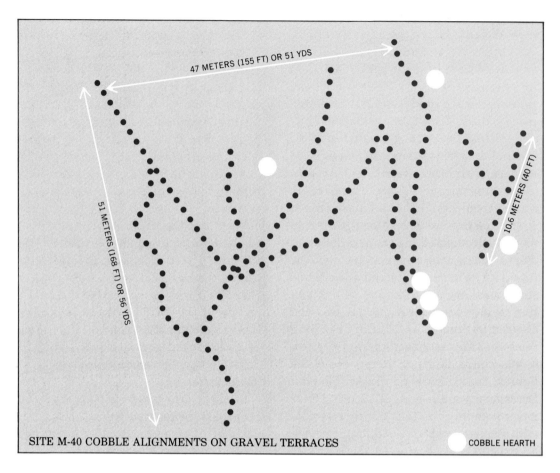

47 METERS (155 FT) OR 51 YDS

10.6 METERS (40 FT)

51 METERS (168 FT) OR 56 YDS

SITE M-40 COBBLE ALIGNMENTS ON GRAVEL TERRACES

COBBLE HEARTH

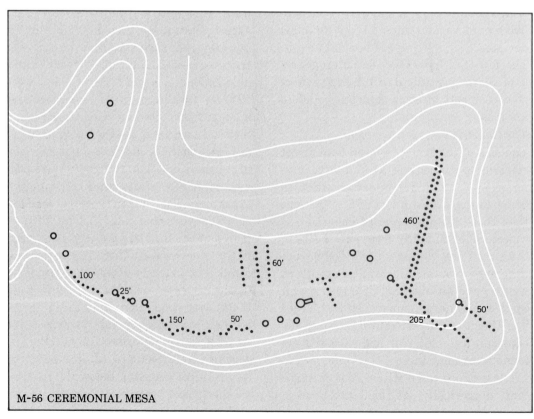

M-56 CEREMONIAL MESA

460'

60'

100'

25'

150'

50'

50'

205'

lies a boulder alignment ceremonial with a few sleeping circles nearby.

There are some aberrant forms which do not meet the qualifications for any of the three major categories. In general they are combinations of parts of two of the standard forms. One variant of the boulder alignment type utilizes small piles of cobbles in place of boulders. Another rare type conforms in design to the intaglio types, except that it is more elaborate. In this one, the pathways were formed by clearing cobbles and boulders from a rocky mesa surface. This type is well exemplified at SDM-A-136, Yuma County, Arizona.

Before leaving the subject, it may be of value to record some additional data relative to the nature of the so-called Mystic

The strange rock alignments of the ancient people of the Far West have been mapped —but no meaning or purposeful design has emerged.

The top sketch shows the alignments on the ceremonial mesa south of Baker in the Mojave Desert and designated by Malcolm Rogers as site M-40.

The area containing the principal alignments is about 168 feet by 155 feet, though there are other cobblestone lines and circles resembling hearths just to the west. The alignments were mapped in 1964 by Clark Brott of the San Diego Museum of Man.

Some distance to the west on a spur of the Cady Mountains is a larger and higher gravel terrace which Rogers mapped and designated as M-56.

Its alignments cover a much greater area and are of different types, though again their meaning is not clear to modern man.

The parallel lines near the tip of the terrace are 460 feet in length. The snake-like lines above them are from fifty to 150 feet long.

The three parallel lines in the center area are sixty feet in length.

Modern day "dune buggy" and motorcycle enthusiasts are racing across the terraces and in many areas rapidly tearing up the creations of prehistoric people.

Maze near Topock, California, which was not included in my 1939 report. Two informants who were familiar with it before the Santa Fe Railroad right-of-way was graded across it in 1893 said the ceremonial extended down onto the twenty-five foot gravel terrace of the Colorado River, and that at this point a very large cobblestone shrine rested. It was looted in the 1880's, and later completely destroyed by railroad grading activities. In the shrine were a number of potsherds, shell and turquoise beads, and several stone axes. Unfortunately, my informants could not remember whether the Yuman offerings were confined to the apex of the shrine or occurred throughout the cairn. If the basal section was barren, the initial stage was probably coeval with the ceremonial.

As Yuman culture does not emphasize religion and cultism it is highly improbable that any shaman could have mustered a sufficient labor force to construct this extensive work of over eighteen acres in area, even if it was built a section at a time over a long term of years. Both the method of construction by raking, and the design remain unique in the entire San Dieguito domain.

A Geoclimatic Problem

The method adopted to present San Dieguito I culture manifestations was chosen because I found it advantageous in my own studies, and I assumed that it would prove of value to others. The purpose of the aspect and phase divisions has been explained. San Dieguito I artifacts of the Central Aspect are considered separately for several artificial geographical zones, the Colorado Desert, the Mojave Desert, and the State of Nevada. In this manner one can quickly grasp the relative archaeological richness or poverty, as well as the regional pattern eccentricities in various areas of one aspect. Using the Central Aspect as an example, it is immediately obvious that in progressing from the Oregon state line in the north, south through the Mojave Desert and into the Colorado Desert, there appears a constant increase of

San Dieguito I phenomena. In studying the distributional richness of the second phase, we find its greatest concentration lies in the Mojave Desert. The third phase pattern, which is strong in the Mojave Desert, is barely represented in the Colorado Desert. Similar conditions prevail in other aspects, and by employing this technique one may be compared with another. If the study is extended to embrace the entire San Dieguito territory, similar inequalities are found. We can assume that this unevenness of frequency is extremely significant, but the cause of it is uncertain. Even in the study of unusual zonal archaeological concentrations, we have no way of determining whether the bulk of artifact representation is the effect of population density or of a small population in long residence.

A peculiarity of San Dieguito I pattern distribution in the Colorado Desert is that nearly one-half the area is devoid of archaeological remains of that period. This barren zone is occupied by the Salton Depression and marginal sand dune terrain. The situation offers no problem, as in the barren zone no old land forms, except for one small unique area, are in evidence. They are covered either with Blake Sea silts or sand dunes, both of post-San Dieguito age. The one exception is a number of flat-topped gravel spurs reaching out to the north from the Superstition Mountains. Their elevations lie beneath the high terrace level (plus forty-five feet) of the Blake Sea, and while the depression was occupied by that great body of water they became buried with lake silts, and their rocky constituents encrusted with lime. A certain amount of worked stone and artifacts as well became encrusted.

The archaeological problem here is a complicated one, for during the Yuman II period the plus thirty-foot shore line was at first occupied and later became inundated for a long period, after the water rose to the plus forty-five-foot level. During this period of submergence, the lime coating was precipitated on both rocks and artifacts. It is a simple matter to eliminate such typical Yuman artifacts as metates, manos, and pestles from the problem. But the flaked lithic patterns of San Dieguito I and Yuman II phases are almost identical, even to the crudity of workmanship. Both utilize the same local green porphyritic cobbles which are strewn over the gravel spurs.

These old land forms were exposed again when post-Blake Sea erosion washed away large areas of the lake silts. The gravels were again worked until the close of the Yuman III phase. Such work, however, can be eliminated because of its sharp, unsandblasted margins.

Some artifacts display incipient and some extreme erosion. It is the latter which may well be of San Dieguito I age, but because of the uncertainty, they have not been used in this study. It is interesting to note that neither San Dieguito II, San Dieguito III, nor Amargosa artifacts are found in this extensive area.

Because of the vast area involved and the slow development of the industry through three phases, I believe that thousands of years, rather than hundreds, are needed to account for the period between the first appearance of the San Dieguito Complex and its final disappearance as an entity. Crude percussion flaking gave place to skilled flaking technique and finally pressure flaking was either developed or introduced from a foreign source. A great time lapse seems obvious enough from the nature of surface geo-archaeological relations, but it is more conclusively demonstrated by the subsurface evidence found in San Diego County, California. These studies are reviewed in the Southwestern Aspect section.

There is uncertainty about the geological time periods concerned, and it must be considered as a possibility that the San Dieguito I pattern, because of its physiographical zoning, usually on terraces away from ancient or modern lakes and streams, is more ancient than has been assumed, and that it may even be of a non-San Dieguito facies. Against this theory is the fact that all its artifacts were carried over into the second phase, and that transitional forms are present. It is unfortunate that in the Southwestern Aspect, where stratigraphical evidence is plentiful, the San Dieguito I phase is not represented.

The geological age of the San Dieguito Complex has been guessed at by some of us in the past. In the Basin and Range province, it must rest on the age of certain extinct lakes, such as Lake Mojave.

CHAPTER IV

SAN DIEGUITO II IN THE CENTRAL ASPECT

A Moist Climate

Reconstruction of geoclimatic conditions during the second phase occupation is probably of greater importance than the individuality of the culture pattern in determining its position in the San Dieguito Complex calendar. For the first time we have definite evidence of San Dieguito association with fossil lakes and stream channels. The lakes are few in number compared with the many extinct stream channels, and they were shallow, with the exception of Owens Lake and Lake Mojave. These two bodies of water were fed by the two major drainage systems of the Mojave Desert. Their size can be accounted for through postulating a minor climatic change resulting in abnormal precipita-

About the time of Christ the later people of the Amargosa culture broke their milling bowls, heaped the fragments in a pile on this dry lake bed, and abandoned camp.

Wind and erosion have scattered the broken stones.

This lake bed has two names, Salt Spring Lake and Silurian Lake, and is located in central San Bernardino County, California, about twenty miles north of Baker.

The first evidence of man which Malcolm Rogers reported he found in this four-square mile area at site M-35 was of the San Dieguito II people.

Beginning with Amargosa I, he found a continuous occupation for many hundreds of years ensued, with the entire Amargosa Complex being present.

The early Amargosa people evidently did not have mortars.

This photograph looks southwest toward the Avawatz Mountains. To the east are the Silurian Hills, and north, the Dumont sand dunes.

tion over a period of perhaps, at the most, a thousand years.

I have yet to see in the Basin and Range province any association of prehistoric camp sites with a Pleistocene lake terrace. Invariably, where archaeological materials are found along fossil lake strands, the lake deposits rest upon more ancient Pleistocene lake silts and clays. In 1953, Clements (Clements, 1953) proposed that the so-called Manly Pleistocene Terrace of Death Valley gives evidence of a former very deep lake with an antiquity of 20,000 years, upon whose shoreline reposed contemporary artifacts of man. I have failed to find any lacustrine features associated with the Manly Terrace. The structure seems to be but one in a series of step-block faulted surfaces on the west flank of the Funeral Range. Regardless of elevation, their surficial stones have served as source material for artifacts made by the different aborigines of the region who lived from San Dieguito I down to the historic Shoshonean period.

Ancient Streams

Regarding extinct (and a few live) water sources associated with archaeological sites, fossil stream channels far outnumber fossil lakes. Judging from the distribution of Early Man camps along stream channels, the streams did not flow continuously over long distances, but were actually drainage channels where an underground flow surfaced in discontinuous stretches. As in the first phase period, San Dieguitoans continued to camp at lower elevations, whether in Nevada, the Mojave Desert, or the Colorado Desert, and shunned high mountain terrain. The high plateau country of western San Bernardino County is devoid of San Dieguito evidence and is nearly sterile of any archaeological materials. Harsh climate was possibly a restricting factor, since in all the San Dieguito periods, low temperatures and heavy precipitation prevailed in this region, with presumably great amounts of snowfall at higher elevations during winters.

Characteristics of San Dieguito II

There are several factors distinguishing the San Dieguito II pattern from that of the initial period. Most notably, the artifacts exhibit a marked improvement in flaking technique. The implements are sufficiently distinct to enable the classifier to type them, in most instances, with more certainty than is the case with the San Dieguito I artifacts. There are fewer nondescript items of uncertain classification. There are also a few new inventions. Unlike San Dieguito I artifacts, San Dieguito II artifacts are not diffuse in their distribution. If the practice of building sleeping circles, stone-outlined ceremonials, and trail shrines was continued, it is impossible to prove it. All that can be recorded is that these exist without association with San Dieguito II implements.

Separation of the two patterns was made by employing the horizontal stratigraphic technique, supplemented with the aid of a few pure San Dieguito II sites. Greater depth of alteration on San Dieguito I items was of some help. The degree of sandblasting was not, as it varies with regional conditions. Where artifacts are found on ferruginous soils, as in certain parts of the Mojave Desert, the presence of ground-patina is observable on both San Dieguito I and San Dieguito II implements, seldom on San Dieguito III and never on Amargosa.

In some mixed sites, elements which are common to both the San Dieguito and Amargosa patterns, such as choppers, chopping tools, and planes, are difficult to assign cultural affiliations. In such instances they have not been utilized in the studies.

Knappers of the first phase were content to use any suitable lithic material which was close at hand, while implements of the second phase testify that their makers were inclined to favor some specific stone, whose source is often some distance from the camps in which the artifacts are found. A characteristic tendency, lasting into the second phase, was to avoid the fine amorphous stones of the region. The only departure was the occasional use of jasper. In seeking an explanation for this strange custom, there are two plausible possibilities. One is a taboo, but that involves thought patterns of the past which are impossible to reconstruct. The other explanation is a convention which perhaps stemmed from success with one medium in the hunt, and the resulting belief that a spear point of the same kind would always insure success. If father handed this belief down to son long enough, it eventually might have become a group idea.

60

CHAPTER V

SAN DIEGUITO III IN THE CENTRAL ASPECT

CHARACTERISTICS OF THE THIRD PHASE

The third and closing phase of the San Dieguito Complex in the Central Aspect is signaled by the appearance of pressure flaking, either as the result of independent invention or through acculturation. At this early period, pressure flaking was an unknown technique to the west in the Pacific Littoral, and to the east it was some 800 miles to the known western boundary of the Clovis and Folsom complexes.***

Artifacts

In a horizontal stratigraphical analysis, the separation of San Dieguito II and San Dieguito III elements presents little difficulty, except for the survival of percussion-flaked heavy duty tools. The establishment of these archaeological divisions rests upon horizontal stratigraphy and geology in the Southwestern Aspect [*discussed in the Southwestern Aspect Chapter, and also in C. Warren, 1966—ed.*]. For the first time, the San Dieguitoans turned strongly to the use of amorphous lithic materials, such as jasper, chalcedony, and where it was available, obsidian, often traveling considerable distances to procure such materials. It is also noticeable that some ancient forms such as bifaces survived from the San Dieguito I period, but with considerable refinement in form and flaking technique. Other basic implements, such as flake scrapers, end scrapers, and concave scrapers, attained perfection as well during this closing phase. It seems obvious that many San Dieguito III projectile types were founded on San Dieguito II biface forms.

After the inception of the third phase, transitional tools undoubtedly lingered on for some time, as well as percussion-flaked heavy duty tools of a San Dieguito II facies. Their San Dieguito III equivalents are indistinguishable, but they have a weakly developed patina, or none at all. As they are so few in number, it is obvious that they were going out of vogue. Hence, the San Dieguito III pattern soon became an almost pure flake industry. The horizontal stratigraphical procedure of keeping separate the yields from different terrace levels of the same extinct lake and channel seems to bear out these contentions.

Other diagnostic features of the closing phase, aside from the discontinuance of certain elements, were innovations such as small projectile points and crescentic stones.

The degree of sandblasting, and especially the degree of patination, have been of some aid as diagnostics. San Dieguito II artifacts from gravel surfaces invariably carry a ground patina on their under surfaces, and San Dieguito III ones none. Patina arising from chemical alteration is present, to a slight degree, on all San Dieguito II artifacts, providing the material employed is not of an acidic nature, but it is found on San Dieguito III implements only occasionally, as a very thin film.

San Dieguito III implements from sandy terrain such as stream margins and lake strands are often so sandblasted that their margins are considerably rounded and their faceting all but obliterated. That such items were formerly artifacts can only be determined through a study of their shapes. On the other hand, San Dieguito I and II artifacts from the same locale, but resting upon or slightly embedded in gravel surfaces, have gone unscathed. From a size study of identical elements from the three phases, it becomes apparent that those from the first phase

are more massive than those of the second and third phases, especially the latter. This factor, combined with degree of patination present, has also been of some aid as a basis of distinction.

Before the end of the San Dieguito occupation of the region, the south half of the Great Basin shows a new cultural manifestation introduced from Utah, the Amargosa, which involved a crude percussion type of flaking. Therefore, these products are not difficult to separate from a surface assemblage of mixed San Dieguito III and Amargosa I artifacts, except for projectile points. However, cruder Amargosa products often cause insurmountable difficulties when classifying the artifacts from dual cultural sites of a San Dieguito II —Amargosa I nature.

The topographical location of sites has helped, both in the cultural separation

Were these crescentic stones used to scarify and tattoo the body of ancient man?

Were they hafted in the center and used as blunt-edged waterfowl arrows? Or were they, as Malcolm Rogers believed, carried by males for use as hunting amulets?

The answer is still a mystery, for very little evidence has been found to indicate what purpose these eccentric artifacts served for Far Western Early Men.

However, the association of crescentic stones with antiquity seems to be well-established. They have been found in early sites from Oregon to Baja California.

A few examples have been unearthed in late Indian deposits, including Cañalino and Luiseño, but these finds can be explained by remembering that every man has a natural curiosity for the unusual. The late Indians probably came upon the crescents on old sites, picked them up out of curiosity, and took them home.

All of the crescents pictured here were found in association with Early Man assemblages. Specimens in the left column, top to bottom, came from Mojave Desert sites. All the remaining examples are from San Diego County sites. (Scale in inches).

problem and in establishing the nature of climates involved. Amargosa I and Amargosa II adulteration of San Dieguito III sites is confined almost entirely to the margins of drainage channels, and is not found on the upper terraces of fossil lakes. As an example, Lake Mojave produced only traces of Amargosa cultural material, as well as some Yuman and Chemehuevi elements, on the low water level locations. The situation may even reflect the presence of a post-Lake Mojave transient lake, as probably do the traces of later cultural debris, such as sherds, arrow points, manos, metates, and an occasional cobblestone hearth.

All the aboriginal groups of the Basin and Range province from early man to historic populations were great wanderers, and representative cultural remains of all are widely distributed. The two exceptions already recorded are the low-elevation restricted habitats of the San Dieguitoans and early Amargosans. Subsequent populations took advantage of the ephemeral lakes which were created from time to time in the more ancient lake basins. Sometimes, through repeated visitations, they left considerable debris on the shores of these lakes. As an example, we may take Ivanpah, as it had, before collectors disturbed the archaeological materials, extensive Chemehuevi camps on its eastern strand. Early mining people who worked in the region in the 1880's told me how the Chemehuevi would camp here as long as a transient lake persisted, for within a few days after a fresh lake was formed, flocks of ducks and even Pacific coast shore birds would appear and provide a bountiful food supply.

On the shore of this dry lake is found cultural material of earlier origin intermixed with the Chemehuevi elements. This situation has been recorded before, and is emphasized again in order to cite the hazards of horizontal stratigraphical interpretation. About the only safeguard a researcher can have is familiarity with all the local culture patterns.

GEOLOGICAL EVIDENCE

In the past, interpretation of channel conditions as they were at the time of early man occupancy has involved the postulation of permanent rivers. Although I argued against this assumption (Rogers, 1939, p. 48) I failed to include in the data one important factor, namely, spotty locations of the camps relative to the lengths of drainage systems. Some lengthy channels have but one archaeological site along their entire courses. This would seem to indicate that subsurface flow surfaced only in certain sections, perhaps by San Dieguito III times, but certainly by Amargosa I times.

The location of San Dieguito III sites would seem to indicate that the lake period in the Great Basin was approaching its close; Lake Mojave, being fed by a major river, could have been one of the last. Even in historic times, its basin has often contained transient lakes of considerable size.***

Other geo-archaeological evidence pertinent to the nature of the climate at the close of the San Dieguito III phase was found at Lake Tonopah, Nevada, where a San Dieguito III camp was found, not on the fossil lake terrace, but in sand dunes overlying the Playa surface (Campbell and Campbell, 1940, pp. 7-11).

RE-USE OF ANCIENT TOOLS

A certain number of San Dieguito implements found throughout the Central Aspect show evidence of resharpening or alteration for different purposes by later peoples, but by whom is a problem. When the study is confined solely to elements which might have been altered by San Dieguitoans of different time periods, some values become apparent. Some San Dieguito I implements have flaked margins whose facets show a patina of less depth than do the original facets, plus a film of desert varnish which is equally weaker. This is considered rather sound evidence for priority of age within the complex. Resharpened artifacts with facets and mar-

gins so fresh in appearance that the work might have been done but yesterday are obviously the work of late protohistoric peoples. It was found that if early Amargosans altered San Dieguito III artifacts, there is no evidence of this through patination studies, for the respective time periods were too close together. In the Southwestern Aspect, where a local felsite which altered readily was in demand by all aboriginal groups there, the study of reworked tools has provided valuable sequential evidence.

ABSENCE OF STRATIGRAPHY
Little Lake Site

To this day no vertical stratigraphy relevant to San Dieguito phase positions in the Central Aspect area, nor their relations to the subsequent Amargosa Complex, has been found except at the Little Lake site (Harrington, 1957), and it has proved somewhat of a disappointment. Here San Dieguito III elements were strongly represented in the same horizon with a much greater number of Amargosa elements, which is most baffling. Obviously there must be some explanation. First it must be realized that for the area of the site, the average archaeological depth is not great, and that its accretion came through the occupancy of the site by peoples of three distinct cultures, San Dieguito III, Amargosa I and II, and Shoshonean; there probably was a fourth, as a few Nevada Basketmaker dart points were present. The digging of house pits, fire pits, deep pits for an unknown purpose, subsurface metate caches, some burial pits, plus rodent and tree root channels may explain the culture admixture.

The implement-bearing section is comprised of two major components of distinctive soil differences, the upper stratum averaging perhaps twenty inches in thickness and the lower one fourteen inches. A solution of the cultural sequence problem might be obtained through stripping a large area down to the basal stratum and carefully exploring that for intrusive elements.

The presence of a few metates in the basal stratum constitutes another problem. These certainly are not of San Dieguito origin, and if they are an Amargosa component, their presence is unique. As the Little Lake site is the most westerly known Amargosa site in the Central Aspect, it is possible that the metate is an acculturated item, having been introduced through Central Californian contacts.

DISTRIBUTION OF
SAN DIEGUITO III SITES

The local distribution of San Dieguito III archaeology is as follows. Beginning in the north at the Oregon State line, it is found to occupy a narrow western band of the state of Nevada, lying east of the base of the Sierra Nevada Mountains. The terrain involved constitutes the lowest part of the state, and perhaps reflects adverse climatic conditions at the time of occupancy in the remaining mountainous two-thirds of the state. The latter area even today has a winter climate which is very cold, given to high winds from the north and storms which produce as much snow as rain.

Progressing southward into the southern tip of the state and into California, the archaeological boundaries mushroom out to the west as far as the Owens River valley, and on the east to the Colorado River valley, although not intruding the valley proper. Absence of the San Dieguito III pattern in the immediate valley of the Colorado is as inexplicable as is the absence of the San Dieguito II pattern.

Further south in the Colorado Desert, distribution follows the same horseshoe-shaped belt as did the San Dieguito II pattern, and like it is meagerly represented. The western limb of the horseshoe joins the boundaries of the Southwestern Aspect in San Diego County without a hiatus in distribution. The eastern limb of its territory fails to cross the Colorado River into either of the states of Arizona or Sonora, Mexico. No San Dieguito III camps were found, and the small number of artifacts from this area were found close to either extinct or live water sources, and on desert trails. It is quite evident that the occupancy of the Colorado Desert was of little permanence. No reason for this is easily assigned. As in Nevada, no evidence of camping and no artifacts were found in the high parts of the Mojave and Colorado deserts. The typical San Dieguito III habitat was of an intermontane basin type.

It was not possible to designate any trail, trail shrine, sleeping circle, or ground pictograph as belonging to this period. As with the preceding two phases, no food bone, hearths, or the method of disposing of the dead was found with this phase.

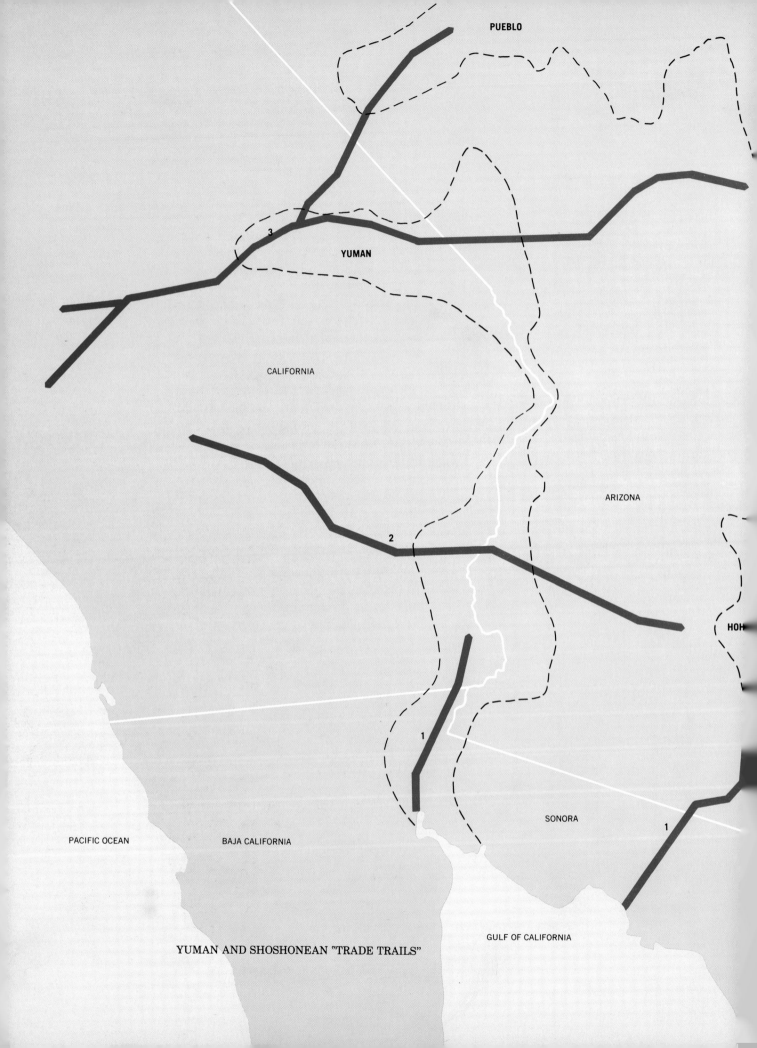

PUEBLO

3

YUMAN

CALIFORNIA

ARIZONA

2

HOH

1

PACIFIC OCEAN

BAJA CALIFORNIA

SONORA

1

GULF OF CALIFORNIA

YUMAN AND SHOSHONEAN "TRADE TRAILS"

CHAPTER VI

THE SOUTHEASTERN ASPECT

THE GEOGRAPHY

It remains to be explained why this division of the San Dieguito domain was made, and why the Southeastern Aspect was set apart from the others. Certain geographical, cultural and climatic factors combined seem to warrant the division. Geographically, it occupies an eastern marginal position; from a cultural standpoint, it appears not to be an early homeland but an infiltration area. If the last assumption is a true one, then the chronology of the cultural phase patterns should fall later than

As the Spaniards learned upon arriving in the Southwest, Indians had well-defined trails by which contact and trade were maintained with different peoples.

The adjoining map shows the principal California-Southwestern trade routes.

They connected the Shoshonean and Yuman peoples of California and the Colorado River region with more inland peoples.

This map by Malcolm Rogers was for a period which may have preceded the arrival of Yuman culture in Southern California coastal areas.

The trails marked 1 were the Gulf Trail which led from the mouth of the Colorado River at the upper end of the Gulf of California, up into Yuman territory, and the one which led from the gulf coast to the edge of the territory of the Hohokam peoples in central Arizona.

Trail 2 crossed the desert and mountains between the Shoshonean people to the west and the Hohokam people to the east.

Trail 3 was the Arizona-Pacific trade route from the Pueblo Indian country in southern Nevada through Utah and northern Arizona, to the coastal area. It had two branches which converged and then separated again.

their equivalents in the Central Aspect.

The only arbitrarily assumed demarcation is the Colorado River. It is of no cultural significance, except that it marks the eastern boundary of the San Dieguito III pattern. Actually, the boundary on the California and Nevada side lies some twenty miles west from the river valley. Neither does the Colorado constitute a cultural dividing line when applied to the San Dieguito I and San Dieguito II phase pattern distributions. Its north to south course merely passes across the geographical arrangement of the two phase patterns, which are present in both California and Arizona, and the southernmost part of Nevada.

San Dieguito I

When the archaeological distribution of the San Dieguito I pattern is mapped, it is apparent that only a narrow strip of northwestern Arizona is involved, and that no widening occurs until a point south of the Bill Williams River in latitude 34°10′ is reached. From this point the boundary turns rather abruptly to the east, to the vicinity of the junction of the Verde and Salt rivers. From here the line turns southeast, and after crossing the Gila River, parallels it on the south to an unknown distance into southwestern New Mexico and northern Chihuahua. Limits of the extreme southerly boundary in Sonora are unknown, as they have not been explored. There seems no reason to believe that the San Dieguito migration halted at any particular point in northwestern Mexico, and it is most probable that when the problem is attacked, the San Dieguito I pattern will be found to disappear into a nebulous zone of acculturation from contact with either a contemporaneous or even an older pattern.

At what point the San Dieguito I incursion into Arizona took place is purely a speculative matter. The first crossing of the Colorado could have taken place from Nevada, just south of Black Canyon, or even farther south. If so, the occupancy was of short duration and did not penetrate far into the interior. In Mojave County, high mountain ranges are immediately met with back from the river, and the Sacramento Wash area is the only low terrain suitable for what seems to have been desirable as a habitat at the time. Farther south, even the lower elevations of the Bill Williams Valley were utilized, but to a minor degree.

While it is most probable that crossings were made in several places, the intensity of occupational debris left in Yuma County may signify that it was in this latitude that the major incursion took place; then again, a prolonged occupation could have produced the same evidence.

San Dieguito II

When one comes to the necessity of restoring the corridor of ingress of the San Dieguito II pattern, whether it was by marginal contact or by actual population movement, we are on firmer ground, because of its geographical position. Its boundaries lie entirely within Yuma County and take the form of an easterly loop, with a western baseline along the Colorado River valley. Because of its latitude and unbroken contact across the river with the San Dieguito II pattern in California, a significant situation is pressing for acceptance.

Because of the restricted area within which the pattern is found, and the small amount of archaeological debris in evidence, the period of occupancy probably was of a short nature. As the pattern of this period does not appear again in the archaeological picture of the Southeastern area, we are confronted with a puzzle of a nature which often faces the re-creator of prehistory: Were the San Dieguito people absorbed or exterminated by the invasion of the Amargosa people from California,

or did they move on, and if so, where? As the solution of this problem is beyond our ability, it is not advanced as a challenge, but simply to point out an existing archaeological interpretive stasis.

The sole pertinent evidence which has been obtained is of the same geoclimatic nature as that found in the Central Aspect, namely, indications of the absence of a time hiatus between the San Dieguito and Amargosa cultures. If the Ventana Cave stratigraphy is not studied critically, it seems to refute this contention because of the geocultural disconformity present. This interruption must be considered a strictly local phenomenon, influenced in the main by the fluctuation of the cave spring flow. It is true that the planed-off capping of the San Dieguito I stratum represents a missing time dimension, but if it could be replaced, it might show, one, a transitional structure reflecting a gradual regional shift from a moist climate to one of semi-aridity; and two, the absence of a time factor of any magnitude existing between the San Dieguito and Amargosa I occupancies of the cave.

The concepts of migrational time-lag, the persistence of phase patterns in marginal areas, and the incursion of Amargosa people into various San Dieguito areas, as chief causative factors of the abrupt ending of the San Dieguito patterns have been discussed before (Rogers, 1939 and 1958).

San Dieguito III

The closing phase of the San Dieguito Complex is not represented in the Southeastern Aspect. Only one definite artifact of a San Dieguito III pattern facies has been found after thirty years' exploration of the territory involved. This is a stemmed point [*the particular type was not indicated in the manuscript, nor could the specimen be found — ed.*], a surface find at site SDM-A-111 in the White Tanks Mountains of Yuma County. It would be futile to attempt to explain its presence. The specimen has one notable quality in that it was made from a local rhyolite commonly used in the area, but also in the Mojave Desert area.

PHYSIOGRAPHY AND CLIMATE

In the main, the positioning of the San Dieguito I archaeology agrees physiographically with that of the Central Aspect. Most of it lies below the 1000-foot contour, and it is not until southeastern Arizona is reached that sites are found at higher elevations. From here on, both to the south and the east, sites are to be found at ever increasing altitudes, especially in southwestern New Mexico and northern Chihuahua. As of the present, Antelope Pass, New Mexico, with an elevation of 4400 feet, is the highest known site.

Desert Pavement

The archaeology is to be found only on ancient land forms, such as the gravel terraces of the Colorado, Gila, and Salt rivers; the terraces of tributary drainage systems; and mesa lands marginal thereto. It is absent from inner terrace sites of an age subsequent to the Little Pluvial (Medithermal). One other land form which has been most productive is the desert pavement area. Geologically it is of the same age as most of the mesa lands, as the latter are merely residual sections which have been sculptured from the pavement during the development of the tributary drainage systems of the Colorado and the Gila. In one basin there may be pavements, residual sections of mesa, and stream terraces standing at different elevations which represent various Pleistocene stages down to the Last Pluvial; yet all are archaeologically involved in that all surfaces of this nature bear San Dieguito I manifestations. The time range separating these similar land features is so great that it has no cultural significance. All of their flattish gravel surfaces are so similar that it seems obvious that their usage was a matter of human selectivity during one period, and that a time sequence of occupation need not be considered. The surfaces universally offer lithic materials suitable to the manufacture of implements.

Arizona is different from the California-Nevada field. In Arizona, desert pavement is more weakly developed, has smaller areal expanses and is much more restricted in its distribution. On the west side of the state it is mostly confined to a narrow strip east of the Colorado River valley, and in the south to the lower part of the Gila River valley. The greatest and least interrupted expanses lie between the Gila and Sonora.

Such zoning must have a geoclimatic significance, as it demands water resources which have not existed in several thousands of years, if immediate channels of the Colorado, Gila, and Salt are excluded. There is one major departure from the generalized norm to be found in the mountains of southeastern Arizona, where San Dieguito I occupation is found in the locality of modern springs and natural reservoirs, colloquially known as tinajas, or tanks. One minor archaeological field of identical nature exists in the Kofa Mountains of central Yuma County. These unusual locations in the vicinity of surviving water holes have been commented on before (Rogers, 1958) with suggested interpretation.

The Migration of Small Bands

The migration of the first-phase people from the Central Aspect into and across the state of Arizona probably was not accomplished in a few hundreds of years. Although the incentive and the reason for the continuance of the movement are perhaps beyond our ability to discern, we have been presented with a *fait accompli* to solve. It has been observed that while hunting peoples move considerable distances within a given year, it is not purposefully directional, with a permanent move intended. It is rather a cyclic movement in the hunt for sustenance within given boundaries. Both the interior of Australia and the Kalahari Desert have provided well documented native patterns of living which seem applicable to the present problem. This is probably a valid comparison although both are concerned with

extreme arid environments, while the San Dieguito period through most of its history was coeval with a modified desert climate and an annual precipitation much above that of today.

Two lines of evidence suggest that the Southeastern Aspect of the San Dieguito I period was both lengthy and in excess of its counterpart in the Central Aspect: one is climatic and the other cultural. The slow withdrawal from the lowlands into the mountains must have resulted from the approach of a period of aridity and climatic changes of some magnitude. The prolongation of the period would have permitted time for pattern enrichment and improvement in flaking technique, two factors which are actually found in the highland sites and nowhere else. Substantiating evidence was found in Ventana

The desert—particularly during the modified conditions experienced by early prehistoric people—was not unkind.

Here and there, even today, are hidden sources of water. They are called "tanks" and are found in rocky mountain areas. Some of them collect large quantities of rainwater.

The Spanish expedition of Juan Bautista de Anza encountered similar rock tanks on their way from northern Mexico to California.

These tanks are in the White Tanks Mountains in southeast central Yuma County, Arizona, at Rogers' site A-111.

They are near a site of prolonged prehistoric occupation dating back to San Dieguito I. It is an area of much camping and many quarries and caves.

On the mesa and on the flanks of the amphitheater surrounding the tanks are about 400 glyphs carved on black lava boulders. On a high vertical cliff above them are about 200 more.

Malcolm Rogers wrote that as usual with the San Dieguito I occupation, each center of concentration would radiate in all directions until another center would be encountered.

Cave, where the San Dieguito I capping by the "red-sand formation" (Amargosa I) was interpreted by Bryan (Bryan, 1950) as reflecting an arid period.

A Geological Summary

As there were Pleistocene and Recent geological factors in the mountains of the southeastern area, deviating to some extent from the rest of the Basin and Range province, and to the degree that they influenced the human habitat millenia afterward, they must be given consideration. This subject, which warrants a separate and voluminous treatise in itself, and which is dealt with in the geoclimatic literature, is beyond the scope of an archaeological report. The following is a simple generalized history of events relevant to archaeological restoration, supplemented with my personal observations.

After the early Pleistocene orogenesis and on down until today, approximately one half of the state received the runoff of the other half, the dividing line having a southeast-northwest strike from the southeast corner of the state to the western end of the Grand Canyon. In the beginning all drainage became impounded in the many low lying centripetal basins of southern Arizona, the major exception being what is now the Bill Williams River valley. Later on, a major crustal tilt to the north, with its hinge near the present International Boundary, ensued. The resulting south to north pitch caused the higher lakes to spill over into lakes of lower elevation, whose combined waters eventually found their way into the great east-west axial depression which the modern Gila occupies today. Here, too, were even larger lakes whose beds were trenched during the genesis of the modern Gila drainage system. At first and for thousands of years afterward there was sufficient volume of flow to deposit extensive beds of river cobbles, which soon after became terraced. Then, either through a subsequent elevation of the river valley or crustal warping, a second set of inner gravel terraces was developed.

The closing history of the Lower Salt and Gila was one of channel alluviation, with consequent meandering over a low gradient. From the confluence of the Salt and Gila to where the Gila joins the Colorado, the loss in elevation is but 800 feet in 160 miles. Because of the meandering nature of the normal river flow, augmented in historic times by flash flooding, the ancient channel of the Gila was cut back considerably on both sides, thus accelerating the phenomenon of channel-choking. The lateral degradation destroyed most of the inner terrace set, and even extensive stretches of the upper set. As both carried all the features of the San Dieguito I pattern, an untold amount of the archaeology of this period, as well as that of later cultures, has been destroyed, thus reducing the archaeological yield proportionately.

THE COCHISE CULTURE

Major tributaries of the Gila, such as the Santa Cruz, San Pedro, and San Simon, did not suffer marginal recession to the degree the Gila did, because of their steeper gradients. Consequently their terraces have produced a greater amount of Early Man archaeology. A geological peculiarity of the Southeastern Aspect is the almost complete absence of undrained fossil lakes and fossil stream channels. Therefore, Lake Cochise with its well-preserved terrace is unique. Antevs (Antevs, 1941) considered the lake to be a manifestation of the Last Pluvial, and in so far as I know is still of that opinion.

In 1958, I reexamined the geology of the lake, and I wish to review briefly my evidence and conclusions here:

The long axis of Lake Cochise lay north and south, and today the exposed features along this line present few salients of value to an historical restoration, except for rather strongly sculptured terraces on the north and northwest sides. The south end of the lake was so shallow that it is difficult to locate the lacustrine features which determined its confines. Although the area covered by the lake is quite impressive, its average depth, which must be considered in estimating the volume of water impounded, is not. The average depth and volume of the impounded water could only be determined through an exhaustive survey of the present basin. From my inspection of all segments of the basin with regard to adjacent terrace elevation above the present playa surface, I am under the impression that the average depth did not exceed eighteen feet.***

An east-west transverse study of the basin discloses some exposures of pre-lake, lake, and post-lake features of considerable historical importance. On the west side, the deepest part of the depression, the post-lake runoff from the Dragoon Mountains broke through the lake terrace in many places and scoured off a great area of the lake sediments. Residual hummocks were left offshore as much as three-quarters of a mile away. The sandy silts at this point attained an average thickness of seven feet. The dissecting of the gravel strand and silts uncovered fanglomerates in a basal position, fans which are continuations of the surficial fans back of the strand, into which the lake beveled a terrace. The fans are undoubtedly of Pleistocene age, but the Lake Cochise etching has all the appearance of extreme youth.

Directly across the basin to the east lies a long north-south exposure of pre-Lake Cochise Pleistocene lake and sediments. These are in an elevated position in relation to the surface level of the last lake, standing as they do some twenty feet higher. They present an abruptly beveled face as a result of Lake Cochise wave action, but the formation can be traced out some distance on the playa surface, indicating that this ancient block of sediments formerly extended well out into the basin. It is not possible at this time to go into their nature, except to note that they are indurated and that the last lake deposits are not.

The geological evidence seems to indicate the presence of a fault with a northwest-southwest strike situated under the west central part of the basin, which resulted in the elevation and tilting to the east of a crustal block lying to the east of the parting line. Whether the older lake was drained by the faulting or suffered extinction through dessication can only be determined through further study.

The geological evidence indicates that Lake Cochise was created and rose to its maximum level in a relatively short period of time, that its duration was short, and that its extinction was not of a halting nature, since it formed no shrinkage strands, which are typical of the fossil lakes of the Great Basin. Archaeological evidence tends to confirm this thinking. The paucity of archaeological material on its strand indicates a brief occupation, when contrasted with the wealth of material from the Lake Mojave strands.

Sayles and Antevs (1941) presented a geological picture which is difficult to understand. If Lake Cochise is of Pluvial age, why is only the Chiricahua (post-Pluvial) stage in evidence at Lake Cochise? The presence of ceramic sites on and back of the strand might be used as arguments for contemporaneity if the age of the ceramic types were not known. The situation merely demands the postulation of one or more small ephemeral lakes in the basin in post-Pleistocene times.

Cochise and San Dieguito Comparisons
In 1958 (Rogers, 1958) the close similarity of the Sulphur Springs stage and the San Dieguito I pattern was demonstrated. Flaked stone artifacts resembling the Sulphur Springs type occur in the San Dieguito I assemblages. However, the San Dieguito I pattern includes at least six elements which either have not been found or have not been presented as components of the Sulphur Springs pattern.

The Pigment Slab (Milling Stone)
When the complete patterns of basic Cochise and San Dieguito are contrasted, an important divergence stands forth in the presence of the milling stone (Sayles), or pigment slab (Rogers), in the former and

its absence in the latter. In the search for an explanation, I have hitherto advanced two theories. One of these, which appeared in print, was to the effect that the grinding slab had perhaps been improperly assigned to an otherwise cohesive pattern; the other was that this bothersome element was the result of acculturation through marginal contact with some as yet unknown culture, either in southern New Mexico or northern Mexico. There is, of course, a third possibility, independent invention. It is of value to note that the slabs were not found in the San Dieguito I (volcanic debris) horizon in Ventana Cave, nor in the next oldest culture level, the Amargosa I stratum. Haury has explained its absence by calling attention to the small amount of midden matter left by the cave visitants of this period, an interpretation with which I am in accord, as otherwise in Arizona the implement is found as an important part of both the Amargosa I and Amargosa II patterns. Several pigment slabs from subsurface positions in Amargosa II territory still retain red ochre in the pores of the grinding surfaces. They are commonly found on the camp sites of the equivalent periods in the California Desert. Once invented, the pigment slab in southern Arizona survived as a component of all subsequent cultures, even after the metate was occasionally put to the same use.

Absence of Burials
After many years of study, I lean strongly to the thesis that basic Cochise and San Dieguito are one and the same, and are perhaps the products of a common stock. There is one other important linking trait. It is obvious that whether we are considering one culture or two, neither inhumation nor cremation was practiced. Normally these would be considered negative traits, but in their absence we must assume that some type of disposal of the dead through exposure was customary. The belief that above-ground disposal (platform or tree-burial) was used and became locally entrenched, is strengthened

by the fact that in subsequent culture horizons (Chiricahua-Amargosa I and San Pedro-Amargosa II) neither inhumation nor cremation was practiced.

ARCHITECTURAL FEATURES OF THE SOUTHEASTERN ASPECT
Trails

The same man-made surface features which are met with throughout the Central Aspect are present throughout the Southeastern Aspect. Area for area, some types are less numerous than in the former, but others are present in about the same numbers.

As in California, the east side of the Colorado River valley terraces retain the imprint of numerous trails leading toward interior regions and in the Lower Gila River valley the same condition obtains on both the north and south sides. Farther up

More than 50,000 stones were placed in this mound, supposedly by individuals passing along the trail running westerly to the Colorado River.

The site is in Arizona between Ehrenberg and Tacna. The mound was identified by Malcolm Rogers as a Yuman shrine, though to him the trail itself probably is pre-Yuman. He listed it as A-29-A.

In the general area he found many cleared circles and came to the conclusion it was old San Dieguito I territory which in later centuries was held by the Amargosans and finally by the Yumans.

The trail meanders to the Colorado River, where washing and flooding have erased any signs of prehistoric habitation. It can be traced, however, for thirty miles in the general direction of the Gila River.

Rogers and a companion excavated the shrine and collected seventy-two trays of marble-size pebbles and 7500 larger rocks.

The original diameter was sixteen feet and the height about thirty inches.

Early men must have passed this shrine 50,000 times and each time placed a stone, presumably in the expectation that the ceremony would help to assure a safe journey.

the Gila and in the Lower Salt River valley, where the rivers are flanked by marginal silt and sandy lands, there probably once existed as many trails as are now apparent in the downstream region. Where gravel terraces and marginal pavements have been preserved, trails leading away from the rivers are numerous.

Again, those of Yuman origin may be differentiated from earlier trails through applying the diagnostics used in the Central Aspect field. They have a profusion of potsherds along their courses, the trail stones carry no desert varnish and they are more deeply trenched. They lead to definite water sources of even the historic period, but through low passes in intervening desert ranges. Exceptions are the few long trade route and war-party trails, which were traversed by man only. Whether they leave the Colorado or the Gila, the trails have this in common: when they reach interior destinations, their association with potsherds halts most abruptly. From there on to their ultimate goals, what little cultural material there is, is predominantly of a foreign nature. These few items, whether they were obtained in trade or through pilfering must have been lost or broken on the return trips. Hohokam sherds are predominant in this category.

A reasonable explanation of the situation would seem to be that the profusion of broken ceramics and other Yuman cultural material, adjacent to the trails for certain distances, was due to family groups engaged in seasonal forays into the hinterlands in search of kinds of sustenance which the river valleys did not provide. Bolstering this theory is the presence of large camps at the points where the abundance of trail potsherds leaves off.

Outside the Yuman sphere, and in the domains of the Hohokam, Pima, and Papago, many of the trails must owe their origins to such groups. They pose an enigma in that one seldom finds a potsherd on their courses.

In the Southeastern Aspect, a problem

of trail assignment similar to that met with in the Central Aspect exists. Some trails must be of Amargosa origin, but no method of proving the assumption has been found.

Shrines and Ceremonials

Attendant to the local San Dieguito trails are the same small cobble cairns met with throughout the Central Aspect. The large ones are located in passes or adjacent to tinajas. They are barren of cultural material, except for a few cairns on trails leading back from the Colorado River valley. These sometimes have a capping of Yuman cultural material, and nondescript man-made flakes below this level.

The cluster type of cairns is also found, generally so arranged that no apparent pattern is evident in the cairn spacing. Also, it is seldom that a trail leads directly to them.

One uniquely situated large offertory shrine exists on a talus trail leading up to Ventana Cave. As it is barren of cultural material, it is impossible to determine who originated it, or if the custom of depositing offerings was carried on down through the centuries by all the various inhabitants of the cave.

In a locational study of the large ceremonial structures, it was found that two were on Amargosa encampments, but San Dieguito I flaking and artifacts were also in evidence. The Yuman trade trail (SDM-A-101) from Ehrenberg on the Colorado to Arlington on the Gila passes near both of them, and, farther to the east, directly over a third (SDM-A-107). Besides the normal amount of trail sherds, there is at this site such an abundance of broken vessels that they must have been purposefully sacrificed. Three of the eight cairns within the boulder-outlined rim had both Yuman and Hohokam sherds on and within their crowns. It seems evident that the Yumans practiced some form of obeisance to this relic of the past. The practice is not so commonly met with on the Arizona side of the Colorado River basin as it is on the California side.

Boulder Alignments

No area of a like size in the entire San Dieguito domain contains so many large boulder alignments as does Yuma County. These alignments differ from others because of the large boulders employed, some weighing up to 200 pounds (not a matter of selectivity, but of immediate availability). The boulders are spaced so that no lines are continuous boulder-to-boulder alignments. Some are of the single line type, but the majority present two parallel lines for some distance, the longest one known being 600 feet long. The rarest type is roughly rectangular, sometimes with one side missing. The intaglio type of ground pictograph without cobble delineation is a rare thing, and those which have been found are on a much smaller scale than those in California. Most ceremonial structures are boulder-outlined, and do not enclose pathways. Usually no zooic figures were reproduced, or if they were, are of such a distorted nature that they are undecipherable. Groups of cairns without pattern and long boulder alignments are the most common types.

In general, no consistent plan of orientation is involved, and no apparent reason for the choice of site locations is observable. Prolonged preservation may have been one factor. If all the rocks had had to be procured and carried some distance, to be arranged on soil land, it would have imposed unnecessary labor to build a structure which would have been impaired in a short time by erosion. Most cobble shrines and ceremonials in the Southeastern Aspect that may be associated with the San Dieguito culture, are away from the immediate valleys of the Colorado and the Gila. Three exceptions are shrines located on the upper terrace of the Colorado in conjunction with well-defined trails leading from the interior of Arizona. One of these was completely barren of cultural evidence and the other two have a slight amount of Yuman material in their upper thirds.

Sleeping Circles

Sleeping-circle architecture departs but little from that of the Central Aspect. No rectilinear shapes were found, and grouping is limited to sites in Yuma County. The boulder-rimmed type is present in approximately the same numbers, and the physiographical placing is the same.

There is no conflicting cultural architecture to confuse identification, as the boulder-rimmed house sites of the Papago, Yavapai, and Walapai have characteristic cultural debris either about or in them, and the wall stones usually carry caliche-encrusted sections, indicating that they had been removed from embedded surface positions at a time too recent for erosion to have removed the caliche.

Since the Ventana Cave site contributes so significantly to the present study, it must be recorded that San Dieguito I sleeping circles occur in the immediate vicinity of the cave.

A SUMMARY NOTE

Undoubtedly numerical class summaries of all architectural features from the various aspects are at this point in order and expected. This I am purposefully avoiding for two reasons: one, because of the cultural affiliation conflict to be found in some instances; and two, because I do not know the totals with any degree of exactitude.

My first experience with the phenomena began in 1919 on the west side of the Colorado Desert. From then on down through the years, as archaeological surveys were extended, an ever increasing number of sites were found and recorded. Quite a few apparent San Dieguito I manifestations were discovered and reported to me by my field associates. I was unable to visit many of these or judge their cultural connections. During the last decade other circles have been located by various amateur and professional archaeologists.

Location work was aided to a slight extent through interviews with old desert men and early ranchers. In general, however, a complete apathy was met with when structures were described and inquiries made. Their sole interest seemed to be directed toward the large cobble shrines.

There was a universal belief that they had been constructed by the Spanish to hide buried treasure, and as a result, many were vandalized long before my time. Many had been trenched through to original surface levels, and at the central point pits two to three feet deep had been laboriously dug into the cemented underlying gravels.

In lieu of class totals, it may be well to provide rough estimates of the same, based on the numbers I have personally seen. In toto, for both the Central and Southeastern Aspects, the trails will approach 500 in number, and the trail shrines twenty. The combined numbers of all types of ceremonial figures which seem to be of definite San Dieguito origin total forty-one. A census of the number of sleeping circles, before it was discontinued in 1943, had attained a figure in excess of 8000.

During walking surveys over such a vast territory as is embraced in this report, thousands of the features dealt with in this section must have gone unobserved.

CHAPTER VII

THE SOUTHWESTERN ASPECT

GENERAL DISCUSSION: CULTURE AND CHRONOLOGY

San Dieguito I

Phase I of the Central Aspect has not been found west of the Peninsular Range of Southern and Baja California. This may mean merely that its meager and simple elements did penetrate the west coast but were lost in the abundance of Phase II materials of the Southwestern Aspect and that its absence is only apparent. This sup-

From these cliffs, for a period of time of perhaps 5000 years, people of the La Jolla culture looked out across the sea.

The cliffs have been retreating before an advancing ocean, exposing their ancient burials and dropping artifacts and cultural debris into the sea.

The cliff area is part of what is known as the Scripps Estate, north of the Scripps Institution of Oceanography in La Jolla, and is known as site W-9.

Evidence indicates that earlier people, identified as San Dieguito III, first visited the site, followed by the La Jollans, who were chiefly seafood gatherers.

Very few La Jolla sites in Southern California and Baja California were situated near constant supplies of food and water, and as the immediate shell fauna was exhausted, the people would move on, to return when the sea had replenished their sources.

This has been proved by changes in species of sea life left at different levels of middens of one period.

Dozens of skeletons have been found in this area, all of them in the customary flexed positions, and generally with the head to the north. The graves often contain shell beads and pendants, and usually are capped by an overturned metate.

position, however, has no supporting evidence. No San Dieguito artifacts carrying a patina equal in depth to that of the San Dieguito I artifacts from the Colorado Desert have been found, nor have the many local San Dieguito II middens yielded any basal pattern of the San Dieguito I facies.

As has been previously pointed out, the San Dieguito I migrational movement from the Colorado Desert pressed on south, into a narrow strip of terrain between the Peninsular Range and the Gulf of California. My early surveys extended no farther south than to Punta Fermin, and on the Pacific side, to San Quentín. Later on, in 1930, Frederick S. Rogers [*father of author — ed.*], archaeologist and a member of the scientific staff attached to the cruise of the *Least Petrel* (Bancroft, 1932) brought back artifacts of a decided San Dieguito I slant from the east coast of the peninsula. These were noted as far south as La Paz.

San Dieguito II

In San Dieguito II times, a westerly movement took place from the Colorado Desert into Southern California and a narrow strip of Mexico, paralleling the International Boundary. This migrational movement seems to have pursued a course through the Jacumba Pass of 3425 feet elevation.

The Kumeyai name is *Hakum*. It is interesting to note that several thousand years later the Yumans used this same pass during their trek to the Pacific Coast. Sections of this trail were still visible along Highway 80 until thirty years ago.

This deduction is based on the presence of a series of archaeological sites leading up from the desert, through the pass and to the west. Substantiating data exists in the absence of San Dieguito sites to the north in the Laguna, Cuyamaca, and other

high connecting ranges as far north as the San Jacinto Mountains. The same condition obtains to the south in the Sierra Juarez Mountains, whose continuations culminate seventy-five miles to the south in the great heights of the San Pedro Martir range.

To the west of the Sierra Juarez lie some intermontane basins whose drainage channels constitute the headwaters of the Rio Tijuana. In them and westerly to the Pacific Coast there are widely separated San Dieguito II camps with a minimum of archaeological debris, in a surficial position. The same conditions prevail on the United States side of the International Boundary.***

During their migration to the west the

Since 1938 when Malcolm Rogers excavated the Harris site, it has been the type locale for the San Dieguito Complex in the Southwestern Aspect.

Crews from the University of California at Los Angeles, San Diego State College, and Idaho State University have undertaken subsequent excavations, and well over 2000 artifacts have been removed from their positions in the ancient river channel.

The oldest level, Locus 1, is a workshop on the southeast bank of the river, and has yielded radiocarbon dates of 6450 and 6990 B.C.

The top row of artifacts, left to right, shows a leaf-shaped point, a crescentic stone, a leaf-shaped knife, and a domed-discoidal scraper.

In the second row are a discoidal scraper and a triangular base-notched point. The six specimens in these two rows are from the Locus 1 trench and belong to the early period.

Specimens in the bottom row are a thin and broad leaf-shaped knife, a triangular trinotched point, and a triangular, quartzite, base-notched point. These three artifacts came from Locus 2, a deposit in the center of the river channel, and are tentatively dated at 2770 B.C., plus or minus 160 years. (Scale in inches).

people fanned out both to the north and the south, to the northwest as far as the San Luis Rey River valley and perhaps beyond, and to the southwest in Baja California a much greater distance.

DISTRIBUTION OF SAN DIEGUITO II SITES

Zone One

In San Diego County San Dieguito II sites fall into three different categories, if grouped according to physiographical zones. The first zone is composed of the high intermontane valleys, although the San Dieguito II people avoided the valley bottoms which were later the favorite abode of the Yumans. San Dieguito II camps are invariably located on the mesas and ridges which framed the valleys, a San Dieguito trait which is also observable in the other two zones and will be discussed later.

Zone Two

The second zone is the area between the Peninsular Range and the Coastal Range, which lies at a much lower elevation than the first. This zone consists in the main of an ancient and greatly eroded peneplain, whereon rolling hills, hogbacks, and interdrainage spurs occur as residual features. On these land forms are found all the San Dieguito II camps and some from the San Dieguito III period. San Dieguito II sites are not found on the margins of streams and rivers.

As the ancient San Dieguito habitat includes much of the agricultural land in this zone, which has been farmed from Spanish times down to the present, it has been subjected to man-created degradation for 150 years. Consequently, many artifacts, even if they originally occupied a subsurface position, are now exposed, except for those which became covered by post-Caucasian alluvium. Some sites which were not of sufficient acreage to warrant clearing for farming are intact and covered with a thin veneer of aeolian deposits which lodged in the chapparal. In such instances a few San Dieguito II horizons attain a depth of eight inches. In the middens, the artifacts and flakes are widely dispersed as a rule, and only occasionally are grouped. It is as though whatever shelters the people possessed were spaced some distance apart. No oxidized soil levels, resulting from fire, have been found.

There is evidence of some antiquity: one, in the depth of the chemical alteration on the surfaces of artifacts; and two, in the long period of degradation which followed abandonment. Many sites were fifty percent destroyed by marginal recession before a new growth of brush took root and captured the aeolian deposits.

Zone Three

The third zone of occupation lies upon the mesa lands between the Coastal Range and the Pacific Coast. This plateau consists of uplifted marine sedimentaries with late Pliocene and early Pleistocene riverine capping.*** The present topography is an apparent condition of four ocean front terraces having been sculptured during the general uplift, but they are all false terraces.

As each bar rose above sea level, it formed a long offshore attenuated key, stretching for miles without much if any interruption. Further crustal uplift drained the sea from behind the keys to the north and south. Draining waters escaped seaward through areas of low elevation. This scouring action was to determine the future courses of San Diego County's major rivers.

Further elevation caused the lateral run-off to sculpture abrupt escarpments on the land side of these fossil bars, the older ones acquiring the boldest reliefs. In the Coastal Belt these eminences were later to become favorite camping sites of the San Dieguito II people.***

Because it is of some archaeological significance, it should be recorded that on the flanks of the major drainage channels a series of terraces can be noted. There are four strongly etched terraces at elevations above sea level of twenty-five feet, sixty feet, 100 feet, and 200 feet. The first two have many La Jolla II middens with an occasional thin veneer of Yuman debris upon their contours, especially the twenty-five-foot terrace. The sixty and 100-foot terraces occasionally present middens of the same two cultures, but to a much lesser degree. In very rare instances there exists evidence of San Dieguito camping, but only if the surfaces are of a sandy loam nature. When they are composed of adobe, which is usually the case, no San Dieguito evidence is found.

All of this geological history, except for the change in sea level, occurred well before the advent of man in the region. It has been reviewed solely to prepare a geological setting, antecedent to the earliest archaeological horizon.

Although the close relationship in any given region between archaeology, geology, and climatology has previously been stressed in presenting the Central Aspect, different regions have their own peculiar problems, sometimes unique.

CULTURAL ASSOCIATION IN THE SOUTHWESTERN ASPECT

In the Southwestern Aspect we find a unique tendency in that the Phase II and Phase III people camped on radically different types of terrain, and their archaeological remains are distributed accordingly. Here we have manifestations of the same material culture, with the pattern deviating only in the acquisition of new inventions and a superior flaking technique, both of which define the San Dieguito III Phase.

There are many stratified middens in the Coastal Zone wherein different cultural levels are represented, and in various combinations. In these are found San Dieguito, La Jolla, Yuman, and Shoshonean horizons. The only combination not found, with either phase of the San Dieguito culture, is an association with La Jolla I. As the latter people camped exclusively on ocean frontage and slough margins, a subsequent rise of sea level has obliterated the major portion of the archaeology of this period. Their middens on the slough margins are not found more than two miles inland from the present coast line. They also avoided the marginal highland mesas which were later frequented by their descendants, the people of La Jolla II period.

La Jolla Associations

Most of the San Dieguito highland sites are thin-bedded, and their maximum depth does not exceed forty-six inches. The average depth of archaeological debris is around ten inches. Although not having impressive vertical depth, their linear extensions sometimes cover an acre. In dual culture sites such as San Dieguito and La Jolla, there is not only a cultural disconformity but a clearly demarked geological one. The San Dieguito II middens have a wavy eroded surface between them and the La Jolla II middens. This feature is much less in evidence in dual cultural sites of the San Dieguito III Phase and the La Jolla II Phase, but it does exist. The geological hiatus probably represents the period and duration of the La Jolla I Phase.

The majority of the San Dieguito horizons consist of a reddish-brown, sandy loam which is indurated to some extent. The minority groups present a soil of gray, sandy loam, not as much indurated as is the ferruginous loam. The two soils are *in situ* and their origins are due in turn to the decomposition of the reddish sandstone and of the gray Pliocene sandstone. Hence, the positions of the two types of camping terrain are dependent on the distribution of the two types of sandstone, although neither is hard enough to be properly termed stone.

The artifacts from both soils, if made of felsite, carry a putty-colored cortex over the green ground mass. In addition to this patina of oxidization, the artifacts from the red loam have an iron-stained surface veneer. No cobblestone hearths of definite provenience have ever been found in a San Dieguito horizon, and the only certain

evidence of fire is finely disseminated charcoal, as if the hunters made small surface fires over which to scorch their meats. Other items which the excavator might expect to find but which are missing are mammal and bird bone, shells and fish bone, and bone tools. This statement must be qualified to a slight degree. From levels which appear to be near the close of the San Dieguito III period, a few clam and pecten shells are uncovered in San Dieguito III middens. Evidently the avoidance of seafood had finally been overcome. Cobble hearths enclosing charcoal appear sparingly in the San Dieguito III horizon, but it has been impossible to determine whether they are of San Dieguito III origin or of a La Jolla II intrusive nature, due to the absence of artifacts within their confines.

The La Jollans of the second phase period constructed numerous cobble hearths and sweathouse pits full of fire-cracked boulders and charcoal. The latter have been found excavated to as much as a depth of twenty-six inches into San Dieguito horizons, and even below them.

No artifact of a foreign origin has been found in a San Dieguito midden, except three instances of metates intrusively cached in an upside down position, probably by people of the La Jolla culture.

Besides the abrupt material cultural break between the middens of the two peoples, there is an easily recognized soil textural and contextual differentiation. La Jolla II middens have a blackish color, which results from a high charcoal content. They also include numerous marine shells of diverse species, fire-broken rock, percussion spawls, and flaked artifacts of an excessive crudity. Although some elements of this culture have their functional counterparts duplicated in the San Dieguito pattern, their technological features fall far short of the sophisticated technique displayed in their San Dieguito predecessors. Furthermore, the La Jollans never mastered pressure flaking. In the ground stone category they were able to produce

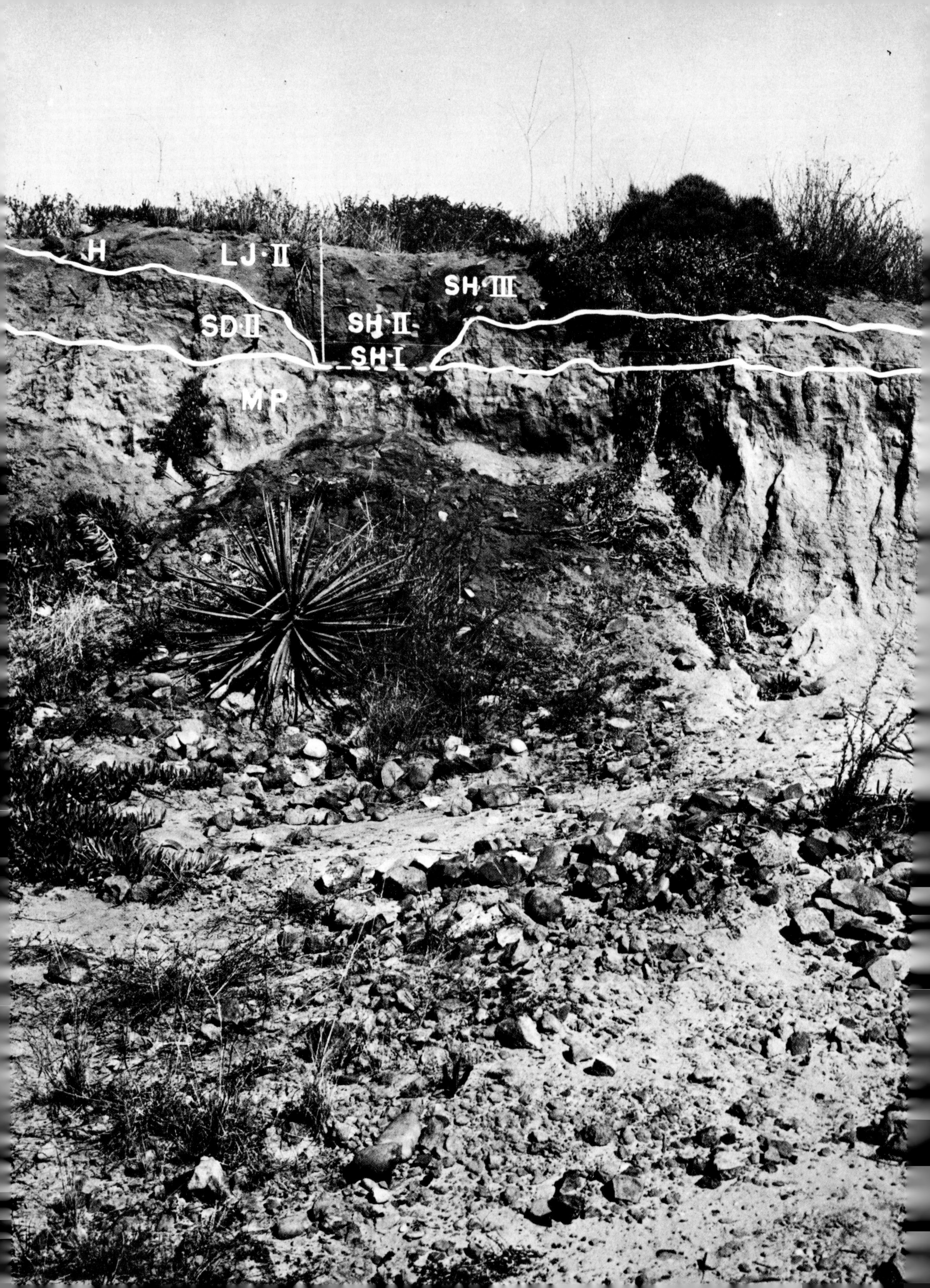
H
LJ·II
SH·III
SD·II
SH·II
SH·I
MP

metates, manos, and small mortars in great numbers. Disposal of the dead was by inhumation. Toward the end of La Jolla II occupancy of the region the first foreign imports appear, either on the surface or a few inches beneath the capping of their middens. These are exclusively of Canalino origin, and consist of spear and arrow points, steatite artifacts, shell jewelry, and shell fish-hooks. The lithic materials employed in the making of the stone artifacts are entirely foreign to San Diego County and Baja California. La Jolla I flaked stone artifacts are more primitive than those of the San Dieguito I pattern in the Central and Eastern Aspects, and even those of the La Jolla II period seldom exceed those of the San Dieguito I in workmanship.

San Dieguito Associations
It is the author's conclusion that the local

This site is situated on a typical fossil marine bar, with an elevation of 200 feet above sea level, at Cardiff, San Diego County.

Erosion has vividly exposed a history which can be read as easily as a book.

The original archaeological area was estimated at slightly in excess of one acre. Malcolm Rogers designated the site as W-167.

At the bottom MP designates an Upper Pliocene formation with a disconformity between it and a midden left by the San Dieguito II people.

Above that is a midden left by people Rogers identified as La Jolla II.

The letter H marks a La Jolla II mussel roasting hearth.

Rogers used the letters SH to designate aboriginal sweathouses.

SH-I marks the site of a La Jolla II sweathouse pit which penetrates the San Dieguito II midden and three inches into the Pliocene formation.

SH-II and III indicate that the pit has been reused.

The picture shows that the two lower sweathouses have suffered four to five feet of vertical displacement.

San Dieguito II Phase was coeval with the last stages of the Pluvial (Anathermal), and the San Dieguito III Phase essentially with the beginning of the Long Drought, although the latter phase developed before the close of the Pluvial, as is testified to by many dual sites in the Coastal Belt highlands.

[*The foregoing sentence was changed to reflect Rogers' final opinion on the subject. It originally read: "...the local San Dieguito II phase was coeval with the Little Pluvial and the San Dieguito III phase essentially with the Little Drought, although the latter phase developed before the close of the Little Pluvial, as is testified to by many dual sites in the Coastal Belt highlands." — ed.*]

The people of this phase were soon after forced to move their camps to the bottom lands of the major river channels in their search for water. During this period there began an exodus into the interior mountains in search of springs and permanent water holes, many of which are still in existence. The easterly movement backtracked on the old corridor of ingress from the Colorado Desert, and stopped only at the mouths of the great gorges which head back into the Peninsular Range. Thus it is that we find the San Dieguitoans camping for the first time in the very bottoms of major stream channels, which would not have been possible even in historic times.

Although quite a few sites of this nature have been located, the classic site is the fossil river channel of the San Dieguito River, because of both the cultural stratigraphy disclosed and the magnitude of the associated historical geology laid bare. The excavations in this fossil channel were conducted in 1938 with a grant-in-aid from the Carnegie Institution. Except for a brief article (Rogers, 1938), this excavation and its findings have not been reported.

[*A full report on this excavation was assembled and edited from Rogers' notes. See San Diego Museum Paper Number 5 (Warren, Claude N., 1966) — ed.*]

Comparing Phases II and III Tools

The San Dieguito trait of stubbornly adhering to the lithic material of their choice for artifact manufacture, no matter how intractable it proved, is again evidenced in the Southwestern Aspect. In this instance, however, they found in the felsite dykes of the Coastal Range an excellent medium. The local felsite, of a highly devitrified nature, is readily subject to chemical alteration, and as a consequence has proved a boon to the archaeologist in the separation of artifacts according to age, and in the establishment of phase patterns.

As would be expected, there exists a considerable residue of a transitional nature, which makes it difficult to assign a specific type of artifact either to the second or the third phase. Many items carry an intermediate degree of alteration, and since a deep or thin patination is one of the criteria for the separation of the tools of the two phases, the classifier is often left in doubt. For the proper allocation of these items one must also determine whether they were percussion or pressure flaked,

San Dieguito people undoubtedly utilized a wide variety of food sources, both plant and animal. Unfortunately, very little evidence, which would aid archaeologists in determining the amount and varieties of plants and animals used, has been unearthed.

The presence of numerous large projectile points and knives in the Southwestern Aspect lends weight to the theory that big game was a source of food.

The top row of artifacts pictured here, left to right, shows six types of San Dieguito points. All came from San Diego County. Presumably, these implements would have been used on darts, with the atlatl, or throwing stick, or they might have been tips for hand-held spears.

Several of these "points" might also have served as knives. The four specimens shown in the bottom row are probably too large and unwieldy for use except as hand-held or hafted knives. (Scale in inches).

the latter technique being the *sine qua non* for admittance to the San Dieguito III classification, but the technique employed is often obscure. However, as in the Central Aspect, we have the same valuable type specimens which set apart San Dieguito II from San Dieguito III, in that only the latter produced a true projectile point, the crescentic stone, and the elongated biface knife. These probably are the best diagnostic forms.

In the third phase the artificers apparently became more interested in the possibility of new mediums, such as porphyry, quartzite, and quartz, although none of the three is as suitable for pressure flaking as is felsite. In Baja California where local felsite is a rarity, they turned to the ancient river and beach cobble deposits for material. These contain felsite cobbles of a foreign origin, a type of felsite which stubbornly resists chemical alteration; therefore, the artifacts from this region can seldom be assigned a cultural position, except on the basis of form and technique employed, unless they are from a subsurface location.

ARCHITECTURAL FEATURES

In the area of the Southwestern Aspect, there are three architectural features missing: cobblestone shrines, gravel pictographs, and circular sleeping platforms. The absence of the first feature is inexplicable. The absence of the second may be accounted for through the unsuitability of the environment for the construction of gravel pictographs, there being no desert pavements nor bare top mesas in the area. Beginning in latitude 30° and extending south into the desert areas of Baja California, conditions are suitable, but insufficient exploration has been carried out to warrant a positive or negative decision.

San Diego County has furnished only one cobble-outlined structure of this nature. It is located on a precipitous spur overlooking the south side of the Escondido Creek Slough (SDM-W-9). In configuration, it is three concentric circles built around the apex of the spur on different contour levels. When first seen in 1924, cirque erosion had already destroyed sections of the three circles on the north side. Subsequent erosion has affected the structure but slightly to this day. As the apex carries a thin veneer of San Dieguito midden, capped by a slightly thicker bed of La Jolla II midden, it is impossible to determine who built the structure.

The boulder-rimmed or cleared sleeping circle was observed, and its purpose defined, by the first Spanish explorers of the southern end of the Baja California peninsula. How much farther north they are to be found as archaeological vestiges is yet to be determined.

DISCUSSING THE OAK GROVE AND TOPANGA SITES

During the past ten to twelve years quite a number of papers have been brought out which purported to establish the presence of San Dieguito culture far north of San Diego County, among which the Oak Grove culture (Rogers, D. B., 1929) and the Topanga Canyon culture (Treganza and Bierman, 1958) were examples. At the time D. B. Rogers published his book, *Prehistoric Man of the Santa Barbara Coast,* I conferred with him both in the field and in the laboratory. In his collections I was surprised to find many boxes of flaked stone artifacts in storage which were not mentioned in the report. My study resulted in the belief that if the Oak Grove culture resembled anything further south, it was the La Jolla culture. There was also the common practice of building cairns of rocks and broken metates over the burials. It is true that there were bifaces to be accounted for, but as the excavations were conducted mostly by high school students, the bifaces might easily have come from the overlying Hunting People horizon.

The Topanga culture, however, in its Phases I and II, presents a seemingly closer affiliation with the San Dieguito Complex. In summation it must be pointed out that only a small portion of the San Dieguito pattern is in evidence; in fact, the poverty of tools of the scraping class is arresting. Also missing are the specialized scrapers and flaking skill of the San Dieguito people. Aberrations, too, occur, such as inhumations, and the metate and mano stone.***

THE METHOD OF PRESENTATION

In presenting the Southwestern Aspect, it was deemed best to divide the area into two parts for several reasons. First of all, the southern California area contains the most complete picture of the development of the two phase patterns, their geological associations and their relations to subsequent culture patterns. San Diego County must be considered the classic focus and diffusional center of the Southwestern Aspect. Nothing was added to the San Dieguito III pattern in Baja California except a few new types of projectile points.

THE GEOLOGY OF THE COAST REGION

The Mesas—Once Under the Sea

It is sufficient for archaeological purposes to deal only with such geology as is relevant to the advent of man in the region, although in preparing this foundation it is necessary to go into pre-man geology to some extent. The extreme western part of San Diego County is composed of an uplifted marine platform, whose surface has retained to the present a remarkably even elevation. Since its emergence, however, it has been deeply trenched from east to west by both small streams and a few major rivers, an action which isolated many sections one from another. As a result, we do not find the Coastal Mesa referred to as an entity, either in the local parlance or in geological literature, but as subdivisions, such as the San Diego Mesa, the Chula Vista Mesa, the Otay Mesa, the Linda Vista Mesa, and others. As the entire coastal mesa is of approximately the same geological age, I shall refer to it as such for the purpose of clarity.

This strip of terrain lies between the Coast Range and the Pacific Ocean. It begins in the northern part of San Diego County and ends slightly south of the International Boundary. It has an average width of nine miles, except where the width is restricted by outlying spurs of Coast Range igneous rocks. It has a mean elevation of 300 feet, and if one stands almost anywhere on its surface and gazes into the distance in any direction, the vista is one of a gently rolling plateau. Where it meets the sea, however, it has a sheer drop of from fifty feet at the north end to 300 feet in places to the south. This almost vertical sea cliff is due in part to some early faulting, but its present state is the result of a rise in sea level which began since the advent of man in the region, and it is still operative. Its destructive effect upon littoral archaeology will be discussed further on.

Sandstone Ridges
The geomorphic history of the surface of the Coastal Mesa subsequent to its emergence is little understood. Its most characteristic feature, perhaps, is the presence of three parallel sandstone ridges, and fragmentary evidences of a fourth, which traverse its surface from the southeast to the northwest. Between their undulations lie extensive expanses of ancient river gravels and sandy clays, which are devoid of San Dieguito archaeology. On their seaward and landside slopes are gravel ramps, the heaviest mantles being found on the seaward side.

As these sandstone ridges support the earliest archaeology, I shall concentrate on their nature and origin. Three different theories have been advanced in attempts to solve their origin. One is that they represent ancient sea level terraces; two, that they are fossil sand dunes; and three, that they are of submarine origin, resulting from the joint action of tides and constant directional currents operating over long periods of time in a shallow sea.

The first theory is the least tenable, since a marine terrace could not be incised

against space. Much time could be spent in presenting the data in support of the different hypotheses and arguing their relative merits, but as this report is essentially an archaeological study I shall refrain from discussing them in detail.

I favor the submarine origin of these ridges, and shall advance supporting evidence for this belief, because it is closely integrated with the archaeology, the latter being found both on their surfaces and within the slope-wash soil derived from the decomposition of the cappings.

It may be that the bars were formed simultaneously or in an alternate manner while the coastal block was in the process of elevation, the one farthest removed from the Pacific being the first to emerge from a regressing sea. As these are purely academic problems in geology and the nature of the archaeology associated with all four is identical, the subject is without value, at least with regard to which ridge was first occupied by man.

As a result of postformative erosion, many deep exposures of longitudinal and cross-section structure are available for study. In the sections, the ridges display unstratified sands of a common lithic nature, with a weathered profile due to ferrugination, which diminishes with depth. The typical capping is a reddish, moderately indurated sandstone. The hematite-stained section quickly softens with depth and diminishes in color intensity until it merges with yellowish, limonite-impregnated sands. These in turn gradually blend into gray sands, which occupy two-thirds or more of a typical vertical section. The weathering is characteristic of a humid climate.

The ridge surfaces are universally strewn with thousands of small ferruginous pellets composed of hematite-cemented sand. In some areas they are incorporated within the sandstone at shallow depths. No conclusive explanation of their origin has been proposed. It seems most probable that they were formed by undulating currents in relatively shallow

water wherein bits of marine flora, acting as nuclei, gathered coatings of sand in being rolled about.

The sandstone capping universally displays roughly geometric systems of crevasses, similar to mud cracks, but on a larger scale. It seems obvious that they represent shrinkage partings formed subsequent to emergence. The crevasses penetrate the surface to a depth of from a few inches to as much as six feet down. They are packed with a lime-cemented gray sand, whose source is most puzzling, unless it was derived from an underlying deposit formed shortly after the crevasse patterns were developed. No evidence of such a formation remains today. Within the crevasse fills, root casts of a calcareous sand nature are commonly found, penetrating to the full depth of the ancient shrinkage cracks. They seem to be pseudomorphs of a terrestrial flora, since marine flora does not have a penetrating root system, merely attaching itself to a ledge or gravel bed. Another form occasionally

Malcolm Rogers reported that natives called this site the "factory."

It is in the sand dunes between Rosarito Beach and Ensenada, in Baja California, near the mouth of the Descanso River, at site LC-26.

It is a narrow strip three-fourths of a mile long and averaging 300 feet in width, much reduced by recession of the sea cliff.

Stones from the beach provided material for all Indian cultures of the southern coast beginning with that of Rogers' San Dieguito III people.

Erosion by wind and rain have continually dropped the debris of later people down upon that of earlier men, causing a considerable cultural admixture.

This photograph shows how sand has been blown away and erosion is cutting at the sandstone and exposing stones worked by human hands centuries, even thousands of years ago.

Green felsite was the most popular material used in the manufacture of artifacts.

found in the red sandstone and down into the yellow sands is a large bulbous cast. These sometimes are attached to an intricate, fossil rootlet system which has been preserved most often by calcite replacement, and more rarely by an opaline mineral. Microscopic examination of the nature of the root casts and crevasse fills eliminates the possibility that the sand was of eolian origin, because of two properties: the pellets were rounded through water transportation, and great lithological selectivity was in evidence. Over ninety percent of the sand was found to be quartzitic, hence it would seem that only the placering action of moving water could have created a concentration of this nature.

The Forces of Erosion

The greatest erosional alteration of the ridges has come about through the extension of the trellis drainage systems associated with the major stream channels. This lateral erosion has produced steep escarpments of considerable height on the east sides of the ridges, especially at their north and south extremities, where deeply trenched river valleys cross their strike from east to west. In their midsections the topography has remained largely unscathed by degradation to the present.

GEOLOGICAL DATING PROBLEMS

Before these factors are considered, an attempt to place the fossil bars in geological time is important because of the associated archaeology. It has been generally accepted that they are of late Pliocene age, but as they are nonfossiliferous, geological positioning is most difficult. Around the flanks of the Coast Range and 100 feet higher than the highest sandstone ridge are a few residual cappings of Upper Pliocene shell in a white sandy marl. This evidence necessitates the assumption that Pleistocene crustal warping had set in previous to the formation of the submarine bars in a regressing sea. Then, too, the bar sands are coarser and of a different lithological nature than those of the fine Pliocene sands. At this time the tilting of the entire Pacific slope seems to have proceeded with such rapidity that hitherto sluggish streams became fast moving on their new and steeper gradients. This resulted in the deposition of extensive beds of gravel and deltaic sands on the lower levels between the sand ridges. These beds too are nonfossiliferous. The combined evidence seems to demand an age for the sand ridges not older than the Lower Pleistocene, and I find even that antiquity difficult to accept, because of the slight geomorphic modification in evidence. There is by no means sufficient surface senility in evidence to warrant the assumption that the bars were raised into a terrestrial position almost a million years ago.

The Artifact Strata

The first evidence of degradation is recorded in an unevenly distributed decomposition of the sandstone *in situ*. The spottiness is due to the uneven thickness of the sandstone. In the valleys between unbroken areas of the caprock lies a residual, sandy loam, which when dry is quite hard. The same formation occurs on the flanks of the ridges as a slope-wash, but is unlaminated and ungullied, indicating a very slow and prolonged period of accretion unaccompanied by sudden precipitation. Since both deposits are of the same nature, they have been combined for convenience under a general term, "red-crag." In some vertical sections, if the slope-wash is observed under a proper cross light, it displays a horizontally bedded structure of a coarse nature, a feature developed by uneven weathering. In this soil, San Dieguito II flakes and artifacts are found throughout, without concentrations. At some sites of this nature, San Dieguito III cultural material is sparingly present on the weathered sandstone surfaces, and to a slight depth in the slope-wash formation.

The cultural material is coeval with the decomposition of the sandstone, but cannot be placed in geological time because of the universal absence of materials such as charcoal, bone and shell, from which radiocarbon dates might be procured. Basal to this in time is the deeply weathered soil profile, which demands a lengthy developmental period, but one for which we have no yardstick.

By using this unsatisfactory evidence, one could postulate that man appeared in the region as early as Middle Pleistocene time, but I am convinced that this could not have been earlier than the Last Pluvial. In such sites there is no evidence of lacunae in the subsequent cultural stratigraphy down until historic time, except for the disconformity between the San Dieguito and La Jolla II strata.

At the close of the San Dieguito period, or shortly afterward, a rejuvenation of the native chapparal shrubs ensued. This permitted wind-transported sand and some slope-wash to lodge on the ridges. In this formation the La Jollans of the second phase period left their cultural debris. Between this stratum and that of the San Dieguitoans, erosional disconformities are commonly observable. Archaeological disconformities are also present, for the La Jollans often cut into the San Dieguito strata in digging hearths and sweathouse pits.

Cirque Erosion

The second degradational inroad upon the sandstone ridges was on a greater scale than the initial period of decomposition, and is archaeologically quite recent. It is manifested by a peculiar type of cirque erosion which takes the form of deep, straight-sided craters within the ridges. They are located both on the east and west flanks but are much more numerous on the east. In proportion to their size, they have remarkably narrow drainage outlets, which suggests the explanation that once an initial break in the hard capping was made, vertical winds operating on the lower and softer sand formation were the major formative factor. Wind is still an operating agent.

The craters are post-La Jolla II in age, as they have all but obliterated many La Jolla II middens, especially where two cirques operating in opposed directions have met at the apex of a site. A few such sites even have a trace of Diegueño cultural material, such as an occasional potsherd or arrow point, upon their crowns. It does not seem possible that these great cirques could have developed in so short a time unless the aborigines burned off the brush, or it died off during a severe and prolonged period of drought.

Diegueños were in the habit of burning areas of high ground in order to keep their trails open. By the historic period the chapparal had reestablished itself upon the sandstone ridges, and erosion has become arrested, to a certain extent. When first seen forty-one years ago, the taluses and bottoms of the craters were literally paved with fire-burned rock derived from the destruction of La Jolla II hearths and sweathouses. They were also rich in San Dieguito II, San Dieguito III, and La Jolla II artifacts, but years of collecting by relic hunters has left almost nothing but the fire-broken rocks.

In Baja California

In the northern third of Baja California the Coastal Mesa of tertiary sedimentaries is not represented. From the mouth of the Rio Tijuana to the south, the coast is flanked by a precipitous range of effusive rocks upon which are sculptured Pleistocene changes of sea level in the way of marine terraces. Upon these are situated La Jolla shell middens, with occasional thin cappings of Yuman midden.

The frontal marine terraces are represented to some degree at corresponding elevations on the sides of some of the major stream valleys. Where their surfaces are not rocky and sandy loam is present, small San Dieguito III sites are occasionally found. At the junction of the main streams with the ocean there are residual blocks of Late Pleistocene estuarine sands at an elevation of twenty-five feet. They are indurated, but far too soft to be classified as sandstone. Upon their surfaces are to be found the largest San Dieguito III sites. These are large in area but they have no archaeological depth. Whatever cultural stratum enclosed the artifacts was carried away after the sites were abandoned, an action which left the artifacts thinly distributed upon a common horizon. As the impacted sand pedestals are ungullied, the destruction of the cultural stratum must have been accomplished during an arid period by wind scour. The San Dieguito III levels are immediately overlaid with La Jolla II shell middens, and as a consequence, San Dieguito III and La Jolla II artifacts are found commingled in the base of some La Jolla middens. How much time span this geoarchaeological disconformity represents is unknown.***

In this part of the Southwestern Aspect, over ninety percent of the San Dieguito archaeological sites are confined to the interior on terrain similar to the two inland zones described for San Diego County. All are of the San Dieguito III period, except for a fringe of San Dieguito II sites just south of the International Boundary. It is rather apparent that the San Dieguito II phase had become defunct before the San Dieguitoans began to move into sites down the peninsula. Neither I nor others have made a study of San Dieguito geological associations south of latitude 30°, and Arnold's work at Laguna Chapala constitutes the present frontier of knowledge. In 1930, F. S. Rogers' field notes established La Jolla II middens to be present as far south as Turtle Bay.

CHAPTER VIII

THE SOUTHWESTERN ASPECT IN BAJA CALIFORNIA

AN UNKNOWN LAND

The international political boundary which separates Upper and Baja California is of no cultural significance when applied to aboriginal cultural boundaries such as the San Dieguito, La Jolla, and Yuman. Both San Dieguito II and San Dieguito III sites and archaeological debris, especially the former, begin to thin out in the southern part of San Diego County, progressively so as one moves south into

These rocks are parts of metates broken in a heap on the sand hills near the seashore not far above the Descanso River in Baja California.

To Malcolm Rogers, they represented a final gesture of a people who "sacrificed" their utensils in some rite, perhaps either of death or departure.

It was his opinion that they had been left there by the La Jollans, or perhaps the early Yumans.

The shifting of the sands and the mixing of artifacts of various peoples obscured the situation.

Curiously, the breaking of a metate seemed to have religious significance to Indians of much later generations.

In a lifetime of association with the modern Indians of Southern California, the late Edward H. Davis obtained from the oldest of their people recollections from their childhoods of cremation ceremonies.

It was a typical gesture to deposit a broken metate on the spot where a relative had been cremated, though this sometimes was done a year afterward.

In one Luiseño rite described to Davis, the surviving relatives, a year after cremation, would pound the calcified bones to a fine powder, dilute it in water and drink it, to acquire the virtues of the departed.

Baja California. It is not until Laguna Chapala is reached that both phases become strongly represented. The interior of the northern third of the peninsula is extremely mountainous, without much intermontane topography which would be attractive to the people of the Phase II period, nor could its wet, Anathermal climate have competed with that of the coastal lowlands.

Early Surveys

Baja California, with an area of 53,280 square miles, excluding the many offshore islands on the Pacific and Gulf sides, is still in the main *terra incognita*, archaeologically speaking. During the 1920's I made archaeological surveys of the interior and Gulf side of the northern third of the peninsula, and in 1929, with the aid of a Smithsonian Institution grant, conducted excavations in Pacific Coast shell middens as far south as San Quentín. Later (Bancroft, 1932) in 1930, F. S. Rogers circumnavigated the peninsula and made surface collections from coastal sites and the main islands. The primary value of this survey was to determine the horizontal distribution of certain artifacts.

Recent Anthropological Studies

In recent times ethnologists and archaeologists have become more and more interested in this region, and as a result, valuable contributions have accrued. Arnold's work at Laguna Chapala has undoubtedly provided us with the most valuable archaeological data of recent times. After studying his report, I have the following comments to make. First, I was rather surprised by the meagerness of the yield from the different lake strands. Had so great a body of water with its long geological history been located in the Great Basin, it would have produced twice

the amount of archaeological materials. It is in so remote an area that one cannot attribute this scarcity to looters alone, but there is that to consider. As early as 1930, relic hunters were showing me arrow points, dart points, and spear points which they had obtained from as far south as La Paz. Unfortunately, looters are prone to pick up only projectile points, knives, drills, and a miscellany of what is to them spectacular. Hence, the professional is left with impoverished and unbalanced patterns with which to struggle.

Laguna Chapala Artifacts

The Chapala artifacts have been divided and presented as three culture patterns, based on flaking technique, weathering, chemical alteration and association with three specific strands. They are designated as the "elongated-biface assemblage," the "scraper-plane assemblage," and the "flake-core-chopper assemblage," and their relative antiquity is placed in this sequence. The terminology is unfor-

The three knives and at lower right the ovate biface in this photograph were collected in 1929 from the Descanso site LC-26 in northwestern Baja California.

They were found on the surface of an eroding midden, mingled with San Dieguito and La Jolla artifacts.

Because these tools resemble Old World artifacts, particularly of the Solutrean period, it was originally thought they might be quite ancient.

When the Harris site was excavated in 1938 and similar implements were found in Locus 2 at that site, Malcolm Rogers concluded these specimens must belong to the San Dieguito Complex.

In 1960 and 1966 radiocarbon dates on materials from Locus 1 and 2 of the Harris site yielded widely separated dates. There are now firm dates of 6450 and 6990 B.C. for Locus I. The Locus II date of 2770 B.C. is still tentative. It would appear then, that the broad and thin leaf-shaped knives and this "coup-de-poing"-shaped ovate belong to the younger period. (Scale in inches).

tunate on several counts. First, flake and core tools are common to all assemblages. Second, the term "scraper-plane assemblage" leaves the reader with the impression that the assemblage is made up entirely of scraper-planes. Such deficiencies could be further cited, but it is more to the point to compliment the researcher for having the foresight to keep the collections from the different terrace levels separated, a practice which in the past was often overlooked in collecting from the strands of fossil lakes in the Great Basin area.

I have no wish to review in detail the Laguna Chapala findings. Nevertheless, I feel that it is incumbent upon me to make some comment. I am familiar with the culture patterns involved, and such a discussion constitutes an integral part of this report.

The oldest assemblage seems definitely of a San Dieguito I facies, even though many elements are apparently missing. If true, this is a unique situation on the Pacific slope, where evidence of this phase has been found only in the narrow strip between the Peninsular Range and the Gulf of California. However, it is only twenty-five air miles from Chapala to this strip.

The second oldest assemblage seems to qualify as a fragmentary San Dieguito II pattern, even though many elements are missing or have not been recorded. There is a possible explanation of this in the fact that even farther north the San Dieguito II pattern was of an impoverished nature when compared with the classic center in San Diego County.

The youngest assemblage is undoubtedly greatly adulterated, probably from reoccupation of the same sites by peoples of diverse cultures. It contains elements of the San Dieguito III, Amargosa II and La Jolla II patterns, the latter being the people who left the true metate. The pigment slabs are characteristic of the Amargosa II phase, as are the finely serrated projectile points. The nearest Amargosa center to Chapala now known is on the

Gulf side of the peninsula.

Apparently Laguna Chapala lake strands differ in no way from the fossil lake and stream terraces of the Great Basin, in that they too carry diverse cultural materials.

In order to deal with the baffling cultural eccentricities of horizontal stratigraphy, one must first of all be equipped with a thorough knowledge of the culture patterns of all the regional cultures. Also, one must be aware that after the extinction of the Pluvial and Little Pluvial lakes, the same basins were reoccupied by transient lakes, in some instances with life periods of several hundreds of years.

The archaeology of the Chapala presents a phenomenon common to all arid regions—the vertical de-elevation of overlying and younger cultural elements to the basal position of an older cultural horizon, without much lateral displacement. This action was caused largely by wind erosion. The phenomenon is also observ-

The points, knives, and crescentic stone pictured here are part of a surface collection from the Descanso midden LC-26 in Baja California.

The specimens could not be arranged in any stratigraphic sequence at that site, because wind erosion had removed most of the midden soil, depositing these artifacts, San Dieguito tools, and La Jolla implements all on the same eroded terrace.

The crescentic stone in the center top row is identical to a specimen recently excavated at the Harris site from the Locus 1 deposit.

The cultural association of the remaining specimens is still not determined.

Present evidence indicates they belong to a distinct, but previously unrecognized, pattern that was in the area by 2700 B.C.

In the top row, left to right, are a knife, crescent, and side-notched point. The second row shows two trinotched points, and the bottom row a side-notched point, a trinotched knife or point, and a serrated-edge knife. (Scale in inches).

able on the Pacific Coast, not far removed from the Chapala basin. A splendid example is shown at the mouth of the Descanso River (SDM-Site No. LC-26). Here a dual San Dieguito III-La Jolla II site has been almost obliterated and the artifacts of the two cultures commingled on a common platform, an elevated section of Pleistocene indurated estuary sands. Many La Jolla II hearths and some burial cairns of broken metates have descended from an unknown height with but little displacement. Judging from a few small residual projections of La Jolla age, these features have descended at least three feet, and perhaps more in some cases.

In the Chapala collection are some scraper-planes which display on the edges and platforms some abrasion of a smoothing nature. If Arnold has correctly interpreted this as wear through usage, it will be the first observed instance in the entire San Dieguito domain.

Arnold presents a very plausible technique for distinguishing between sandblast and water erosion in his studies of the local material. It does not, however, account for the great amount of material from the Mojave Desert, artifacts which have never been under water and yet do not retain a single vestige of man-made shaping except a profile. It must also be realized that an artifact can gain a silt and sand sheen polish after emergence from a position under water.

In Summary

Again, in this territory the position in time of the San Dieguito and La Jolla cultures is not in conflict, at least as far south as the latitude of Laguna Chapala, beyond which I am unfamiliar with the archaeology. Sufficient vertical stratigraphy has been found to prove the position of the two and to disclose no existing geological disconformity between them.

The La Jollans in their southerly drift down the Pacific Coast continued to make many shell middens, adhered to the coastal belt, and practiced the same frozen economy, that of a seafood and seed-gathering nature. Judging from the archaeological remains, their material culture had made no progress with time, and pressure flaking was still unknown to them. Therefore their implements cannot be confused with those of the San Dieguitoans. As an example, their lithic pattern still did not include a refined scraping tool. They certainly were the first to introduce the metate into Baja California, but how far south is still a moot question.

SAN DIEGUITO IV IN BAJA CALIFORNIA

The Pericu

A fourth developmental phase of the San Dieguito Complex and its persistence in the southern third of the peninsula down into historic time has been previously postulated (Rogers, 1939). This hypothesis opened up not only a view of events unique in the field concerned, but a plausible explanation of what became of a certain segment of the San Dieguito people. Additional evidence gathered through the ensuing years has been affirmative rather than negative.

The theory is not that the Spanish found a pure San Dieguito racial and linguistic culture pattern resident in the Pericu of the 16th Century, but a residue of that ancient heritage. Because subsequent peoples with diverse cultures pushed ever southward down through this narrow corridor, eventually to become dammed up in a *cul de sac,* a late ethnic melange was inevitable. When the archaeology of the south half of the peninsula is worked out, I predict that a basal San Dieguito horizon will be found with overlying levels becoming more and more diluted with the passing of time.

Burial Practices

As an example, Massey's work (Massey, 1947) disclosed three different types of interment in the Cape Region: secondary, extended, and flexed. Furthermore, he presents historical evidence that the Pericu practiced cremation in Hispanic times. The last recording is more puzzling, in that the Yumans, who practiced cremation, never took over more than the northern third of the peninsula.

No evidence, after over thirty years of field research, has thrown light on how either the San Dieguitoans or the Amargosans disposed of their dead, but the La Jolla method (flexed burials) is known.

Secondary burial (the term is inaccurate in that if exposure abandonment was practiced, there could have been no primary burial) perhaps yields a clue to an ancient San Dieguito practice, wherein the dead were abandoned where they died. Then, had a more demanding respect for the dead become engendered with time, perhaps inculcated by a shamanistic cult, collection and disposal of surviving large bones might have resulted.

The most southerly known La Jolla burial comes from San Quentín, but the characteristic lithic pattern has been traced in the middens down to Turtle Bay. Also, Arnold's work (Arnold, 1957) substantiates the presence of the La Jolla pattern around the Bahia de Santa Rosalillita. The most northerly known record of cave caches of human bone is at Refugio, inland from Rocky Point.

Sleeping Circles

The cleared sleeping circle, a trait going back to San Dieguito I times in the Central Aspect (from which a narrow southerly projection has been traced down the Gulf side of the peninsula), does not appear on the Pacific slope until the arid regions are reached. I do not record this as evidence of a positive geographical break in the distribution of the sleeping circle, but to point out that it has not yet been found in other than the arid regions. Its absence, as well as its preservation or destruction, may be due in part to variations in climatic conditions.

The two types of sleeping circles, the simple clearing and the boulder-rimmed type, have beeen previously described by Rogers (Rogers, 1939) and much earlier by both Venegas (1759) and Clavigero (1787).

Rock Alignments

To date we have only one recording of another San Dieguito trait, the ground pictograph or gravel outlined figure. This was observed by F. S. Rogers (Bancroft, 1932) in 1930 on a mesa back of Turtle Bay on the seventy-five-foot terrace. Unfortunately, there is no available photograph or sketch of the structure. A third trait, the cobblestone cairn, is still unrecorded from the peninsula.

In the future particular attention must be directed toward discovery of pure La Jolla and Amargosa horizons and their relationship to the older San Dieguito culture, as well as to how far south they penetrated before they disappeared, either through acculturation or extinction.

CHAPTER IX

THE WESTERN ASPECT

BORAX LAKE, CALIFORNIA

Adjacent to the Central Aspect, and lying westerly to it, is an extension of San Dieguito archaeology in northern California. Even at this late time, it is still best exemplified at the classic Borax Lake site in Clear Lake County, which was excavated and reported upon by M. R. Harrington in 1948. Although the cultural horizon here has considerable depth, it is unfortunate that it was located on an erosional cone of alluvium, which failed to become stabilized during the period of human occupancy. The history of this inversion fan seems to have been one of alternating periods of degradation and alluviation. Because of such action, ancient artifacts were transported from their origi-

In each aspect of the San Dieguito Complex, there are distinctive variations of tool types which help separate one region from another. The phases within the aspects also exhibit differences, with the pattern becoming richer and more refined with time.

Basically, however, the San Dieguito Complex embodies a tool manufacturing co-tradition which is consistent from region to region and from the earliest man to the most recent Indians. The use of heavy planes, side-struck flakes, and a scarcity of blades all seem characteristic of this tradition.

Shown here are three kinds of artifacts: small domed discoidal scrapers, ovate bifaces, and blades. (Scale in inches).

The left column of tools, top to bottom, are classified as San Dieguito I in the Central Aspect.

The second column contains San Dieguito II-III implements from Lake Mojave.

At the right are three San Dieguito II-III specimens from San Diego County.

nal positions on the high part of the cone, to become reburied or deposited on the surface farther down the cone, where its pitch became more gentle and storm waters lost their velocity. Since the site is agricultural land and has been cultivated for years, the surface and near-surface archaeology has been further confused.

It seems impossible otherwise to interpret the topsy-turvy archaeological history, wherein elements of the San Dieguito and Amargosa industries as well as Pomo derivatives are found commingled upon or near the surface. Here too, at the same level, were found types of artifacts which also occurred at the very base of the midden. It is also interesting to note that the greatest number of channeled points were found on the surface, or in close proximity thereto.

Those who first studied the geological age of the fan and its accompanying archaeology agreed as to its late Pleistocene age, namely the Last Pluvial or Provo stage, pointing out that only the excessive precipitation of that period could have created the fan. In justice to Antevs, it must be recorded that he later re-evaluated the archaeology's place in time, grading it upward and making it coeval with his Altithermal period, with a time-span between 5000 and 2500 B.C. (Antevs, 1952).***

From the beginning I took an opposite view as to what climatic conditions were necessary to produce the structure and its contained archaeology. First, if the fan had been built during the Last Pluvial, the constant runoff would have rendered the terrain uninhabitable, or at least so unsatisfactory for habitation that the aborigines would have sought a better-drained camp site. Second, the fan has all the attributes of the typical western detrital structure associated with a canyon debouchment, a phenomenon which is universally observable in the process of formation during the present period of aridity, during which there are long periods wherein no runoff occurs, followed at intervals by sudden localized freshets during cyclonic storms. This type of runoff may incise a single major channel near the head of the deltaic cone, but when the detrital load becomes out of proportion to the suspending body of water, a damming action ensues, and the main stream ramifies into many laterals. From that point on, and progressively so, alluviation supersedes degradation and becomes the major factor in the cycle. It seems certain that some of the depth of the cultural horizon here was built in this manner.

If the theory that the San Dieguito III period in the Western Aspect was coeval, or at least survived into a dry period, as it did in the Southwestern Aspect, we have the choice of two established climates, either the Great Drought (Altithermal) or the Little Drought, which immediately followed the Little Pluvial (Medithermal). In the Central Aspect, because of the dessication of Lake Mojave, there is evidence that the climate of the San Dieguito III period was altering from moist to dry, and in the Southwestern Aspect the nature of the evidence is even more conclusive.

At Borax Lake there exists an erosional disconformity between the lacustrine deposits and the overlying midden. Evidence of man's presence was found below the disconformity, and, if Pluvial man is involved, it would seem that these interspersed beds of clay, sand, and gravel are the ones concerned and not the midden.

Comparison of the Artifacts

Shortly after the completion of the 1938 excavations at the Borax Lake site, I had the opportunity to go over the material and data derived therefrom with Harrington. Later on he came to the San Diego Museum of Man to study the San Dieguito collections at that institution. As a result of the two conferences, we were in accord as to the basic similarity of the two lithic industries involved, but Harrington wished to retain the Borax Lake complex as a separate and distinctive entity. In 1958 I was privileged to make a restudy of the material and data, and came away more convinced than ever that it represented a marginal manifestation of the San Dieguito Complex.

Harrington's Analysis

If I understand Harrington's archaeological interpretation correctly, it is this. At first there was a resident, indigenous settlement, for which we have as yet no well-defined culture pattern. During their occupancy, "the whole artifact-bearing deposit at Borax Lake was laid down within a relatively short time, perhaps within a few centuries" (Harrington, 1948, p. 118).

This concept of a short Pluvial occupation demands an archaeological lacuna between it and the protohistoric Pomo occupation of 6000 to 7000 years. No evidence of such a lengthy abandonment of the site has been provided.

We are left to conclude that during this brief period, visitors from many undefined geographical centers visited this occidental Mecca, either to leave or to make projectile points of their characteristic and diverse cultures. Among the visitors were the Lake Mojave Point, the Silver Lake Point, the Pinto Point, the "Yuma" Point, and the "Folsom" Point peoples. The Borax Lake Point people were considered to be native.

Apropos of the so-called local Folsom points, the Borax Lake channeled points present all the evolutionary stages from a simple basal-notched point to ones with multiple basal faceting, as well as points with a single side facet. Even the latter were usually given a final basal notch retouch.

An Unsolved Problem

The mortar, metate, and charmstone, elements of a non-San Dieguito nature in all

104

other Aspects, occurred at considerable depths, and therefore have created a problem of some magnitude. Through Heizer's work (Heizer, 1949, 1953) all three were found to be components of the Central California Early Horizon. In striving for a solution, it would seem that there are three avenues of approach. One is that the Borax Lake culture is the more ancient and that the three items had their origins in that culture. The second possibility is that the Early Horizon is locally the older and they owe their presence to acculturation. The third explanation is that the two cultures were contemporary and the three elements were trade intrusives. Whichever explanation may eventually be proved correct, it is of great significance to the problem that Heizer (Heizer 1949, p. 39) suggests the modest beginning date of 2500 B.C. for the Early Horizon.

DISTRIBUTION OF THE
WESTERN ASPECT

Subsequent to the exploration and diagnosis of the Borax Lake site, the findings of the California Archaeological Survey began to widen the orbit of distribution of the pattern, in northerly and southerly directions. At no site was the complete pattern represented, and even the fragmented patterns displayed some degree of dissimilarity from site to site. Most important was the fact that when stratigraphy was available they occupied basal positions in relation to the Early Horizon.

It is quite improbable that the local San Dieguito archaeology is confined by modern political boundaries, such as the state divisions of California, Oregon and Nevada. In the arid eastern part of Oregon, field research in the past has produced some elements of this complex, but as yet no one has found, or at any rate reported, a near complete assemblage for any of the three phase patterns.

Evidence Supporting the Comparison
It seems quite evident that the pattern under consideration is mainly of a San Dieguito III nature. The Silver Lake points,

Lake Mojave points, gravers, concave scrapers, tools with serrated margins, and above all the crescent proclaim it so. If the San Dieguito II phase or the younger Amargosa Complex are represented, the problem can be solved only through a reappraisal of the nature of all the artifacts and associated data, especially with regard to type frequencies in depth, implemented with studies of alteration and flaking technique.

The study of the flaking techniques employed here is made particularly difficult, because the industrial medium is almost entirely of obsidian. A skilled percussion flaker can produce artifacts in obsidian, which I think will defy anyone to distinguish from many pressure-flaked equivalents. Then, too, apprentices in the latter field probably produced many confusing artifacts of an in between nature.

In summation, it is perhaps in order to venture an opinion regarding the location of the homeland of this western extension of San Dieguito people, and the pathway pursued in their migration. It is suggested that the corridor of ingress from the Great Basin was near the point where the two states of California and Nevada corner on the Oregon state line, rather than over the high Sierra Nevada range. Had the east-to-west movement been over the Sierras, it would seem that by this time some occupational evidence in the intervening Sacramento River valley would have been found.

THE PROBLEM OF THE
GRINDING SLAB

At Borax Lake and Danger Cave
The metate of the Pacific Littoral, which is an indigenous, independently invented implement, is of considerable antiquity. It appears in the Early Horizon, to the south in the Oak Grove culture and even farther south, it is a component of the La Jolla culture. In the latter culture, Carbon 14 dating from shell has provided it with an age of 1950 B.C., plus or minus 200 years. (L J-I, Hubbs, 1960). Therefore, it is not surprising to find it at depth in the Borax

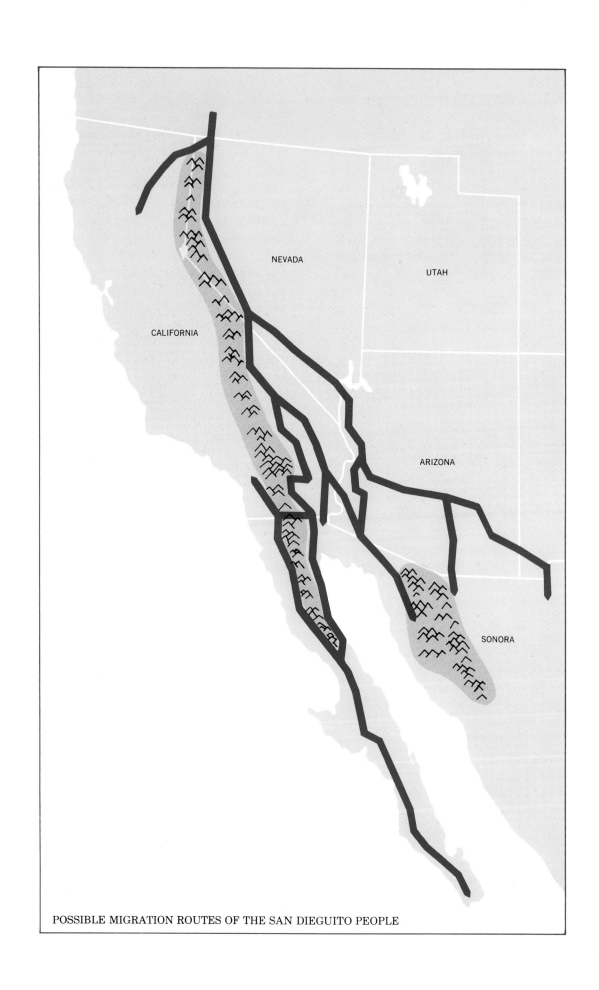

POSSIBLE MIGRATION ROUTES OF THE SAN DIEGUITO PEOPLE

Lake site, even though I am not satisfied that we are dealing with seed milling implements, either here or in Danger Cave (lower levels) and other early cave deposits of the northern Great Basin. Harrington noted that his handstones occasionally exhibited a red pigment in the pores, but Jennings (Jennings, 1957) makes no such comment regarding the manos and grinding slabs found in Danger Cave. The latter situation is difficult to understand, as dry cave deposits offer near-perfect conditions for the preservation of such evidence, as witnessed by the number of pigment-bearing slabs found in Ventana Cave.

Seed Mill vs. Pigment Slab

Because of the confusion which is quite apparent in archaeological reporting, as to whether an object should be identified as a seed mill or a pigment mill, it may be

When the San Dieguito people came into the Great Basin, and by what route, is not known for certain.

Malcolm Rogers offered some tentative suggestions as to their migration routes which he based in part on geography and on the distribution of artifacts.

For a time it was the thought that their ingress might have been from Wyoming through the low pass in the Continental Divide leading into the Great Salt Lake basin.

But Rogers found an unbroken line of archaeological sites extending north up through Nevada to the Oregon state line.

This suggested that the main corridor was down through central Washington and eastern Oregon.

There were many questions left unanswered, however.

How far into the Mexican mainland did they penetrate?

Did they gradually drift all the way down the peninsula of Lower California?

All the evidence so far indicates that in the beginning the peopling of the American continent was from north to south and the first to arrive certainly came over the now submerged Bering Straits.

of help to enumerate some diagnostic approaches to the problem. First, there is an obvious selective factor involved. All peoples living under a seed-gathering or agricultural economy tried to obtain coarse-grained igneous slabs for their metates, because of their superior milling properties. On the other hand, for pigment grinding they chose fine-grained stone of a sedimentary or metamorphic nature, such as sandstone, limestone, quartzite, slate, or schist. Another distinguishing property is the one of dimension. The average pigment mill has one half or less the thickness and one half the surface area of the average metate, and considerably less grinding area. Perhaps the most convincing evidence of a practical nature would be experimental attempts to reduce some hard seeds to a meal on one of these small, flattish slabs, and keep the seeds, the half-reduced seeds, and the meal all on the slab at the same time. We do have, however, some historical data gathered from Great Basin tribes to the effect that they overcame the difficulty of using flat slabs or shallow-basined slabs for seed milling by placing them on hides to catch the spill, a laborious task of replacing the grist many times (Loud and Harrington, 1929, p. 140).***

Grinding Slabs in the Pinto Basin

The presence of the metate as a component of the Amargosa culture was instigated in 1935 (Campbell and Campbell, 1935) in the Pinto Basin site report, when the entire archaeological yield from the basin, except for potsherds, was presented as a cultural entity. Actually, the archaeology is an admixture of San Dieguito, Amargosa, Yuman, and Cahuilla cultural materials. The last-named two left but traces and these are of such an obvious cultural nature that we need not be concerned, except for the presence of three large thick slabs, and a few large manos. These are characteristic implements of both the desert Yuman and Cahuilla cultures.

Concern should be given more to the relatively large group of intact and fragmented small thin slabs and the accompanying small unshaped handstones. In 1939 I attempted to correct the confusion which existed between the two distinctive implements, pointing out that only the small, thin slab belonged to the Pinto-Gypsum, or the Amargosa II culture, and that the majority of Pinto-Gypsum sites produced nothing that could be construed as being a metate. At that time, I provided the suggestion, a faulty one, that these small slabs were planing platforms, upon which small hides were fleshed or pulpy leaves were scraped in order to separate the fibers therefrom. Several years later, when several similar slabs were recovered from sub-surface positions with red pigment in their pores, their true nature became apparent.

PART III WHEN DID MAN COME TO NORTH AMERICA?

H. M. WORMINGTON

PART III

A SUMMARY OF WHAT WE KNOW TODAY

With the ever increasing knowledge that is being gained concerning the ancient inhabitants of this continent due to the rapidly growing interest in early preceramic cultures, it is easy to forget how little was known and how much pioneering effort lay ahead when Malcolm Rogers began his investigations of lithic industries in 1920. The discoveries at Folsom, New Mexico, that were to provide the first clear proof of the antiquity of man in North America were still six years in the future.

Not until 1932 would a find, made at Dent, Colorado, show that primitive hunters had killed mammoths in the New World as well as the Old. Radiocarbon dating was still undreamed of. The technique of fluorine dating was known, but was not being utilized. Excavation techniques and stratigraphic studies were far indeed from the present level of development. Few investigators were concerned with problems of Early Man, and publications on this subject were very limited. Even as recently as 1939 a fairly complete bibliography contained less than one hundred items.

The progress that has been made in less than fifty years is truly remarkable. More and more archaeologists are devoting themselves to the study of the early inhabitants of North America. A comprehensive bibliography would contain thousands of references, and even for the

This peaceful scene is in the San Dieguito River Valley of San Diego County.

Over a period of thirty-five years archaeologists have been digging trenches along the banks of the river in this area, at W-198, known as the Harris site for the ranch on which it is situated.

It is just outside a deep gorge which the river has trenched through the Coast Range on its way to the Pacific Ocean, nine miles to the west.

At this point the river valley widens to form a small basin and at its lower end it becomes restricted again where it passes through a narrow gorge known as the Narrows.

Alternate river flows have built layers of deposits.

A flood in 1926 scoured the channel sufficiently to peel back some of the layers and revealed evidence of long occupation by prehistoric people.

A trench turned up what Malcolm Rogers classified as an entire tool factory of the San Dieguito III phase.

In the last year another trench yielded the first firm dates in the effort to determine the time scale of the San Dieguitoans.

111

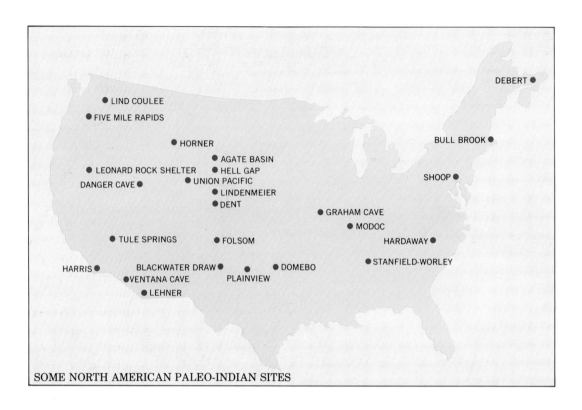

SOME NORTH AMERICAN PALEO-INDIAN SITES

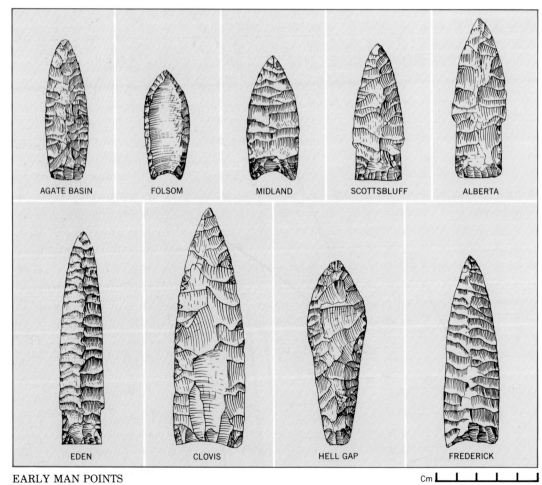

AGATE BASIN   FOLSOM   MIDLAND   SCOTTSBLUFF   ALBERTA

EDEN   CLOVIS   HELL GAP   FREDERICK

EARLY MAN POINTS   Cm

specialist it is difficult to keep up with the flow of publications. Of these, many that represent significant contributions have come not only from archaeologists, but from geologists, paleontologists, and palynologists. Specialists in a variety of disciplines have cooperated with prehistorians in interdisciplinary studies that have provided valuable information relating to past environment.

Of the utmost importance is the development of the radiocarbon method of dating. Before this extraordinarily useful tool became available fifteen years ago, archaeologists seeking to date early sites were

Only a few decades ago, before radiocarbon dating, it was difficult for archaeologists to accept the evidence of their own eyes.

In 1932 at Dent, Colorado, came the first find that indicated man had been on the Great Plains early enough to have hunted mammoths.

Now it is known that in the Plains the most common prey of primitive hunters was the mammoth, and most of them made large, finely flaked fluted projectile points of a type called Clovis, shown in the accompanying illustration.

Since the development of radiocarbon dating twelve Early Man sites between 9000 and 10,000 B.C. have been found and all of them but one contained bones of the extinct mammoths.

The wide distribution of some major North American Early Man sites is shown in the map, drawn by Arminta Neal. Also shown is a variety of Paleo-Indian projectile points of the Plains, shown in half natural size.

While some skeletons of the La Jolla Man may go back as much as 5000 to 7000 years, much remains to be learned about the appearance of Early Men on the rest of the North American continent.

Only three partial skeletons have been found — in Texas, Colorado and Tepexpan, near Mexico City — which can be attributed with some confidence to a very early period of occupation.

largely dependent on the estimates of geologists who could place archaeological phenomena only in broad general time ranges. Today, we have vastly more information concerning the time spans of geological phases of the terminal Pleistocene and early Recent, as well as dates for specific sites.

The use of heavy equipment, undeveloped in the Twenties and Thirties, has opened new vistas, and the greater availability of funds has made possible investigations that would have seemed in the realm of fantasy some twenty years ago. Studies of stratigraphy and methods of excavation have grown increasingly sophisticated. A growing knowledge and interest in technology have made it possible to gain new insights into the development of different lithic traditions.

In a brief space it is quite impossible to cover, in any detail, the vast mass of data that has been gathered by workers concerned with Early Man in North America. Any reasonably comprehensive summary would require hundreds of pages. All that can be attempted here is to provide a summary of the broad overall picture as we know it now.

Physical Remains of Early Man

Despite all that has been accomplished, much remains to be learned about the early inhabitants of North America. As yet, we know virtually nothing about the people themselves. Only three partial skeletons have been found which can be attributed with some confidence to an early period of occupation. Parts of a skull, some metacarpals, and some broken ribs found near Midland, Texas, may date back to about 9000 B.C. A skull and parts of a human skeleton found at Tepexpan near Mexico City (De Terra, Romero, and Stewart, 1949) are, according to fluorine tests, of the same age as mammoth remains found in the vicinity.

Recently the greater part of a human skeleton has been found on a tributary of Gordon Creek, Roosevelt National Forest, Colorado. It lay in a burial pit and

113

was covered with red ochre. Charcoal found in the pit produced a radiocarbon date of 7750 B.C., plus or minus 250 years. Associated artifacts consisted of one large and two small bifacially flaked ovoid objects that appear to be blanks or preforms, a smoothed stone, a hammerstone, a broken end scraper, and some utilized flakes (Anderson, 1966).

Most archaeologists now feel that "Minnesota Man," the skeleton of an adolescent girl found near Pelican Rapids, Minnesota (Jenks, 1936), is not of the same age as the ancient deposits in which it was found. The discovery was made by a highway road crew unfamiliar with scientific methods of excavation.

The Earliest Dates

One of the greatest problems facing students of Early Man in the New World is that it is still impossible to say when men first left Siberia and crossed the Bering Strait to enter America. We do know that there were times in the past when they could have passed from one hemisphere to another by crossing a broad land bridge that linked Siberia and Alaska (Haag, 1962). It is quite certain that the first entry was well before 10,000 B.C. There are firm dates for human occupation in the Plains and in the Southwest in the tenth millennium B.C., and the implements represented include sophisticated projectile points of types that must have developed in the New World. Futhermore, during the ninth millennium B.C. men were living in Patagonia and Brazil and it must have taken considerable time for the newcomers to this hemisphere to reach these distant lands.

A few sites have suggested an age of 30,000 to 40,000 or more years, but in no case was there incontrovertible evidence that these could be linked with the presence of man. Localities in California, Texas Street, Scripps Service Yard (Carter, 1957), and Santa Rosa Island (Orr, 1956a, 1960), have yielded dates of great age, but human occupation during so early a period has not been regarded as proven

by the great majority of archaeologists. Santa Rosa Island would certainly merit further investigation. There is need for exposure of preserved land surfaces on a broad horizontal basis. Bones found in very old deposits in Potter Creek Cave are not artifacts in the opinion of the author. Viewed with the naked eye, some do seem to be of human manufacture, but seen under a microscope and compared with true bone tools, they do not appear to have been shaped by man. Excavations in the very ancient deposits of the Calico Hills locality in the Manix Lake area (Simpson, 1958) are still continuing and cannot be evaluated at this time.

Radiocarbon assays of charred vegetal matter from the Lewisville site near Dallas, Texas (Crook, 1958), have consistently produced dates in excess of 35,000 B.C., but the presence of a well-made fluted point, which could not possibly be of this age, has left the chronological position of the site open to question. It is regretable that this site is now covered by a lake and that further investigations cannot be undertaken.

To many archaeologists, the writer among them, the Tule Springs site in southern Nevada was the most promising of putatively early sites, for limited excavations undertaken by the Southwest Museum had produced a bone tool, a stone scraper, and apparent hearths and burned bones, in deposits believed, on the basis of Carbon 14 dates, to be more than 28,000 years old (Harrington, and Simpson, 1961). In 1962 and 1963 when excavations on an unprecedented scale were undertaken by Richard Shutler, Jr. and a number of specialists in other disciplines, it became apparent that there was no evidence of the presence of man at an exceptionally early date. When large stratigraphic sections were exposed and detailed geological studies were undertaken by C. Vance Haynes, Jr. a vastly complicated geological sequence of alluvial and lacustrine sediments separated by soils and erosional contacts was revealed. It became apparent that the samples used for the earlier radiocarbon assays were mixtures of materials collected from two deposits of quite different ages, although on the basis of the first limited excavations it had been entirely reasonable to believe that a single deposit was represented. Dates obtained from such a mixture are, of course, meaningless.

During the 1962-1963 excavations no hearths, burned bones, or burned earth were found, and it seems possible that those reported earlier may have been the result of organic decay and staining, rather than burning. The previously reported scraper appears to have been derived from a rill that dates back to probably less than 4000 B.C. Three bones found in a unit that is between 14,000 and 11,500 years old may have been modified by man, but they cannot be regarded as unmistakably artifacts. In a unit dated at 9250 B.C. to 8000 B.C. the only incontrovertible evidence of human occupation was found. It consisted of a scraper and some flakes.

Artifacts of the 10th millennium B.C. previously found in the Plains and in the Southwest have, up until now, constituted the earliest firmly established evidence of human activity in North America. Now there appears to be a breakthrough with the release of two dates obtained from bone samples from two strata at Wilson Butte Cave in the Snake River Plain of southern Idaho, which was excavated by Ruth Gruhn (Gruhn, 1961). A sample from a stratum that contained bones of horse and two kinds of camelids produced a date of 15,000, plus or minus 800 years (13,050 B.C.). Evidence for the presence of man at the time when this deposit was formed is not entirely conclusive. It consists of two fragments of bone that bear what appear to be scars of knife cuts. Also, large mammal bones were broken in a manner that suggests smashing by man. In a higher stratum, however, there is clear, though scanty, evidence of human activity, and a sample taken from there yielded a radio-carbon date of 14,450, plus or minus 500 years (12,500 B.C.) (Gruhn, personal communication). Three stone artifacts and two fragments of bone that may have been modified by man were recovered.

The stone artifacts consist of a bifacially flaked leaf-shaped point of basalt, a utilized flake, and a blade of chalcedony. It is most important to note that the term blade here, and throughout this section, is used in a technological sense to indicate a parallel-sided, usually prismatic flake struck from a prepared core and more than twice as long as it is wide. The length is measured along the axis of the detachment blow, and the width, at right angles to the axis.

One might expect that some of the oldest traces of man would be found in the Arctic, the area closest to the Asiatic homeland of the earliest Americans and the first to be reached. As yet, though, we have no fully acceptable evidence for very early occupation of the far north. At Cape Krusenstern, at a site called the Palisades, which lies on a terrace some distance from the sea, the late J. L. Giddings (1961) found crudely flaked stones, including choppers or axes and a fragmentary stemmed point made of chalcedony that showed strong chemical alteration. It is reasonable to assume that it must have taken a long time for this material to be so altered, but there is no way of knowing just how long a time period may be involved.

The British Mountain level of the Engigstiak site on the Firth River excavated by Richard MacNeish (1956) and the Kogruk site at Anaktuvak Pass reported by John Campbell (1961) may be quite old, but the stratigraphy of the former is not clear, and the latter is a surface find. Both do contain artifacts that show use of a Lavallois technique, but this is not necessarily significant, for the use of this technique persisted to some extent until Choris times, about 1000 B.C. (Giddings, 1963). The phenomenon that has been called "Arctic retardation" (Collins, 1964) must

be constantly kept in mind in evaluating undated materials. Points of types that were being made in the Plains in the 6th to 7th millennia B.C. were being produced in Alaska between 2500 and 1500 B.C. Side-notched points are old in the Arctic, and were produced at an early period at Cape Krusenstern and at Onion Portage (Giddings, 1966). At the latter site on the Kobuk River, where excavations are still in progress, thirty culture-bearing layers divided into eight bands have been revealed. They constitute a long sequence that includes pre-Denbigh material, some of which predates 6000 B.C. There are radiocarbon dates in the 7th millennium for a site on Anangula Island that produced flakes and blades (Laughlin and Marsh, 1954). In general, finds so far made in the Arctic represent specialized traditions, and throw little light on problems relating to the peopling of the rest of the continent.

Paleo-Eastern and Paleo-Western
The Plains area of the United States has

Countless generations of men have sought shelter in Ventana Cave in Arizona.

This photograph shows its small, dark opening in a butte in the Castle Mountains on the Papago Indian reservation. The site is south of Phoenix and west of Tucson.

An internal spring provided water for prehistoric animals as well as Early Men. The legend of the cave may have survived in a song of thirst and distant water of Papago Indians.

It was a meeting place of many cultures and the finding of San Dieguito I artifacts below the midden of Amargosa I and II aided Malcolm Rogers to verify his postulations on culture phases of the Far West.

Emil W. Haury's report on Ventana Cave stated that the vertebrate assemblages included a high proportion of animals now extinct and that their extinction came after man had become established in Arizona.

Archaeologists have assigned a date of at least 8000 B.C. for what they call the Ventana Complex.

provided the longest, clear, stratigraphic sequences and, before the release of the Wilson Butte dates, the earliest acceptable dates obtained in North America. Here, and in the Southwest, we know that during the 10th millennium B.C. men were hunting animals which are now extinct. The most common prey was the mammoth, and most of the hunters made the large, finely flaked fluted projectile points of the type that bears the name Clovis.

Twelve radiocarbon dates from six sites fall between 9000 and 10,000 B.C. These sites include Dent, Colorado; Lehner and Ventana Cave, Arizona; Blackwater Draw, New Mexico; Domebo, Oklahoma; and Union Pacific, Wyoming (Haynes n. d.). All yielded extinct fauna, and all but Ventana Cave contained mammoth bones. Fluted points were lacking only in Ventana Cave and the Union Pacific site. The latter, however, produced a leaf-shaped biface that may be a knife or a preform, an end scraper on a blade, a strangled blade with an end scraper, a retouched blade, and a perforator and, because these are tools found elsewhere with Clovis points, it would seem possible that, although proof is lacking, this may well be a Clovis site (Irwin, Irwin and Agogino, 1961).

The lowest level of Ventana Cave, Arizona, (Haury et al., 1950), has provided evidence of the contemporaneity of man and extinct horse, ground sloth, tapir, jaguar, and wolf. The bulk of the artifacts found here are quite unlike those represented in the other sites that fall in this time range. One unfluted leaf-shaped point with a concave base that, in general outline, resembles a Clovis was found, but the associated artifacts were not like those normally associated with Clovis. They included choppers, planes, keeled and discoidal scrapers, and knives and scrapers made from side-struck flakes, commonly found in the extreme western United States, but not characteristic of complexes to the east of the Rocky Mountains. This is of great interest because, as we shall see, during later periods, there was a

117

strong dichotomy between the dominant lithic traditions to the east and to the west of the mountains, and it would appear that the Paleo-Western tradition has greater time depth than has been established by dates from a pure site, such as the Harris site.

At present, we do not understand the significance of the dichotomy between the traditions that have been called Paleo-Eastern and Paleo-Western. It could be that both traditions developed from a common, as yet unknown, base in response to different environmental conditions. It is also possible that two different traditions were introduced from Asia. The Western one with its choppers and core tools is certainly most like that of southeastern Asia; and the Eastern, which has a blade technology, is reminiscent of the Upper Paleolithic of Siberia.

Blackwater Draw locality in New Mexico, excavated at intervals since 1932 by a number of individuals (Howard, 1935; Cotter, 1937, 1938; Sellards, 1952; Agogino, n.d.; Hester, n.d.) is of extraordinary significance for it was occupied for thousands of years and the sequence runs from Clovis to Archaic. Of major importance is the fact that the Clovis horizon represents a habitation, as well as a kill site, and as a result, it has been possible to learn quite a bit about tools other than projectile points. Of particular interest is the extensive use of a blade technology (Green, 1963; Warnica, 1966). This is in sharp contrast to assemblages found farther west. Side scrapers were the most common tool type. There were also many end scrapers. Knives were large, very thin bifacially flaked ovoids. Many specimens with tiny, finely worked spurs commonly called "gravers" were found. Some had only a single spur, but a large number had multiple spurs.

Their function is not known with certainty, but experiments conducted by Donald Crabtree and Henry Irwin have suggested some interesting possibilities. They have found that it is possible to manufac-ture eyed bone needles using only the so-called gravers and small polishing stones. The author has examined a needle manufactured by Irwin and has found it to be exactly like those found at the Lindenmeier Folsom site and in the Agate Basin level at the Hell Gap site.

The Paleo-Eastern Tradition

There is a type of early point which is sometimes fluted, but more often is not. It is called Sandia after the cave of that name in New Mexico (Hibben, 1941). Sandia points are characterized by an inset on one side only, which produces a single shoulder. Few Sandia points have been found, and they appear to have a limited distribution, largely confined to the southern Plains. There are no firm dates for Sandia points, but recent geological investigations in the type station by C. Vance Haynes and George Agogino indicate that Sandia points fall in the general 7000 to 11,000 B.C. time range (Haynes, n.d.).

The deep, stratified site with three locations near Guernsey, Wyoming, called Hell Gap, excavated during the past five years by Henry Irwin, Cynthia Irwin-Williams, and George Agogino (1966), has provided much information concerning developments in Paleo-Indian times. The stratified Blackwater Draw and Hell Gap sites, and others that have only a single component, have shown that during the 8th and 9th millennia B.C. more sites were occupied and there were a number of distinctive lithic complexes, most, and probably all of which evolved from Clovis. By this time, mammoth, horse, and camel had disappeared and the primary dependence of the ancient hunters was now on extinct species of bison, larger than present day buffalo. The practice of killing great numbers of animals by impounding them, or driving them over cliffs was already well-established (Dibble, 1965). It may go back still further in time, for at the Dent site, there is evidence that suggests that Clovis hunters may have driven mammoth over the edge of a cliff.

Folsom points characterize the most famous complex of the 9th millennium B.C. They are smaller and more refined versions of the Clovis points, which must have been ancestral to them. One extensive habitation site of Folsom man, the Lindenmeier site in Colorado (Roberts, 1935, 1936) has been found. It has produced a radiocarbon date of 8820 B.C., plus or minus 375 years (Haynes and Agogino, 1960). End scrapers were more commonly used than in Clovis times; large, thin biface knives continued to be made. The implements with small spurs, called gravers, were more often single than multiple. The beveled edges of end scrapers often had a spur on one side.

Two other point types of the same general period as Folsom have shapes very like Clovis, but they are unfluted. They bear the names of the sites in Texas where they were first recognized, Plainview (Sellards, Evans and Mead, 1947) and Midland (Wendorf, Krieger, Abritton and Stewart, 1955). In recent years, it has become increasingly apparent that the complex called Agate Basin was of major importance at about this time in the northern Plains of the United States and in western Canada, and some have been found in Alaska. The site is named after the type station in Wyoming (Roberts, 1943, 1961). Later work at the Brewster site, an extension of the original locality, has provided additional data and a radiocarbon date of 7400 B.C. for an upper level, and 8040 B.C. for a lower one (Agogino and Frankforter, 1960a). Contrary to earlier interpretations, the bones associated with Agate Basin points appear to be those of extinct, rather than modern bison.

Characteristic points are long, slender, lanceolate forms with straight or slightly convex, or, rarely, slightly concave bases. Many are completely unfluted, but a few have a very narrow flute removed from one face. The Agate Basin horizon at the Hell Gap site and the Frazier site in Colorado, where excavations begun in 1966 will be continued in 1967, show an interesting use of a blade technology in the pro-

duction of scrapers, which is reminiscent of Clovis. In Agate Basin, as in Folsom, there is a greater use of end scrapers than in Clovis. Small spurred objects continued to be made, and spurs were present on end scrapers.

At Hell Gap, in a slightly higher level than the Agate Basin Horizon, were found examples of the point that bears the site name. These resemble the Agate Basin type, but are so markedly constricted at the base that they may be regarded as essentially stemmed forms. Of approximately the same age are Alberta points which are definitely stemmed. Higher in the sequence, in a layer dated at 6640 B.C., plus or minus 600 years, are Eden points, a component of the Cody Complex.

Elsewhere, Eden points have been found only in sites that have also yielded Scottsbluff points, although the latter have been found unaccompanied by Edens. Scottsbluff points have broad stems, small shoulders, and triangular or parallel sided blades. Eden points are narrower relative to their length, and are less markedly stemmed. At the Horner site in Wyoming (Jepsen, 1953) was first recognized the Cody Complex which includes not only Scottsbluff and Eden points, but a highly distinctive type of knife with a stem on one side and an oblique blade. Radiocarbon dates indicate that the bison hunters who produced these beautifully flaked points and implements occupied the site during the 7th millennium B.C. Only slightly more recent than the Cody Complex is one identified at Hell Gap and tentatively designated Frederick, which has lanceolate points characterized by oblique parallel flaking.

Until recently, it had been assumed that all notched forms found in the Plains were of relatively recent age. A discovery made at the Simonson site near Quimby, Iowa, however, has shown that side-notched weapon tips were used in hunting an extinct form of bison. The site produced a radiocarbon date of 6480 B.C. Similar points found in the Logan Creek site, Nebraska, are probably of roughly comparable age.

Sites in the Eastern United States

In the eastern United States, fluted points have been found in great quantities. Many are like the Clovis points of the Plains and Southwest, but there is great variation in shape, and some are essentially triangular, some have markedly convex sides, and others have constricted bases and flaring ears. Here, as in the Plains, fluted points constitute the earliest types yet recognized. Somewhere, though, there must be unfluted prototypes from which these forms developed, for fluting was not used in the Old World. Where in America this technique first came into use remains a matter of conjecture. In the East, as farther west, tools associated with fluted points were often made on blades. The spurred tools that have been called "gravers" are well represented.

In the northeast, glacial ice had begun to retreat, and occupation was feasible any time after 15,000 B.C. It would have been possible for it to have begun still earlier farther south. Paleogeographic studies suggest that fluted points in the East and in the Plains and Southwest are of essentially comparable age (Mason, 1962), but in the northeastern and southeastern states there have been no associations of artifacts with remains of extinct animals, and few sites have lent themselves to radiocarbon dating. Such eastern fluted sites as Shoop, Pennsylvania (Witthoft, 1952); Williamson, Virginia (McCary, 1951); Quad, Alabama (Soday, 1954); and Reagan, Vermont (Ritchie, 1953), are known from surface collecting, and no material was obtained suitable for dating.

The Bull Brook site in Massachusetts did produce some charcoal (Byers, 1959) which gave a date of about 7000 B.C., but the site may well be older, for this material did not come from an occupation surface or a fireplace. In the course of recent excavations at the Debert site in Nova Scotia, fluted points with deeply concave bases and other implements were found.

A series of radiocarbon samples produced an average date of 8600 B.C. (Douglas Byers, personal communication).

In the Northeast Woodlands area, after fluted points were no longer produced, there came into use points that are quite similar to those made in the Plains between about 8000 and 6000 B.C., notably points of the Cody Complex and Agate Basin. No radiocarbon dates are available, and efforts to estimate dates on the basis of correlating sites with changing levels of the Great Lakes have provided contradictory results. At the Renier site in Wisconsin a cremation burial, which contained Scottsbluff and Eden and one side-notched point, was found (Mason and Irwin, 1960). In Ohio, square-based points that resemble Scottsbluff points are frequently found associated with unfluted lanceolate points which are very like the Agate Basin points of the Plains. Some archaeologists attribute the use of these points to a gradual stylistic change that marked the beginning of a series of regional adaptations that were characteristic of the Archaic period (Griffin, 1965). Others believe that point traditions characteristic of the Plains came into the northeast from the west, probably as the result of some population movement (Prufer and Baby, 1963). The writer, while agreeing that there is basic continuity between Paleo-Indian and Archaic, favors the latter hypothesis as a means of explaining the presence of points that resemble those of the Cody and Agate Basin Complexes.

In the southeastern United States, such large numbers of fluted points have been found, and there is such diversity of form as to have suggested to some writers (Griffin, 1965) that this tradition may have first developed here, and later spread northward and westward. None, however, has been found in a datable context.

In recent years, it has become apparent that the point type called Dalton, essentially the same that is called Meserve in the Plains, provides a useful horizon marker for the beginning of the period which follows that of Clovis and related fluted forms. These are points that are parallel-sided in the lower portion and triangular in the upper. The upper part is commonly characterized by an alternate bevel. There is considerable variation, and different subtypes are beginning to be recognized. Daltons are found over a wide area, and are represented in early levels in the Modoc Rock Shelter in Illinois (Fowler, 1959) and Graham Cave, Missouri (Logan, 1952) At the Stanfield-Worley site in Alabama (Dejarnette, Kurjack and Cambron, 1962) Dalton points and associated tools have been found in strata that have produced dates that fall in the 8th millennium B.C. They are associated with large side-notched points called Big Sandy. On the Carolina Piedmont, Daltons are the earliest points found in excavated sites (Coe, 1964). There is evidence of their development into a side-notched type with flaring bases. Marked basal thinning suggests the survival of a form of fluting. In the southeast, in general, there is no evidence to suggest the introduction of new traits from outside; rather there appears to be gradual change from early fluted points to later unfluted types.

Evidence from the Far West

In the area to the west of the Rocky Mountains, outside of the Southwest, there is no evidence for a widespread dispersal of makers of fluted points on the earliest time level now recognized. Some discoveries of points of this type have been reported, but none is firmly dated and most consist of sporadic, isolated finds. The discovery of a pure fluted point site has been reported in Nevada, but no detailed information has been published (Campbell and Campbell, 1940). At Borax Lake (Harrington, 1938), fluted points were found with artifacts of relatively recent age and their chronological position is uncertain. West of the Rocky Mountains the earliest dates so far obtained, which fall between 10,000 and 9000 B.C., come from rock shelters. In Fishbone Cave, Nevada, were found two large flint choppers which lay on a bed of juniper

fiber dated at about 9200 B.C. (Orr, 1956b). Of essentially the same age is the Humboldt Culture, represented in the lowest level at Leonard Rock Shelter, Nevada (Heizer, 1951). Here were found a knife, flakes, and olivella shells. The latter could have come only from California. Another site in Nevada, Gypsum Cave, produced points with diamond-shaped blades and small tapering stems that have been given the name of the site (Harrington, 1933). The earliest Carbon 14 date, 8500 B.C., came from sloth dung samples. It may be of the same age as the artifacts, but better evidence could be obtained if an assay were made of one of the wooden artifacts found there.

The term "Desert Culture" is often applied to the pattern recognized in the Great Basin and in portions of the Southwest for the period beginning about 7000 B.C. Desert Culture people did not depend largely on one resource, but exploited every possibility for obtaining food and utilized many vegetal products. In southern Arizona is recognized a manifestation of the Desert Culture called Cochise (Sayles and Antevs, 1941). Radiocarbon dates indicate an age of only about 7000 to 6000 B.C. for the earliest stage, despite the association of tools with extinct fauna, including mammoth, horse, and dire wolf. Flaked tools of the Cochise people were largely flaked by percussion and included choppers and domed and keeled scrapers and planes made from large flakes and cores that show similarities to forms found farther to the west and that are quite unlike the tools of the big game hunters previously discussed. Doubtless some animal foods were used, but projectile points were not of major importance. The most common Cochise tools were grinding stones, thin flat milling stones and cobble manos, used in the preparation of seeds.

Danger Cave, a deep stratified site in Utah, has provided valuable information concerning the Desert Culture during the period from about 9000 B.C. until the Christian Era (Jennings, 1957). Only

121

scanty material was found in the oldest zone, but there was a rich inventory for a zone with dates falling in the 7th and 8th millennia B.C. It is of particular interest that as early as 7000 B.C. there was use of grinding stones and basketry made by a twining technique. Most projectile points were corner or side-notched forms with a notch at the base, but there were some small lanceolate forms somewhat reminiscent of Mojave points. Choppers, planes, crudely flaked triangular and ovoid bifaces, and retouched flakes are also similar to San Dieguito forms. Here, too, blades were so rare as to suggest that the few found may have been produced fortuitously.

In the northern part of the western United States lanceolate points are the earliest type known. Scattered finds of points similar to types found in the Plains suggest that some big game hunters penetrated the area, but there are no fluted point sites, nor sites with finely flaked unfluted points of a somewhat later period, sometimes grouped under the name Plano. At the Lind Coulee site in Washington (Daugherty, 1956) there is evidence of early bison hunters, but the assemblage found there is, in general, unlike those known in the Plains. The most common point type has a long, tapered stem. Associated implements include: crescentic implements, common in the west but not used east of the mountains; side and end scrapers made on flakes, some of which have concave sides; domed and keeled scrapers and choppers. Stones, ground through usage, were used in the preparation of pigments. The average radiocarbon date is 6750 B.C.

Bipointed, leaf-shaped points, usually made on blades, are characteristic of an early occupation in Idaho and the Pacific northwest. They are commonly called Cascade points and are attributed by B. Robert Butler (1961) to a culture designated the Old Cordilleran. This area has also provided evidence for the use of notching at an early date. Finds made in the Upper Klamath area (Cressman, 1956), indicate that notched points came into use there prior to 5000 B.C. At the Five Mile Rapids site, which may have been occupied as early as 9000 B.C., bipointed, leaf-shaped forms, and those with constricted stems were the earliest types. Notched forms were introduced later. At the Marmes Rock Shelter in Washington, points found below volcanic ash deposited about 4500 B.C. were bifacial foliates (Fryxell and Daugherty, 1963). Side-notched points were made after the period of ash deposition. Another cave site that contains a layer of pumice has provided important data. In Fort Rock Cave, Oregon, (Cressman, 1951), charred sandals that lay below the volcanic material were dated at about 7000 B.C.

Richard D. Daugherty (1962) has introduced the concept of an Intermontane Tradition in the region that lies between the

For a long time, Gypsum Cave, on a spur of the Limestone Mountains sixteen miles east of Las Vegas in Nevada, was well known to the local Paiute Indians and to White residents of Las Vegas.

To the Paiute, it was a sacred place of mystery at which their medicine men deposited offerings.

In 1929 and 1930 Southwest Museum expeditions led by M. R. Harrington began archaeological explorations revealing bones and atlatl dart shafts. This opened up the probability that Early Man in the Southwest had been contemporary with prehistoric animals now long extinct.

The cave entrance measures about seventy feet across and about fifteen feet in height.

Inside, the floor was found to slant sharply downward.

The roof was badly shattered and crumbling dangerously in spots, the results of many earth movements.

The descent disclosed five rooms, and the adjoining photograph shows Room 2, looking west.

Overall, the cave measures about 300 feet in length, the widest spot being about 120 feet, with the lowest point sixty-two feet below the entrance.

Cascade and Sierra Nevada ranges on the west and the Rocky Mountains on the east. There was a diversified economy, based on food gathering, hunting and fishing during the early period that began about 9000 B.C. and lasted until about 6000 B.C. Lanceolate points and crescentic implements were common. A period of markedly increasing specialization followed, and notched forms came into use. Earl H. Swanson (1962) recognizes three basic cultures, to an extent sequential, but with some chronological overlap: the earliest, the Old Cordilleran with bipointed, leaf-shaped points, is followed by the Mountain Plains characterized by points reminiscent of, but not entirely like, Plano forms, and the Bitter Root with side-notched points.

In California, there has been general agreement that there was a wide-spread culture horizon characterized by an extensive use of milling stones dating back to about 6000-5000 B.C. (Wallace, 1954; Meighan, 1965). There has, however, been controversy concerning the age of the earlier San Dieguito and Lake Mojave (Campbell and Campbell, 1937) materials which include large projectile points suggesting that hunting was of considerable importance. There have been no associations of artifacts with extinct fauna. Only surface finds were represented at Lake Mojave, so no radiocarbon dates for materials associated with artifacts could be obtained. The fact that artifacts were found on high beach levels suggested, but did not prove, that occupation dated back to an early period when the lake was filled with water.

A radiocarbon date of 7690 B.C. was obtained for the high shore line. Investigations in the Panamint Valley by Emma Lou Davis indicated a date of about 8500-8000 B.C. for a time of high water, but there was no precise correlation between the Mojave materials recovered there and the lake.

Now, however, we are on firmer ground for the Harris site, the type station for San Dieguito. It has produced a radiocarbon date of 6990 B.C., plus or minus 350 years, and two of 6450 B.C., plus or minus 400 years, for the levels containing San Dieguito implements (Claude Warren, personal communication). A date of 9340 B.C. for the lowest level at Ventana Cave, which contains material similar to San Dieguito, suggests that still earlier sites of this complex may yet be found. The report on the later excavations at the Harris site by Claude Warren and D. L. True (1960) has provided valuable data and now, with the publication of this volume, it will be possible to evaluate Malcolm Rogers' interpretations and reclassification.

It is reasonable to assume that interest in the early inhabitants of the New World will continue and, quite probably, increase. Even a few years from now, the most superficial summary of our knowledge of Early Man will be vastly more complicated and quite different from this one. There will be answers to many questions for which none can be found at present, and there will be new questions for which we shall be seeking answers.

PART IV HOW DID THEY LIVE
AND HOW LONG AGO?

E. L. DAVIS

PART IV

THE SAN DIEGUITO PEOPLE: SOME ETHNOGRAPHIC COMPARISONS

As one reads these pages, it is natural to wonder about the people: who were the San Dieguitoans and how did they live? In archaeology, it is all too easy to lose sight of human beings by concentrating on artifacts, to forget that we have been collecting the scanty but all-important remnants of a way of life.

The Economy

We can do no more than speculate about the customs and appearance of these early California Indians, basing such speculations on our knowledge of recent desert peoples of the Great Basin (Steward, 1938), Owens Valley (Steward, 1933), the Sierra Nevada (Davis, 1965), the Paiute as reported by Kelly (1932, 1964), and the Cochimí of central Baja California (Aschman, 1959), Using these analogies, we can suggest that San Dieguito people spent most of the year in small, migratory bands of fifteen or twenty persons, related to one another by descent or marriage. The bands moved about a territory known to most of them from childhood, enabling the men to predict the location and seasonal migrations of game.

In the same manner, a wise and experienced old woman would know the country like the back of her hand and could instruct and direct the more flighty girls in the lore of berry picking, root grubbing,

The diversity of Indian tribes and practices surprised the early Spanish explorers venturing far up into what is now the United States, even as it had the explorers along the North American coast.

Unlike the hunters and collectors of ancient times, and most American Indians, Southwest aborigines had made a settled life by converting a semi-desert country into a permanent source of food.

The Papagos were a Pima-speaking people living south of the Gila River.

The report of the United States and Mexico Boundary Survey of 1857 found the Papago Indians then "comparatively well

off in worldly goods" and planting and growing corn.

The practice of agriculture by the people of the Colorado River region was an obvious cultural link shared with the Aztecs and other peoples in Central Mexico.

However, the Boundary Survey reported that while they raised crops they lived some distance from water, "as there seems to be a superstition about living near it."

The women had to carry the water supply in ollas, or earthen vessels, for a long way, bearing it on their heads, and large ollas were kept filled and sunk in the ground.

127

and the harvesting of greens, nuts, and numerous seasonal food plants. Perhaps, like the Mono Lake Paiute (Davis, 1965) they relished grubs, crickets, and larvae and were not averse to stocking the larder with an occasional snake or lizard in addition to rodents and rabbits.

However, the San Dieguitoans appear to have relied on hunting more than did recent Indians and they apparently did not develop stone-on-stone milling to prepare small, hard seeds as flour or gruel. They pursued a lifeway of generalized hunting and collecting, if we have correctly interpreted their tool kit of well-made stone implements, which is all that time has left us.

They moved frequently, following natural crops. Primitive hunter-collectors do

How the ancient San Dieguito people lived can be surmised only in a general way by the knowledge gained of customs of recent desert Indians.

Among these desert people are the Paiute.

The accompanying photograph of a Paiute woman of Inyo County, California, with her seed shaker, was taken before 1900 by the famed photographer, C. C. Pierce.

The photograph is in the Southwest Museum collection.

There was no organized living on a large scale and in all probability the San Dieguitoans spent most of the year roaming in small migratory and closely related bands.

Their territory would have been known to them all their lives and they would be familiar with the seasonal migrations of game.

While they were primarily hunters, archaeologists believe that, just as among the historic Paiute, a wise and experienced old San Dieguito woman might have known her territory like the back of her hand and could have instructed young girls in the lore of berry picking, root grubbing and the harvesting of greens, nuts, and numerous seasonal plants.

They probably never reached the stage of exploiting a permanent source of food.

not live for long periods in a centralized village. A sedentary way of life can develop only after people have discovered a permanent source of food, such as the sea, and have learned to exploit it. The San Dieguito bands may not have reached this stage, although several hundred years later, La Jolla people collected and ate shellfish. Later still, California coastal Indian groups became expert boatmen and fishers.

So it is probable that the little San Dieguito bands were only occasional visitors at any one spot. An example of such an occasional camp is the C. W. Harris site on the San Dieguito River in San Diego County.

Because the face of the earth has changed considerably with passage of the ages, early camps have been washed away or deeply buried, making San Dieguito traces rare and difficult to find.

Band Leadership

It is reasonable to presume that leadership of the bands was vested in a senior man, trusted for his experience as a hunter and respected for his ability to deal with people. Gatherers at this simple level do not have ranks and royalties, but are bound together by ties of kinship and are governed by tradition and consent.

The bands may have been patrilineal, a common way of reckoning descent among hunting peoples whose menfolk occupy an important position in the economy. In this case a boy would grow up with a sense of territoriality and of inherited hunting rights within a certain range.

However, if plant collecting were of major importance, it is possible their group membership, like our own, was inherited bilaterally, equal importance being placed on relationship through the mother's as well as the father's side of the family. Bilateral descent has certain advantages for people whose subsistence is marginal: in the event of a drought or failure of the food supply, a bilateral kinship system provides twice as many close relatives to offer help and shelter during the lean periods.

Appearance of the People

Since no San Dieguito burials have so far been discovered, we do not know whether these people were tall and long of limb like recent Mojaves or whether they were short and stocky, like the Paiute. Clothing was probably minimal among them, as it seems to have been considered largely unnecessary by other Indians living in the mild, coastal and desert areas of Southern California and Baja California. Men of the tribes observed by early missionaries and explorers were frequently naked except for a few ornaments, although strong sandals, woven or braided from agave fiber, were worn to protect the feet from thorns. Women wore little aprons or pubic covers. During the cold weather, Great Basin peoples such as the Paiute and Shoshone used fur-string robes, woven by the men. These poncho-like garments served as robes by day and as bedding by night. A Mono Lake Paiute informant related his memories of being put to bed as a child on a pile of such skins and enjoying burying his nose in the softness and warmth, which smelled of rabbit.

Desert Indians who are known from ethnographic accounts, tattooed themselves, particularly the chins of women, and painted their faces and bodies. Since the human body seems to have been the earliest vehicle of the painter's art, we can presume that the ancient San Dieguitoans decorated themselves, at least occasionally, with colored earths and finery.

Religion and Folklore

Folklore and religion are difficult to read archaeologically and therefore we do not know any details of San Dieguito ritual. However it is certain that, like all people, they must have had a system of beliefs explaining the unknown as well as the powers of nature, together with magical procedures for controlling these powers. The ethical and spiritual values of very simple people can be surprisingly mystical and complex, as illustrated by the secret, male religions of some Australians. There seems to be no one-to-one relation between technological advancement and ritual sophistication. Each people has its own style of living, its own particular history of customs. Environmentally impoverished Great Basin groups had a simple ceremonial life, but the Cochimí of the even more impoverished Central Desert of Baja California had both elaborate rituals and paraphernalia (Aschmann, 1959). Arts, beliefs, and technology are independent variables. It seems likely that the great cave paintings recently reported by Meighan in Baja California were made by men whose subsistence and material goods were meager in the extreme (Meighan, 1966).

Festivities

If we continue to extrapolate, cautiously, from the historical present and from known lifeways of recent Indians of Alta and Baja California, it seems likely that large scale group activities were only occasionally made feasible by good harvests or seasons of plenty. As an example, the annual harvest of pitahaya cactus fruit enabled the Cochimí of Baja California to gather in sizable congregations to celebrate their good fortune and engage in social mischief. In the same manner, Northern Paiute came together in numbers when pine nuts were plentiful. These festivals were occasions for feasting, gambling, dancing, and wife-stealing.

Beyond these few parallels and comparisons we cannot venture. It is not possible to make any statements with certainty about the long-vanished San Dieguito people. We can only assume that they were competent and intelligent humans, skilled enough to wrest a living from the mountains, meadows, and streams of ancient California; but their esoteric customs, their appearance, and their language remain unknown.

NEW PROSPECTS FOR DATING ANCIENT MAN

In order to understand Malcolm Rogers' work, it is necessary to know something of the problems he faced in trying to place his early Californians in time. Did they live hundreds or tens of thousands of years ago? Rogers was careful and conservative, his conservatism leading him to place the three stages of San Dieguito culture (Rogers 1950, pp. 193, 537) at a point in time much too close to the present.

Just before his death, Rogers revised his estimated dates, and now much new evidence has developed to further substantiate his revisions. A test excavation on the shoreline of the extinct lake in Panamint Valley, California, which appeared to be associated with San Dieguito II and III camp sites, has yielded material from which radiocarbon dates of 8000 and 8500 B.C. have been obtained. In his own excavations at the Harris site in San Dieguito Valley, Claude N. Warren of Idaho State University has reported radiocarbon dates for the San Dieguito culture in San Diego County at 6990 B.C., plus or minus 350 years, and 6450 B.C., plus or minus 400 years.

It is not easy to change one's mind on a major issue one has defended for years, and great credit is due Rogers for his intellectual effort and honesty. Many a scientist, renowned in his day, has not been able to be so impartial and, blindly championing his own past mistakes, has temporarily impeded the flow of learning. Even the late Aleš Hrdlička, as curator of the United States National Museum, found it hard to believe a growing body of evidence that man in the New World had a tenure of longer than 4000 years. This view was almost as fixed and biased as the doctrine of Bishop Ussher, who in the 18th Century believed that the world itself was created in 4004 B.C.

As the second half of the 20th Century slowly unwinds, the reconstruction of geological, climatic, and archaeological situations, as well as their position in time, becomes the task of teams of experts. An archaeologist in particular can no longer work alone, as Rogers was obliged to do, but must have the cooperation of a geologist, a pedologist who is a specialist in soil morphology, a palynologist who can reconstruct previous flora of the locality from pollen deposits, a naturalist or paleontologist to identify the fauna from bone, and the resources of a laboratory which can process his datable materials.

Great strides have been taken in recent years in those geophysical techniques of dating which can be applied in archaeology. So far as chronology is concerned, Rogers was obliged to work in the dark. During the Twenties and Thirties of this century, there was little except geological events of estimated date and sequence which could be applied to the task of procuring dates for human events and sequences. Varve series and relative dating of the fluorine content of bone were also understood at the time, but in Rogers' case, the Colorado Desert sites had no varves and negligible quantities of bone.

This situation creates problems for an archaeologist in the New World, where the entire span of human occupancy may not exceed 15,000 years. Geology is too vast. There are too many figures to the left of the decimal point and the huge perspectives cannot be scaled down to a mere ten millenia or so. Rogers knew this.

In making a study of dating techniques, a first step is to understand the differences between an event and a date, as well as the difference between dates which are absolute and those which are only relative. An event is a known occurrence—the advance or retreat of a glacier, a volcanic eruption or a forest fire. However, an event in itself hangs in time without coordinates to fix it until it has been dated.

A date is a calculated point in time or a known span of time. As an example, we

now know that the last glaciers on this continent reached a maximum at about 19,000 years ago and that, since 11,000 years ago, the climate has slowly become warmer and drier (Broecker, 1966; Broecker and Kaufman, 1965). This is a known span of time which can be related accurately to the present. Individual, pin-point dates of high reliability are much harder to arrive at, and the techniques which will supply them are few. Under limited conditions, an outstanding technique is dendrochronology, or tree-ring dating, described below, which may make it possible to date to the year the cutting of a beam in a long-abandoned pueblo.

A date of this precision is an absolute date, as is also the broader, or span date given to the glacier above. An absolute date enables us to use our own time as a

This is an air view of a section of Panamint Valley which lies west of Death Valley.

It is a dry, hot valley bordered on the west by the Sierra Nevada and on the east by the Panamint Mountains.

The hill, known as Lake Hill, jutting up from the white bed of an ancient lake, may once have been an island on whose shore camped prehistoric men.

Trenches bull-dozed on the shore and at the foot of the Panamint Mountains have revealed the original shore line, long since buried by the effects of erosion and other geologic changes.

The trenching disclosed a "buried" site of the San Dieguito people, yielding their tools and weapons and perishable material for dating studies.

One of the trenches can be seen in the photograph as a thin dark line at the base of the hill.

Dr. E. L. Davis, of the University of California Archaeological Survey, has announced that radiocarbon dates obtained at this site are 8000 and 8500 B.C. However, the precise correlation between the time of the prehistoric camp and the deposit of the datable material has not been established.

fixed referent and to measure back from this datum almost as though we used a steel tape.

A relative date has no such chronologically fixed position in a terrestrial river of time. Relative dates apply only locally or regionally. Fluorine dating of bone, also described below, illustrates this more circumscribed kind of association. Similar fluorine content will demonstrate contemporaneity of two pieces of bone in one soil layer, but it cannot be stretched to include bone from another soil a thousand miles away. For such a correlation, absolute dates are required.

ABSOLUTE DATING

Dates which range from several hundred to several million years into the past can now be assigned by measurements of the decay of radioisotopes. Isotopes are forms of a chemical element having the same chemical properties but different atomic weights (Fergusson, 1964), due to different numbers of neutrons associated with their nuclei. Decay of such isotopes proceeds at a constant rate until a stable end product, such as lead, is reached. It is this average constancy of decay rate which makes measurement feasible. During the decay process, different kinds of particles are emitted, as one element transforms into another:

1) Alpha-particles — two bound protons like a helium nucleus.
2) Beta-particles — identical to electrons.
3) Gamma-particles — Xrays of varying energies.

It can be seen that each radioisotope is unstable and for each there is a calculated "half-life" ($T \frac{1}{2}$) — that length of time during which half the atoms present in a sample will probably have ejected a particle, thereby decaying to another stage.

Potassium-argon Dating

Potassium and its radioisotope potassium 40 (K^{40}) are present in most rocks, including those suddenly produced by volcanic activity. Since the processes of decay commence as soon as the rock has cooled, an-

133

cient lava flows can be dated by measuring the amount of decay from potassium 40 to argon 40 (K^{40}-Ar^{40}) which has taken place. The method has been considered applicable only to flows of great age of hundreds of thousands and millions of years, due to the very long half-life of potassium 40 (which is 1.35×10^9 years). Evernden and Curtis, however, now claim dates as recent as 5000 to 10,000 years obtained by this method, which they have also used to date Lower and Middle Paleolithic cultures. Their claims are subject to some question (Schwab, 1964; Evernden and Curtis, 1965).

Uranium, Actinium and Thorium Series

The closely related elements uranium 238, uranium 235, and thorium 232 decay into three different, stable isotopes of lead via three different chains. A look at the tables in Schwab (1964, pp. 338-339) gives a startling picture of our new understanding of matter—a far cry from the concepts of basic substance of the Aristotelian world where rock was rock, and solid to boot. Matter is dissolving before our eyes into transient states of transformation. The unstable elements protactinium 231 and thorium 230 have half-lives of 34,000 and 80,000 years respectively (Butzer, 1964) and are useful in dating materials beyond the range of radiocarbon measurement. Recently, Broecker and Kaufman (1965, p. 557) have used measurements of uranium 234 to thorium 230 (U^{234}-Th^{230}) to supplement radiocarbon dates of fluctuations in the water levels of late Pleistocene lakes Lahontan and Bonneville II.

Radioactive Carbon Dating

Dating organic material by radiocarbon measurement is probably the most widely-known and most widely used of absolute dating methods. Archaeologists have relied upon it since it was first developed some fifteen years ago by Willard Libby, who won a Nobel Prize for this contribution. Radioactive carbon, or carbon 14 (C^{14}), is continually being formed in the upper atmosphere through bombardment of nitrogen atoms by cosmic rays. This production is constant over time, and is a

thorough mixing of the carbon 14 isotope with seas and atmosphere. Therefore, living organisms, now and in the past, have had equal opportunity to absorb radiocarbon. When an organism dies, replacement of radioactive carbon ceases and the carbon clock starts running down. It is possible to measure how far the running down has proceeded and thus know how many years have elapsed since the plant or animal was alive (Libby, 1961).

Radioactive carbon has a half-life of approximately 5730 years. Five thousand years is a relatively short span of time, so that this isotope can only be used to date charcoal, bone, wood, and so on, within a time range of 100 to 50,000 years old (Schwab 1964, p. 346). For older dates, uranium-thorium or potassium-argon methods are required. However, the three methods permit trustworthy dating of events from the beginning of our era backward for millions of years.

Fission-track Dating

This method was used recently to check the reliability of potassium-argon dates on very ancient hominid remains at Olduvai Gorge in Tanganyika, Africa. A date of 1,750,000 years had been questioned because of a possibility that the sample had already contained radiogenic argon at the time of crystallization and it was therefore considered advisable to use a different dating method as well—one not dependent on the presence of argon (Fleischer, 1965).

Fission-track dating is accomplished by counting the number of tracks—tiny scars left within crystal or glass by spontaneous fission of uranium 238 during the life of the sample. While wrong dates can be gotten from fission-track readings, the source of error is different from the source of wrong-age results in the potassium-argon method, and the two techniques can be used to cross-check one another. In the Olduvai Gorge case, after correcting the fission-track age and allowing for a standard deviation, it was found to be in good agreement with the slightly lower age obtained by the potassium-argon decay method.

Moving even closer to the present, absolute dates can be extended upward to recent times by the use of two methods which are independent of radioactivity—tree-ring comparison and glacial varve comparison.

Dendrochronology

In 1914 A. E. Douglass, while making a study of sun-spot cycles, began analysis of tree-ring patterns to see if they reflected cycles of solar radiation. As an outgrowth of this work, he developed a method of correlating the various wide and narrow sequences of rings and was able to construct a time scale, written in tree rings. This scale now has been extended backward for more than 2000 years in the southwestern United States.

Despite its accuracy, tree-ring dating has a number of limitations (Butzer, 1964). It is applicable only in certain climatic areas, and only certain kinds of wood can be used. Correlation, or "teleconnection," is possible within small areas but cannot as yet be extrapolated. However, dendrochronology has been extensively and successfully employed to date pueblos in the Southwest by using corings from pine beams and partially burned firewood.

Glacial Varve Comparison

Varves are water-deposited layers of glacial clays and silts. They are paired and represent the spring run-off (coarse silt) and summer run-off (finer clays) of melted water from retreating glaciers. When this water is discharged in a still lake or other natural settling-tank, the materials are deposited in thin layers each year. Varve thicknesses can be measured and teleconnected, and a datable sequence has been constructed for almost 10,000 years in Europe. Varve dating has been less successful in North America. (De Geer, 1912; Oakley, 1964).

Astronomic Correlations

A very ingenious means of dating, which did not work, was developed by Milankovitch (Oakley, 1964; Zeuner, 1962), by calculation of the varying amount of solar heat received on earth. Insolation fluctuates over long periods and is controlled by complicated inter-relations of three variables, each with its own cycle. These controls are:

1) Obliquity of the ecliptic—the angle of the earth's axis of rotation to the plane of its orbit. This angle wobbles through about three degrees of tilt.
2) Eccentricity of that orbit which brings the earth closer to the sun at some periods than at others.
3) Precession of the equinoxes—slight shifts in the onsets of the seasons.

To put this into simple language, when the tilt of the poles toward the sun coincides with an orbit which also brings the planet closer to the sun at some point, then more heat is received and polar and continental ice melts, producing an interglacial stage. When the reverse combination occurs, the beginning of an ice age is triggered. When the controlling variables occur out of phase, they nullify one another.

This complex system of calculations did not prove to fit the picture of glacial events as actually known. Recently, Broecker (1966) has proposed a correction factor which may make astronomic dating workable. This factor considers the damping action of the earth's two thermal blankets, the ocean and the atmosphere, and their effects in creating a lag of glaciations and interstadials past the astronomic phenomena which cause them.

RELATIVE DATING

Relative dates are those which correlate a group of phenomena in a limited region and over a limited time, but which do not provide an exact measurement in years before the present. Fluorine dating of bone is the best example of this, making use of a chemical method.

Fluorine Dating

Bone lying in the earth is slowly altered, both through chemical loss and through chemical substitution. If the surrounding soil contains salts of the element fluorine, the fluorine will gradually become incorporated into the bone, amounts of this element increasing with the centuries and millenia. Because of this slow absorption, it is possible to determine whether various bones within the same deposit are contemporaneous. If two bone fragments contain like amounts of fluorine, then they were deposited at the same time; but if the amounts differ, then one bone is younger or older than the other (Oakley, 1955).

Fluorine dating was an important instrument which, along with a battery of other modern techniques, made it possible to expose the famous Piltdown Man hoax (Oakley 1955, pp. 573-583) where the jaw of a modern orangutan, a fragment of a Neolithic skull and some assorted teeth and bones were fobbed off on the scientific world as an astonishing "ape-man."

Stratigraphy and Pedology

Rocks, and soils which are rocks weathering into loose dirt, are deposited layer (stratum) upon layer. When down-cutting or erosion takes place, this process is reversed, or the erosion may slice through at an angle, making way for what is called a disconformity. However, it is not uncommon for recent layers of deposit to lie, stacked upward from older to younger, in orderly succession. Thus, it may be found that, over an area of several hundred yards or several miles, there will be a stratum sequence from bottom to top, such as: 1) bedrock; 2) sorted gravels; 3) marl; and 4) inter-fingering clays and silts, generally found in a single physiographic setting as, for example, around the foot of a peninsula.

Ideally, it could be assumed that artifacts found in stratum 2 would be older than those in 3, while those in layer 3 would be older than the artifacts in 4. However, the earth is unquiet. Faulting moves and tilts layers, erosion can remove old soils from a ridge, redepositing them lower down and on top of newer material.

Caves, which trusting archaeologists would like to accept as stratigraphic bibles, are prone to many kinds of hard-to-detect disturbances. The ancient inhabitants dug holes in the floors for their grass beds; their children dug holes because this is a thing all children do; fireplaces and storage pits were sometimes excavated; cave fill is frequently dry and lies loosely around rocks so that material works its way down through cracks. Last of all, if a 4000-year-ago Indian used handfuls of a 16,000-year-ago pack-rat nest plus 4000-year-ago kindling to start his fire in a cave, the archaeologist's radiocarbon date on charcoal from that hearth may come out as 12,000 years before the present. This can look very strange when it accompanies artifacts which should have been made at about the time the Greeks were beginning their march upward to a great civilization.

Weathering, Hydration and Patination

Sun heat, water, and chemicals slowly change the surface characteristics of a stone artifact. The most usual alterations of this nature are: 1) hydration (obsidian only), and 2) patination or "desert varnish" (most apparent on rocks rich in iron and manganese, on desert surfaces).

Obsidian, which is a volcanic glass, can be dated within a local sequence by the thickness in microns of the outer rind, visibly altered by absorption of water (Clark, 1964). This hydration layer gradually increases in thickness over the centuries, average temperatures appearing to be the most significant factor. Zeuner (1960) expresses grave doubts about the consistency and reliability of this process. However, it is currently being used at the University of California Los Angeles with promising results (Michels, 1965).

Basalt and some quartzites slowly turn a dark and lustrous mahogany color when exposed in the desert sun. Artifacts made of identical material and supported by the same surface of a very limited area can be compared, cautiously, as being more or less patinated. However, there is a recorded case in which stones beside a new road-cut acquired a varnish or patina within twenty-five years (Engel, 1958). Rates of patina formation seem to vary. A dark coating may be deposited in twenty-five years, or 2500, or 25,000; or it may form and be dissolved a number of times. Patina is a clue to relative age, but one which must be used with judgment and caution.

Faunal Shifts

Just as glaciers have advanced and retreated over our continent during the past two or three million years, groups of animals have moved southward or northward, following boreal or temperate climates as they preferred (Hibbard et al. 1965, Table 2 and Fig. 3). A good example of this shifting is a comparison of present distribution of the muskox, *Ovibos moschatus,* with late Pleistocene distribution. Today, muskoxen are found only along the polar edges of this continent in the extreme north. However, during periods of glaciation, these cold-adapted animals ranged south through the central states as far as the Texas Panhandle.

Because we know the present habits and habitat of muskoxen, the presence of fossil muskox remains in a Texas or Kansas site gives this site a relative date "somewhere" during a glacial period. However, the question of just which period this might be can be answered only by getting an absolute date on the bone or the surrounding matrix.

Faunal Extinction

Remains of animals which have become extinct can be used to assign relative dates to the deposits which contain them; however, within the last 10,000 years such "dates" are vague. It is interesting that we know elephant, camel, ground sloth, horse, and dire wolf lived in North America until sometime after 10,000 years ago and then died out. Yet the "how" and "when" of these extinctions are poorly understood. Did climatic change destroy this megafauna, or were human predators, armed with such lethal inventions as fluted points, the villains?

However, despite conflicting opinions and insufficiency of radiocarbon dates (Hester, 1960), the presence of extinct fauna in an archaeological site places that site in an early or Paleo-Indian horizon, one which lies near in time to the close of recent glaciations.

Palynology

Each year, flowering trees and plants shed their pollen into the wind, and it is spread far and wide, pine pollen being a particularly long-distance traveler. The pollen grains of each plant have a distinctive size, shape, and minor detailing, making it possible to segregate and count them under a microscope (Martin and Mehringer, 1965).

The chief story they tell is one of climatic change or stability, although various animals, particularly men, can spread, restrict, or decimate plant populations. When left to their own devices, plants respond to conditions of soil, temperature, insolation, and moisture. Therefore changes in rainfall or mean annual temperatures, or even shifts of rainfall maxima from one season to a different season, will be reflected in the vegetation cover of an area.

As an example, corn requires summer rainfall and therefore Pueblo Indians were able to grow it successfully in a semi-arid climate because the scanty rains fell at a time when the corn was in growth. Cooler summers with curtailment of cloud-building and thunderstorm activity could make it impossible for corn-farmers to raise crops, and this has been offered as one explanation of the 13th Century abandonment of Mesa Verde and the "Four Corners" area.

Therefore, pollen associations from deep within old lake beds, straticuts, or archaeological excavations can be interpreted as pictures of warmer or cooler, wetter or drier climatic periods. During much of the Wisconsin stadial, spruce, *Picea*, grew on what is now the dry San Augustin Plains of New Mexico (Martin and Mehringer 1965, Fig. 2). This points to a prolonged period when the climate was both cooler and wetter.

There are, of course, difficulties inherent in the use of pollen for relative dating and climatic reconstruction. Because pollen is carried far abroad, the pollen rain at any one spot may not be entirely representative of local vegetation. Dust storms transport the pollen of xerophytic plants from desert to conifer forests about mountain lakes, while pine may account for forty percent of the total pollen in some desert soils (Martin and Mehringer, 1965). However, when pollen can be found and if interpreted by an expert, it gives excellent, relative information on sequences of warm and cool climates related to changing vegetation. As with other relative dating procedures, some sort of absolute date is needed to pin these events in time.

It is easy to see that considerable advances have been made in correlating natural and cultural events and fixing them in chronologies. Like everything else in society, archaeology is growing apace, amassing a body of theoretical and technical tools which serve teams of specialists.

Therefore, Rogers' work stands as a great contribution, in spite of lacking all these advantages. Working alone, driving over the hostile deserts with an old car, he still was able to lay the basis for the only comprehensive study of early people which has yet been undertaken in California.

PART V HOW STONES BECAME TOOLS AND WEAPONS

CLARK W. BROTT

TIME	CENTRAL ASPECT	SOUTHEASTERN ASPECT	SOUTHWESTERN ASPECT
PRESENT	PAIUTE, MOJAVE, ETC.	PIMA, PAPAGO, ETC.	DIEGUENO, LUISENO, ETC.
1500		?	PREHISTORIC YUMAN AND SHOSHONEAN GROUPS
1000	PREHISTORIC YUMAN AND SHOSHONEAN GROUPS		
500	PUEBLO II	HOHOKAM AND MOGOLLON	
	BASKETMAKER III		
A.D. 1			
	AMARGOSA III ?	SAN PEDRO-AMARGOSA III	
1000			
2000			LA JOLLA COMPLEX
3000	AMARGOSA II (PINTO-GYPSUM) ?	CHIRICAHUA-AMARGOSA II	AMARGOSA II-LIKE PATTERN IN AREA AT 2500 B.C. ?
4000			
5000	AMARGOSA I ?	VENTANA-AMARGOSA I	LA JOLLA COMPLEX (5,500 B.C.)
6000	?	?	?
7000			SAN DIEGUITO III (6,990 B.C.)
8000	SAN DIEGUITO II-III (8,000 B.C. ?)		?
B.C. 9000	SAN DIEGUITO I ?	SAN DIEGUITO I-II (VENTANA COMPLEX)	

POSTULATED CORRELATION OF WESTERN CULTURES

TENTATIVE GRAPHS OF TEMPERATURE AND MOISTURE.
MAIN TIME DIVISIONS OF DEGLACIAL AND NEOTHERMAL AGES.

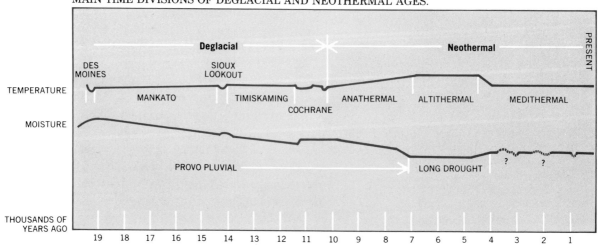

PART V

ARTIFACTS OF THE SAN DIEGUITO COMPLEX

We may often look upon projectile points, scrapers, or other tools as "Indian relics" or curiosities somehow not really related to us or the way we live. However, when found *in situ* at an archaeological site, artifacts constitute the most valuable evidence the scholar has for solving mysteries about people who lived prior to our time. Unfortunately, relic hunters and the advance of civilization are destroying this valuable information faster than it can be found or studied.

Archaeologists are not ready to come to definite conclusions about the precise functions of all the stone implements associated with the San Dieguito Complex. But

the collections made by Malcolm Rogers and other archaeologists at ancient camp sites and primitive workshops indicate the people were in a broad sense skilled technicians. The shapes of the tools themselves often suggest ways they might have been used.

Primitive quarry workshops in a fault-scarp of Panamint Valley have been examined by the University of California Archaeological Survey. This was in connection with the test excavation of the former shore line of Lake Panamint which Dr. E. L. Davis reported yielded material dated at 8000 and 8500 B.C. The shore line appeared to be associated with a San

The upper chart is a postulated correlation of Western cultures based upon recent radiocarbon dates and previous geological and cultural comparative estimates.

It has been worked out by the scientific staff of the San Diego Museum of Man and emphasizes how much is yet to be learned in American archaeology.

It covers a span of about 11,000 years.

The dates for the La Jolla Complex and San Dieguito III in the Southwestern Aspect are firm ones, from the Harris site.

All others are estimated dates, or the analysis has not yet been completed.

Also, the dotted lines between the cul-

tural levels means that the beginning and closing dates are unknown and only are suggested here.

Question marks too must be used to indicate that conclusive data is lacking, or the analysis is still at a hypothetical stage.

The lower chart presents time scales for temperature and moisture conditions influencing the study of early man in the Far West, as suggested by Ernst Antevs.

It shows that a Great Pluvial period came to a final end perhaps 7000 years ago and was followed by a Long Drought and it in turn was followed by several indefinite wet periods.

Dieguito camp site, with artifacts resembling those found at Lake Mojave. However, precise correlations of lake and culture remain to be determined.

In her report Dr. Davis wrote that the collections from the nearby workshops and from others distributed from Wyoming to Baja California, indicated the existence of a western lithic co-tradition of considerable time depth:

This arose from a Paleo-western base quite distinctive from the blade-making Paleo-eastern tradition of Clovis and Folsom.

It seems likely that all the workshops ...were scenes of woodworking and other activities...In addition to the primary business of making stone tools, the presence of planes, spokeshaves, choppers, chopping tools, and numerous adaptable ovate bifaces suggest manufacture of gear made of wood.

Dr. Davis' postulation of a western lithic tradition distinct from the eastern Paleo Indian pattern was based upon an analysis of manufacturing techniques. In the Great Plains or eastern area, emphasis is upon tools made from blades and other flakes struck from prepared cores. In the West greater use was made of side-struck flakes and heavy core tools.

The correlation of artifacts with datable material at ancient camp sites is difficult and often impossible. The Harris site, on the San Dieguito River in San Diego County, for example, only now is yielding dates which begin to bring some light on the age of the tools and weapons of the San Dieguito people.

Several dates which Claude N. Warren, archaeologist for Idaho State University, has provided, come from the Locus I area of the Harris site. The dating analysis was run by the Geochronology Laboratories of the University of Arizona. A date of 6990 B.C., plus or minus 350 years, was taken from a carbonaceous residue, and two dates of 6450 B.C., plus or minus 400 years, were taken from charcoal. All three dates are from the San Dieguito level.

Charcoal lying above the San Dieguito level and probably associated with the La Jolla component was dated at 5580 B.C.

There is an overlap in the San Dieguito and La Jolla settlement patterns in western San Diego County and northwestern Baja California, and there are many stratified sites, with both cultures represented.

An impressive collection and sequence of dates have been derived from shell and charcoal samples taken from La Jolla shell middens, with dates ranging from 5500 B.C. for several sites on the Scripps-Torrey Pines Plateau to as late as 300 A.D. for at least one site in the same area (Bright, 1965). In his 1938 excavation of the Harris site (Warren, 1966), Rogers established rather clearly that the San Dieguito Complex preceded the La Jolla culture. His stratigraphy studies on other coastal sites indicated a consistency in this San Dieguito-La Jolla sequence.

It appears, then, as Warren and True concluded in 1961, that the San Dieguito complex thus seems to be an early population, relatively small in number, whose primary activity was hunting. They probably entered the San Diego coastal area, from the southern Great Basin, about 10,000 years ago and persisted until 8500 to 7500 years ago, when the La Jolla Complex made its appearance.

THE CENTRAL ASPECT

In the main body of his text and in his manuscript describing the artifacts, Rogers separated the second and third phases of the San Dieguito Complex. In the final version prepared for this book, it was not possible or desirable to present Phase II and III artifacts as separate entities. Phase I, however, is a clearly distinct pattern and is described as such.

The two most critical sites used by Rogers to study horizontal stratigraphy in the Central Aspect are M-110, south Granite Dry Lake, and M-115, ancient Lake Mojave. Both site areas are subdivided into occupation concentrations. According to the data in Rogers' notes, nearly all of the sites contain more than one cultural pattern, most being a combination of San Dieguito II and III. Of the Soda and Silver lakes, the Lake Mojave sites, Rogers wrote:

The bulk of the San Dieguito II pattern was confined to the highest strand, elevation 943 feet to 946 feet. A small amount of San Dieguito II material occurred on the 937-foot strand, which consists of a fossil back-wash wave terrace and bay bars at that elevation. On the 937-foot level, San Dieguito III implements occurred in great numbers, and a small quantity was found on the strand and spits having an elevation of 930 feet, which were devoid of San Dieguito II material.

While assembling the data for the site summaries, it was found that San Dieguito II material is confined to the upper terraces of the lake, but San Dieguito III artifacts actually have been found at all terrace levels. It is not possible with any surety, on the basis of Rogers' notes, to separate the surface collections from these sites into Phase II or Phase III. There are sites in the Central Aspect which Rogers concluded were pure San Dieguito II, but the collections from these sites contain only a few rather undiagnostic artifacts and flakes, which he indicated could occur in either period.

Furthermore, when Rogers laid out the San Dieguito Type Collection, shortly before his death, he selected only partial patterns for Phases II and III, and, perhaps because he had not finished his work, there was some mixing of specimens between the two phases, leaving doubt as to their exact phase association. Rogers wrote:

The San Dieguito III pattern deviates from the San Dieguito II pattern only in the acquisition of new inventions and an improved flaking technique. In the Central Aspect, type specimens which set apart San Dieguito III from San Dieguito II are a true projectile point, the crescentic stone, and the long point-knives. These are probably the best diagnostic forms.

THE SOUTHWESTERN ASPECT

Color Variation of Felsite Artifacts

The various green felsite porphyries of San Diego County were the favorite sources of raw material for San Dieguito tools. In very simple terms, these felsite artifacts are found in three colors: 1) dark green or blue-green, the natural color of the felsite when freshly flaked; 2) gray-green or putty color, a type of chemical alteration forming on the surface of the artifact; and 3) a rust-colored "scum" or stain, which may form over either of the other two colors. There are variations and shadings between each of the color groups, but Rogers thought this chemical alteration or "patina" was of some use as an age indicator when employed in a general way with large numbers of artifacts within a given site.

San Dieguito Settlement Patterns

Another kind of evidence used was the geographical location of San Dieguito sites, which Rogers interpreted as indicating chronologically separate culture patterns. Sixty-five sites in San Diego County yielded San Dieguito artifacts, and, based upon depth of patina on artifacts, location of the site, and the artifact typology, Rogers assigned particular sites to Phase II or Phase III. Twenty-one Phase II sites are on "highland terraces," which are terraces, ridges, or mesa spurs 200 feet or more above sea level. Two Phase II assemblages come from "low terraces," defined as a terrace, ridge, or bay bar less than 150 feet above sea level.

Eight Phase III sites are on highland terraces, while three San Dieguito III collections come from low terraces. Five high terraces and two low terraces have yielded such poor assemblages that the particular phase pattern cannot be defined.

This picture is confused, however, because Rogers found thirty-five sites which he reported contained both Phase II and III patterns. Twenty of these dual sites are on highland terraces, eleven on low terraces, and four located in the lower

143

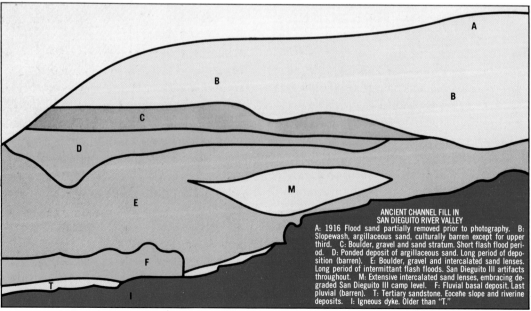

**ANCIENT CHANNEL FILL IN
SAN DIEGUITO RIVER VALLEY**
A: 1916 Flood sand partially removed prior to photography. B:
Slopewash, argillaceous sand, culturally barren except for upper
third. C: Boulder, gravel and sand stratum. Short flash flood period. D: Ponded deposit of argillaceous sand. Long period of deposition (barren). E: Boulder, gravel and intercalated sand lenses.
Long period of intermittant flash floods. San Dieguito III artifacts
throughout. M: Extensive intercalated sand lenses, embracing de-
graded San Dieguito III camp level. F: Fluvial basal deposit. Last
pluvial (barren). T: Tertiary sandstone. Eoceñe slope and riverine
deposits. I: Igneous dyke. Older than "T."

HARRIS SITE 1938; LOCUS I, TRENCH 1

elevations of "highland valleys." In such instances, the main criteria for pattern separation seem to be artifact typology and patina depth.

There is no doubt that Rogers was never thoroughly convinced he had correctly interpreted the evidence indicating some sort of Phase II-Phase III distinction. One of his chief disappointments was the failure to find any clear-cut stratigraphy between the two patterns. Most of the collections were gathered from the surface, where they were found eroding out of thin-bedded highland terrace sites. In the several surface sites containing more than one culture pattern, no definable stratigraphy, including the horizontal, was noted, with the possible exception of the Harris Site, where San Dieguito II material occurred on the upper terraces of the valley, above the river bank where the Phase III material was buried.

Malcolm Rogers, in the foreground, stands in a trench at the site which after his death yielded carbonaceous earth from which came some of the first firm dates indicating the age of the San Dieguito people.

This is at the Harris site, W-198, in the San Dieguito River valley, and is identified as Trench 1, Locus 1.

The basin itself originated well back in early Pleistocene time and Rogers noted in his site reports that it owed its physiography to the meandering of the river at different elevations over partially indurated, marine Tertiary sandstone and shale.

Behind Rogers is the late Dr. E. L. Hardy, former director of the San Diego Museum of Man.

Rogers is pointing to Stratum E, a flash-flood deposited boulder lens with San Dieguito artifacts scattered throughout.

The older terraces and even the mesa tops, 400 feet above the basin, yielded both San Dieguito and La Jolla archaeology.

The chart at the bottom shows the various levels as charted by Rogers at the time of excavation. Studies at this site are continuing.

Reinterpretation of the Harris Site

Rogers' excavation of the Harris site was well-controlled and fairly extensive. Using the analytical tools of the day, he drew certain conclusions from the evidence that influenced his interpretation of the San Dieguito Complex from that point on. According to Warren, two of these conclusions are now open to reinterpretation. Warren excavated the site in 1958, 1959, and 1965, and he thoroughly analyzed Rogers' data.

The first conclusion bearing re-examination is the concept of a geochronological sequence of Phase II and Phase III. According to Warren, the geological evidence available at this time does not support a chronological separation between the two patterns (Warren, 1966).

The other interpretation now in serious doubt is Rogers' belief that Locus I at the Harris site, or the river-bank workshop, is contemporary with Locus 2, the center of the channel midden. Rogers was surprised by the first radiocarbon date to come from what he had defined as a San Dieguito III camp at Locus 2, even though this level did not actually underlie a La Jolla stratum. The Locus 2 date, taken from shell collected by Rogers in 1938, is 2770 B.C. A La Jolla stratum from the same site, but overlying Rogers' Locus I area, was dated at 4350 B.C. (Warren and True, 1961).

A reinterpretation of the geology by H. T. Ore and Warren in 1965-66, indicates the Locus 2 material probably is younger than the Locus I assemblage. This evidence may eventually help clear the picture, because several of the surface sites Rogers identifies as San Dieguito III, with artifacts exhibiting little or no patina, are typologically related to the Locus 2 assemblage. This assemblage is characterized by trinotched points and broad, leaf-shaped knives.

The Locus 2 material may represent either a younger stage of the San Dieguito Complex, or it may be a separate, as yet undefined culture pattern.

METHOD OF PRESENTATION
Site Numbers and Maps
The Museum of Man site numbering system was started in 1922 when good maps were not available for many areas of the Far West. Rogers used geographical areas to demarcate blocks of sites. For example, A stands for Arizona, C for the Colorado Desert, LC for Lower California, M for the Mojave Desert, N for Nevada, and W for western San Diego County. Under this system, then, C-70 is the seventieth site discovered by Rogers in the Colorado Desert. If the site is extensive or contains distinctive parts, Rogers subdivided it A, B, C, et cetera.

Included in each artifact description are the numbers of sites represented by specimens in the San Dieguito Type Collection. A great quantity of sites were used in his study, but artifacts from many of them were not placed in the type collection. Site

These artifacts from San Diego County sites represent one of the most perplexing of unsolved mysteries in the archaeology of the Far West.

Until recently, these specimens, and several hundred others like them from the Southwestern Aspect, were included in the San Dieguito Complex pattern.

They are typologically related to material from Locus 2 at the Harris site.

Because recent dating evidence and a re-analysis of the Harris site geology indicate that the Locus 1 pattern is older than the Locus 2 assemblage, it appears that archaeologists are faced with yet another culture pattern, which may have been developing in San Diego County about 2770 B.C.

Elsewhere in the Far West, similar artifacts are found in parts of Baja California, in the Amargosa II culture of the Mojave Desert, and in the Chiricahua-Amargosa material from Arizona.

The large specimen on the left is a thin, percussion-flaked knife. The six items on the right are dart points or haftable knife blades. (Scale in inches).

numbers are also used in the identification of pictures throughout the book and in the descriptive summaries. The site distribution maps show the location of sites with respect to the overall complex.

Descriptive Summaries of Sites
Too many sites were involved in this study to describe every one in detail, and archaeologists interested in a greater depth of information must resort to the archives of the San Diego Museum of Man. However, it was felt useful to select certain sites for brief descriptions. These sites are typical of the San Dieguito pattern, and they cover the known varieties. The summaries are compiled from site records, field notes, maps, photographs, and artifact collections made by Rogers between 1922 and 1960.

The Artifacts
Phase I artifacts from the Central Aspect are treated as a separate section in the artifact descriptions. The settlement patterns and the typological differences require Phase I be viewed as a distinct assemblage.

The Western Aspect is not represented by any material in the San Diego Museum of Man as Rogers studied the Southwest Museum's collection. Descriptive texts of those artifacts have not been included.

Rogers died before he could finish analyzing the artifacts from the Southeastern Aspect, and he had selected only a few specimens for study. In view of the small number of items representing such a large area, no attempt at an artifact classification was made. A selection from the material was photographed and included with the site summaries.

In the Central and Southwestern aspects, all of the forms found in a San Dieguito II pattern can be duplicated in a San Dieguito III pattern. Consequently, it was found more desirable to describe the types in each aspect as a cultural entity rather than repeat them for each phase. Because Rogers regarded points, crescents, and point-knives as diagnostic forms of the third phase, such artifacts are presented near the end of each chapter.

Material, like trinotched points and broad-leaf knives, which are typologically related to Locus 2 Harris site artifacts, are not presented in the Southwestern Aspect section since their cultural association is still in question. Rogers' culture classifications of the various sites are listed in the site summaries enabling the reader, with a little effort, to make a few of his own comparisons.

In the spring of 1966, Dr. H. M. Wormington and Dr. E. L. Davis were invited to San Diego to study the collection. The terminology and type groupings used herein are based upon their recommendations and also upon published types. The artifact typology was worked out, using 1051 specimens, not including unmodified flakes, and selected by Rogers as being suitable for illustration or exhibition and now assembled as the San Dieguito Type Collection in the museum. The type collection was drawn from 5121 specimens Rogers associated with the San Dieguito Complex and used in his study for this book. All artifacts and Rogers' original manuscript are on file at the San Diego Museum of Man.

There are more than three dozen artifact types in the San Dieguito Complex, and to present these simply and clearly requires a change in the usual format. Instead of describing projectile points first and grading out to the less refined tools, the order is reversed. As each aspect and phase is discussed, those artifacts shared by all the other aspects and phases, which happen to be the less refined types, are treated first. Artifact types peculiar to a particular aspect or phase will come at the end of that section. As we progress from San Dieguito I in the Central Aspect through San Dieguito III of the Southwestern Aspect, the order is not changed, it is only enriched.

THE CENTRAL ASPECT

SITE SUMMARIES

The Colorado Desert

C-1

Location: Black Mesa Pass, Imperial County, California. *Cultures:* San Dieguito I and II and Yuman. *Type:* Trails. *Architecture:* San Dieguito Trail running north and south; Yuman trails in same area with trail shrines. Some camping evidence along the trails.

C-4

Location: West entrance to Midway Well Pass, Eastern Imperial County, California. *Cultures:* San Dieguito I. *Type:* General camping area on desert pavement terraces. *Architecture:* Many trails and hundreds of sleeping circles.

C-22

Location: Northeastern Imperial County, California, on the 40-foot level of the Colorado River terrace; along a 2-mile strip. *Cultures:* San Dieguito I and some Yuman. *Type:* Gravel mesa land; scattered camps. *Architecture:* San Dieguito I cleared circles, a few boulder-rimmed. Yuman architecture consists of house pits 8 inches deep. Yuman caves in area.

C-23-A

Location: Chuckawalla Wells, Southeastern Riverside County, California. *Cultures:* San Dieguito I, Yuman. *Type:* Sandy wash beach for the Yuman; desert pavement for the San Dieguito people. *Architecture:* Yuman hearths; San Dieguito cleared circles, some boulder-lined. Trail shrine.

C-27-A

Location: Eastern Imperial County, California, near Colorado River. *Cultures:* San Dieguito I. *Type:* Gravel terraces. *Architecture:* San Dieguito I cleared circles, but most destroyed by modern activity.

C-28

Location: Southeastern Imperial County, California, near the Colorado River. *Cultures:* San Dieguito I. *Type:* River terrace. *Architecture:* Many cleared circles without cobble rims. As late as 1926, there were three gravel alignments.

C-40-A

Location: Arrowweed Springs basin, northeastern Riverside County, California. *Cultures:* San Dieguito I and II. *Type:* Gravel mesa lands; scattered camps. *Architecture:* San Dieguito I clearings.

C-41

Location: Junction of Arroyo Seco and Colorado River, eastern Riverside County, California. C-41 is a 5-mile strip of the west bank of the Colorado River extending inland for one mile. *Cultures:* San Dieguito I. *Type:* Gravel terraces of the Colorado River. *Architecture:* San Dieguito I circular clearings of both the non-rimmed and boulder-rimmed type. Several gravel alignments present.

C-43

Location: Black Mesa, eastern Imperial County, California. *Cultures:* San Dieguito I and II. *Type:* Quarry site covering 2 acres. *Architecture:* None.

C-45

Location: Eight-mile strip along Colorado River, eastern Imperial County, California. *Cultures:* San Dieguito I and Yuman. *Type:* Gravel river terraces. *Architecture:* San Dieguito I cleared circles on the 50-foot terrace.

C-63

Location: Maria Mesa on the Colorado River, eastern Imperial County, California. *Cultures:* San Dieguito I and II and Yuman. *Type:* Colorado River terraces. *Architecture:* Ten gravel alignments have been recorded to date (Rogers) on the gravel area between Maria Point and the Riverside Mountains on the north. This is the

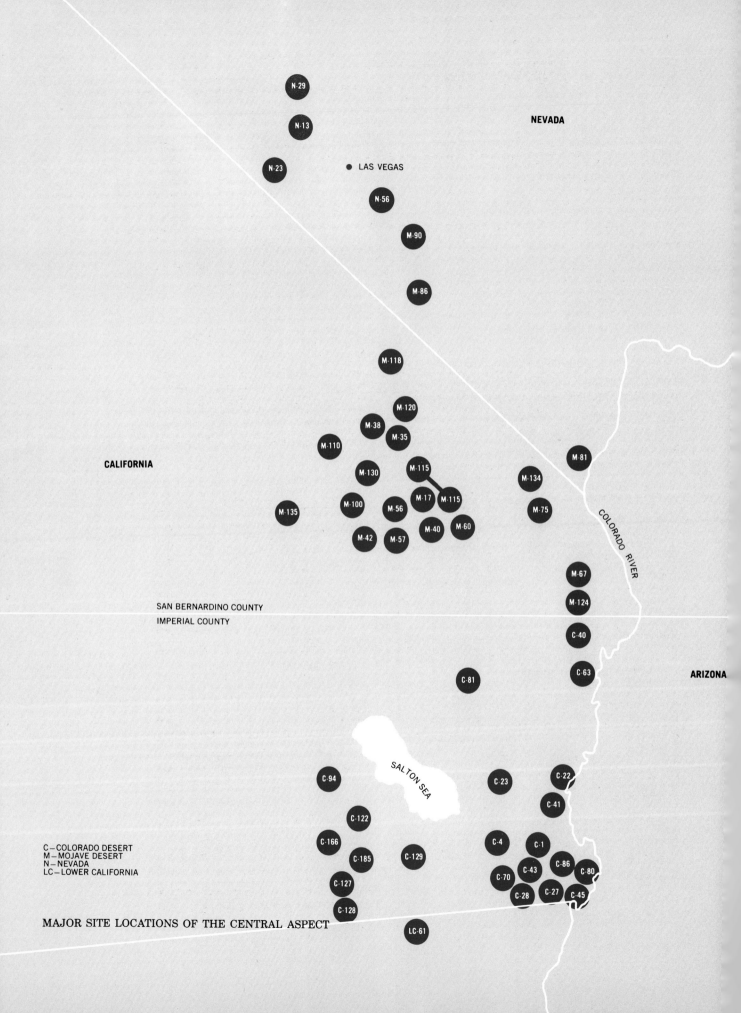

NEVADA

N-29

N-13

N-23

● LAS VEGAS

N-56

M-90

M-86

M-118

M-120

M-38

M-35

CALIFORNIA

M-110

M-81

M-130

M-115

M-134

M-135

M-100

M-56

M-17

M-115

M-75

M-42

M-57

M-40

M-60

M-67

M-124

SAN BERNARDINO COUNTY

IMPERIAL COUNTY

C-40

C-81

C-63

ARIZONA

SALTON SEA

C-94

C-23

C-22

C-41

C-122

C-166

C-4

C-1

C-185

C-129

C-86

C-70

C-43

C-80

C-127

C-28

C-27

C-45

C-128

C—COLORADO DESERT
M—MOJAVE DESERT
N—NEVADA
LC—LOWER CALIFORNIA

LC-61

MAJOR SITE LOCATIONS OF THE CENTRAL ASPECT

greatest gravel pictograph area in the Colorado Basin. Rogers attributed them to both San Dieguito and Yuman.

C-70-C

Location: Eastern Imperial County, California. *Cultures:* San Dieguito I. *Type:* Desert pavement. *Architecture:* Two small trail shrines. Numerous boulder-rimmed and unrimmed circular clearings.

C-80-P, S

Location: This is a trail 16 miles long, the "Inner Picacho Trail." It leaves the Yuma Valley and bears northwest 8 miles, then due north until it strikes the Colorado River. *Cultures:* San Dieguito I and Yuman. C-80-P is a factory site or camp site 1 mile south of Picacho Pass (San Dieguito 1). *Type:* Trail over stony mesas. *Architecture:* Some San Dieguito I shrines with Yuman and Mexican capping.

C-81

Location: Lower Pinto Basin, northern Riverside County, California. *Cultures:* San Dieguito I and II, and Amargosa II. *Type:* Extinct lake and stream banks. *Architecture:* San Dieguito I cleared circles on mesas; the San Dieguito II and Amargosa II occupation is represented by disturbed cobble hearths.

C-86

Location: Southeast Imperial County, California. Begins on Colorado River and goes almost due south to the delta passing Pilot Knob 1½ miles east of it; "Outer Picacho Trail" which is 22 miles long. *Cultures:* San Dieguito I and Yuman. *Type:* Trail and scattered camps on desert pavement. *Architecture:* Along the course of this trail are many San Dieguito I circles; rock alignments, five trail shrines.

C-94

Location: Seventeen Palms, northeastern San Diego County, California. *Cultures:* San Dieguito I and Yuman. *Type:* Clay hill badlands capped with gravel mesas with scattered camps of San Dieguito I;

Yuman in small palm-filled canyon. *Architecture:* None except for some San Dieguito circles, scattered about on the mesas.

C-122

Location: Carrizo Wash, east central San Diego County, California. *Cultures:* San Dieguito I and Yuman. *Type:* Stony mesas and desert pavement. *Architecture:* San Dieguito I cleared circles and boulder-rimmed circles in the gravel capping of residual mesa blocks. This is the greatest concentration of the structures in the entire San Dieguito I domain (at least 364).

C-127

Location: Dos Cabezas Spring, southeast San Diego County, California. *Cultures:* San Dieguito I and Yuman at C-127 and San Dieguito II at C-127-A about 2 miles away. *Type:* Sand and gravel mesas. *Architecture:* A few San Dieguito cleared circles in the area, with a few Yuman rock shelters.

C-128-A

Location: Base of Jacumba Pass, southeast San Diego County, California. *Cultures:* San Dieguito II and Yuman. *Type:* Mountain rock shelter for Yuman; gravel and sand valley terraces for San Dieguito II. According to Rogers, this site lies in the principal corridor for the San Dieguito II migrations from the Desert into western San Diego County. Quarries and camps. *Architecture:* None.

C-129-B

Location: At the east end of Fish Creek Mountains, Imperial County, California. *Cultures:* San Dieguito I and Yuman. *Type:* Trails and general camping area on a gravel terrace; the Yuman is concentrated in one small temporary campsite and along one trail; the San Dieguito material is spread over 4 acres of desert pavement. *Architecture:* Yuman trail with potsherds scattered along its margins; older trails on slopes above the gravel terrace may be San Dieguito; four sleeping circles and three ancient stone-lined pits, which may have been roasting pits. All are set well into the desert pavement.

C-166

Location: Lower Split Mountain Area, eastern San Diego County, California. *Cultures:* San Dieguito I and Yuman. *Type:* Gravel bench above dry arroyo. *Architecture:* A few San Dieguito I stone circles; Yuman hearths and house pits.

C-185-A

Location: Coquina Mesa, west end of Split Mountain in San Diego County, California. *Cultures:* San Dieguito II and Yuman. *Type:* Scattered camps. *Architecture:* Yuman boulder-rimmed house pits.

Baja California
LC-61

Location: Due south of Coyote Wells, Imperial County, California, and two miles south of the border in Baja California; Cantu Petrified Forest; several square miles in area. *Cultures:* San Dieguito I and Yuman. *Type:* Quarry. *Architecture:* Scattered San Dieguito circles on surrounding mesas.

The Mojave Desert
M-17

Location: Rasor, north central San Bernardino County, California. *Cultures:* San Dieguito I and II. *Type:* Soda Lake terraces and adjacent mesas; sand dunes and silt floor of the Sink; scattered camps. *Architecture:* Cleared circles, some boulder-rimmed on the mesas on the margin of Soda Lake terrace.

M-35

Location: Salt Springs Dry Lake, north San Bernardino County, California. Area of 4 square miles involved with closely spaced campsites. *Cultures:* This is primarily an Amargosa site, with all phases represented. There are also traces of San Dieguito and Chemehuevi. *Type:* Playa residual humps, fossil dunes and late

dune camps. *Architecture:* Amargosa hearths.

M-38

Location: Denning Spring, Avawatz Mountain, central San Bernardino County, California. *Cultures:* San Dieguito I and II and early Mojave. *Type:* Stony mesas above a spring. *Architecture:* Some boulder-rimmed San Dieguito I circles present on the mesa.

M-40

Location: Mesquite Hills dry lake, east central San Bernardino County, California. *Cultures:* San Dieguito I, Amargosa I and early Mojave. *Type:* Silt and gravel benches above a playa and playa dunes. *Architecture:* Cobble hearths at early Mojave main camp. San Dieguito I circles on gravel terrace on south side of the playa; rock alignment on north terrace.

M-42

Location: Cady Wash, central San Bernardino County, California. *Cultures:* San Dieguito I and II. *Type:* High stony terace of Mojave River. *Architecture:* At the south end of the terraces are a few San Dieguito I stone circles averaging 6 feet in diameter; also late petroglyphs.

M-56

Location: Cady Mesa, north central San Bernardino County, California, 4000 feet by 500 feet. *Cultures:* San Dieguito I, Amargosa I and early Mojave. *Type:* Rocky mesa top. *Architecture:* A few San Dieguito I boulder-rimmed circles present; large rock alignment.

M-57

Location: Fossil Spring, north central San Bernardino County, California. Total area is 1 square mile, intensive occupation covers an area 2500 feet by 500 feet. *Cultures:* San Dieguito I and II, Amargosa I and II, early Mojave. *Type:* Pluvial lake deposits covered with out-wash from Cady Mountains to form a boulder and gravel-capped mesa with dunes at the base. *Architecture:* San Dieguito I cleared circles and a few Amargosa and Mojave cobble hearths; two large boulder shrines.

M-60

Location: North central San Bernardino County, California, at the southern end of ancient Lake Mojave. *Cultures:* San Dieguito I and II. *Type:* Scattered camps on a stony mesa, marginal to the south abayment of Mojave Sink. *Architecture:* Several boulder-rimmed circles in the desert pavement of the mesa top.

M-67

Location: West Well, southeastern San Bernardino County, California. *Cultures:* San Dieguito I and II and Yuman. *Type:* Stony upper and lower wash terraces. *Architecture:* Sixty cleared circles in terrace surfaces (about twenty have boulder rims) In the sandy, gravely areas of the lower terrace the boulders have been carried some distance to build the rims of the San Dieguito II circles. Both types are generally grouped in twos, threes, fours or fives. Rimless clearings are smaller than the boulder-rimmed ones and the latter are most often linked together. Two rectangular boulder-rimmed circles are present.

M-75-A

Location: Paiute Creek, east margin of San Bernardino County, California. *Cultures:* San Dieguito I and II and Amargosa II. *Type:* On a Pleistocene residual mesa of lacustrine deposits. *Architecture:* A few San Dieguito I cleared circles are present. M-75 is a great petroglyph site.

M-81

Location: South end of Clark County, Nevada, on the west bank of the Colorado River. *Cultures:* San Dieguito I. *Type:* Ancient river terraces; San Dieguito I occupation debris occurs on the two lowest terraces, and camps are scattered along a 6-mile strip of the Colorado River. *Architecture:* Rimless circular clearings in the river terrace gravels.

M-86

Location: Searchlight Wash, Clark County, Nevada. *Cultures:* San Dieguito I and Yuman. *Type:* Gravel river terraces of the Colorado River. *Architecture:* Scattered and isolated San Dieguito I cleared circles in the terrace surfaces, especially on the 50-foot terrace. The only boulder-rimmed circles in the area were noticed at the junction of Searchlight Wash and the Colorado River.

M-90

Location: Eldorado Wash, southern Clark County, Nevada. *Cultures:* San Dieguito I and some Yuman. *Type:* Forty-foot gravel terrace and the 60-foot terrace of the Colorado River. *Architecture:* Occasional San Dieguito I cleared house circles in the terrace gravels.

M-100

Location: Mannix Lake Terrace, central west San Bernardino County, California (Mannix Quarries). *Cultures:* San Dieguito Complex and Amargosa Complex, and possibly some Shoshonean. This site was utilized by every group who inhabited the Mojave Desert from San Dieguito to Vanyume and Chemehuevi. *Type:* Extensive quarries on gravel terraces. *Architecture:* None.

M-110

Location: Granite (dry) Lake in northwestern San Bernardino County, California. *Cultures:* San Dieguito II and III, Amargosa I and trace of Yuman or Panamint. *Type:* Pluvial lake terrace open site on Pleistocene lake silts. *Architecture:* None.

M-110-A

Location: Same as M-110. *Cultures:* San Dieguito III and Amargosa I. *Type:* Mesa back of talus slope, covers 2 acres, mostly covered with sand. *Architecture:* None.

M-110-B

Location: Same as M-110. *Cultures:* San

Dieguito, Amargosa I and late occupation. The San Dieguito occupational strip was eroded down into the lake. *Type:* Quarry; covers 4 acres. *Architecture:* None.

M-115

Location: Ancient Lake Mojave; central San Bernardino County, California. *Area:* Sixty miles of shore line. *Cultures:* San Dieguito I, II and III, trace of Amargosa I and Mojave. *Type:* Camps on lake terraces, bay bars and spits. *Architecture:* San Dieguito I and II stone circles; cobble hearths. *General Remarks:* This is a large and extremely complex series of sites covering a great number of components and phases. Rogers defined the shore line features and the actual shore line of the lake (now extinct) and divided the area into twelve zones (A-K) based on areas of concentration.

Zones:
M-115
West shore site of Silver Lake on 33-foot terrace; material all back of wave terrace except some which has washed down; hearths present on 10-foot terrace. *Cultures:* San Dieguito II and III.

M-115-A
A 33-foot terrace site, Silver Lake; all traces of hearths washed away; no metate evidence. Previous collecting has upset the picture. Artifacts are sandblasted. This is a bay terrace connecting an island with the shore. *Cultures:* San Dieguito II and III.

M-115-B
A 33-foot terrace site, Silver Lake. Terrain of the desert pavement type with artifacts set into surface. Had not previously been disturbed. Artifacts not blasted like those at M-115-A. A few washed-out hearths present on talus slopes. *Cultures:* San Dieguito I, II and III.

M-115-C
A 33-foot terrace, Silver Lake; has been collected from previously. Artifacts show

tremendous sand blasting and are distinguishable only in profile. No metate evidence. Anadonta shell present at all sites. *Cultures:* San Dieguito II and III.

M-115-D
East terrace of Soda Lake; one residual section 130-feet long and several short disconnected sections to the north and south. This is a storm terrace. *Cultures:* San Dieguito II.

M-115-E
Large section of Soda Lake terrace located northwest of Soda Station. Stratified deposits of gravel and sand washed into Lake Mojave for a great distance. Mussel deposits in this flat mesa-like formation indicate that it was built out for at least 600 feet before man appeared. The artifacts are scarce and scattered. Three cobble hearths are exposed at the back of the site about 20 feet apart, arranged in a triangle. *Cultures:* San Dieguito III.

M-115-F
Soda Station site. Located on terraced lake fill which connects the base of the Soda Mountains with an outlying marble hill. A slight amount of occupation is present back of the site on the high level-terrace. One Gypsum Point found here and a little late Indian material, including two arrow-points and a few Mojave sherds. Two sherds were found 12 inches underground in the fill between two bars. *Cultures:* San Dieguito III, Amargosa II, Mojave.

M-115-G
Located around the Black Hills on the east shore line of Soda Lake. No occupation found on the highest terrace or back of it except for a few cobble hearths. This site is on a very long lake fill and mostly on the sandy parts. The stony terraces produce very little material. *Cultures:* San Dieguito II and III.

M-115-H
Covers the area from the Black Hills to as far north as the town of Baker. This is a

long low bay bar which was uncovered after the lake had reduced its elevation 6 feet. *Cultures:* San Dieguito II.

M-115-I
Gravel terraces on the south and east sides of a hill on the west shore opposite Baker. Very slightly occupied. *Cultures:* San Dieguito III.

M-115-J
Upper terrace in a small northwest corner of Soda Lake. Not a densely occupied site. *Cultures:* San Dieguito II.

M-118
Location: Amargosa Valley, southeast Inyo County, California. *Cultures:* San Dieguito I and II and Amargosa I. *Type:* Gravel terraces along Amargosa River. *Architecture:* Cleared circles.

M-120
Location: North Salt Spring Dry Lake, north central San Bernardino County, California. M-120 is four separate sites covering a total acreage of 6 acres. M-120-A is an area about the margins of the north end of the lake. *Cultures:* San Dieguito II, Amargosa I, and late Indian. *Type:* Dry Lake surface camps; fossil dunes. *Architecture:* Cobble hearths of early Mojave or Panamint, and the crater and raised rim of a dug well.

M-124
Location: Mopi Canyon-Turtle Mountains, southeastern San Bernardino County, California. *Cultures:* San Dieguito I. *Type:* Mesa camp in the forks of a mountain drainage system. *Architecture:* No evidence of circles but surface is greatly disturbed by post-occupation erosion.

M-130-A, C.
Location: Tietfort Basin, central northwestern San Bernardino County, California. Intensive occupation involves 5 acres. *Cultures:* San Dieguito II, Amargosa I and early Mojave. *Type:* Four large encampments on ancient lake residual humps of

silt covered in part by sand dunes; scattered occupation. *Architecture:* Disturbed Amargosa hearths.

M-134
Location: Marl Lake basin, northeastern San Bernardino County, California. *Cultures:* San Dieguito I and II. *Type:* Drainage channel terrace for both San Dieguito I and II, but San Dieguito II is on a lower level. *Architecture:* San Dieguito I cleared circles on the gravel terrace flanking the west side of the present drainage system which cuts through the Pleistocene Marl Lake beds.

M-135
Location: Harper Dry Lake, central western San Bernardino County, California. *Cultures:* Main occupation was early Mojave, with San Dieguito II present. *Type:* Scattered camps on a large residual block of Upper Pleistocene lake deposits. *Architecture:* Cobble hearths and winter-beds, probably early Mojave.

Southwestern Nevada
N-13
Location: Mesquite Springs, Charleston Mountains pediment, elevation 3270 feet, Nye County, Nevada. *Cultures:* N-13 is San Dieguito I. N-13-A is San Dieguito III, Amargosa III, and Paiute. *Type:* Mountain talus slope with springs at base; detached camps over 4 acres. *Architecture:* Disturbed boulders suggest circles.

N-23
Location: Pahrump Escarpment at the base of the Spring Mountains, Clark County, Nevada. *Cultures:* San Dieguito I and, at N-23-A, Paiute. *Type:* Fault escarpment terraces; quarries and small camps near live or fossil springs (from base of lowest terrace). *Architecture:* None.

N-29
Location: Quartz Spring, Lincoln County, Nevada in northwest end of the Pintwater Range. Elevation 4500 feet. *Cultures:* San Dieguito I and Basketmaker. *Type:* Mar-

gins of a steep-sided canyon; scattered camps. *Architecture:* Possibly San Dieguito I cleared circles, boulder rims indefinite.

N-56

Location: Las Vegas Wash, Clark County, Nevada. *Cultures:* San Dieguito I and Amargosa III. *Type:* Stony terraces. *Architecture:* San Dieguito I stone circles on upper levels; possibly Amargosa III circles or roasting hearths at lower levels.

ARTIFACTS, PHASE I
Cores

Three basic variations in cores occur in the San Dieguito Complex: amorphous shapes, prepared-platform cores, and "tortoise" cores (described under San Dieguito III, Southwestern Aspect). Amorphous cores have flakes removed from a number of faces, and no pattern can be discerned. Such workshop evidence has been found on nearly every San Dieguito I site in the Central Aspect. Amorphous core types are from sites C-23-A, C-45, M-57, and M-75A. Rogers noted:

Apparently, it was more practical to make tools on the spot, use them, and discard them, than it was to carry around a kit of heavy implements in some sort of receptacle.

"Tortoise" cores have not been found in the San Dieguito I phase, but crude versions of prepared-platform cores occur in rare instances in Central Aspect collec-

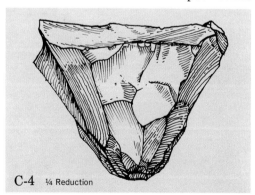

C-4 ¼ Reduction

tions. The illustrated specimen is from site C-4, and it has an irregular platform with part of the cortical surface remaining on it and on one side. The specimen resembles

a keeled scraper, but shows no sign of wear, and it is triangular in cross-section.
Hammers

Several items in the San Dieguito I collections which might have been used as hammers are small cobbles (usually about fist-size) with battered ends and margins. None of them show prolonged use.

In the same category are small implements Dr. E. L. Davis terms "fabricators" because they resemble miniature tabular core hammers with a platform at both ends. Davis suggests they might have been used to sharpen the edges of finished tools. Type specimens are from sites C-43-A, C-70-C, and N-56.
Flakes

Three kinds of more or less unmodified flakes in the collections are: trimming flakes, "Teshoa" flakes, and blades. As with amorphous cores, trimming flakes were found on nearly every San Dieguito I site. Many of them make good cutting

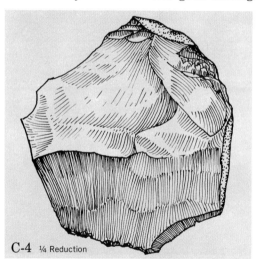

C-4 ¼ Reduction

tools. Illustrated is a specimen showing signs of use from site C-4. Rogers noted:

They occur in such great numbers that wastage alone cannot account for them, and, by inference, one may deduce that their makers considered them to be finished products.

A Teshoa flake is a plano-convex flake with a cortical back, struck from one end of an elongated cobble. Rogers noted:

The name is the Ute term applied to them, and such items occur as occasional ele-

ments in many Far Western patterns from the advent of man on down to the historic Ute (Leidy, 1873).

Almost every type of San Dieguito artifact has a considerable size range, and teshoas are no exception. The smallest, from C-86-S, is 1½ inches in diameter, while the largest, from C-22, is 4½ inches in diameter. Type specimens from M-81 and M-90 show wear from being used as scrapers. Other type specimens are from C-41, C-63, and C-80-S.

The San Dieguito Complex made great use of flake and core tools, but true blades or tools made from blades seem to have played a minor role. A true blade is a long, thin prismatic flake, essentially parallel-sided, struck from a prepared-platform core. Most San Dieguito I sites in the Central Aspect average one or two such specimens, but they are shorter, wider (no more than 2 to 1, length-width ratio), and poorly done when compared with eastern North American or European specimens. Type specimens are from C-40-A, C-43-A, C-

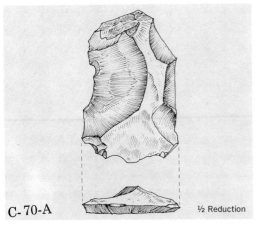

C-70-A   ½ Reduction

70-A (illustrated), M-56, and N-23. Malcolm Rogers compared such flakes to similar specimens made by Australian Aborigines, who haft the blades for knives and spears (unpublished notes, MJR).

Ovate Bifaces and Biface Preforms

The ovate biface seems to be the closest the San Dieguito I people came to a stone knife form. The type specimens are all crude, bifacial, percussion-flaked, ovoid in outline, and lenticular in cross-section. A few specimens may be derived from

thick flakes, but most are decidedly core tools. The type collection contains specimens from C-23-A, C-43-A, C-43-B, C-70-

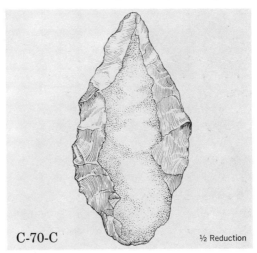

C-70-C   ½ Reduction

C (illustrated), C-80-S,P, M-40-A, M-90, and N-13. They average 3¼ inches long by 2½ inches wide.

Preforms are an unfinished version of the biface. Type specimens come from C-4, C-27-A, C-70-C, C-80-P, LC-61, M-56, M-57, and N-29.

Choppers and Chopping Tools

Choppers of the simplest variety were made by percussion flaking one face of one end of an oval river cobble. A thick unifacially-flaked primary flake was also used. Quartzite is one of the common types of stone employed in the manufacture of choppers. Chopper types were found at C-22, C-28, C-45 (illustrated), M-90, and M-124.

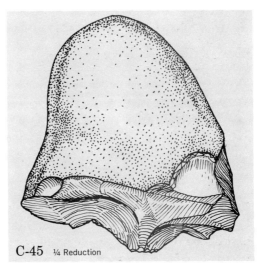

C-45   ¼ Reduction

Bifacially percussion-flaked "chopping tools" were also made, and once again, oval river cobbles or thick primary flakes served as the basis for these tools. Each specimen made from a thick flake is flaked around its entire perimeter. Another type, from M-86, is an elongated cobble bifacially flaked at both ends. The flaking could easily have been made while using the cobble as a hammerstone. Bifacial chopping tool type specimens come from C-4,

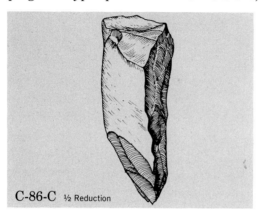

C-86-C ½ Reduction

C-43-A, C-45, C-70-C, C-86-C (illustrated), C-122, M-40-A, M-57, M-86, M-134, N-13, and N-23.

Gravers

Only two items showing possible use as engraving tools are in the San Dieguito I

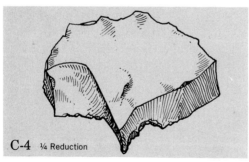

C-4 ¼ Reduction

Type Collection. One, from C-4 (illustrated) is made from an amorphous trimming flake, and it has a sharp point on one side. The opposite side was used as a side scraper. The other specimen, from C-43-A, is essentially an end scraper made from a small flake. It has a sharp-pointed beak extending from its scraping margin. Chisel gravers, like those of the San Dieguito II and III phases, have not been found on Phase I sites.

Planes

Planes and discoidal scrapers, which are often treated as being functionally similar, are separated in this typology on the basis of the rake-angle of the working edge. If the angle is greater than 45°, the tool is classified as a plane. Implements with a working edge having less than a 45° angle fall into the discoidal scraper class (San Dieguito II or III). A further subdivision is based upon the size of the tool. Large planes average 3 inches in diameter by 2 inches high. Small planes average about half the size of the large ones. It is not known if size had any effect on the function of the tool. With the exception

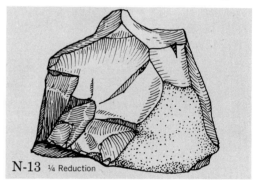

N-13 ¼ Reduction

of one plane which is made on a core (illustrated) from N-13, all of the planes are percussion-flaked from thick flakes. They have an irregular outline and are plano-convex in cross-section. They usually are step-flaked along the working edge, giving them a D-shape, or "pony-hoof" shape. Type specimens are from C-43-A, C-122, M-40-A, M-57, and M-81.

Small planes in the Type Collection are from C-23-A (illustrated), C-43-A, C-70-C, M-57, M-124, and N-23.

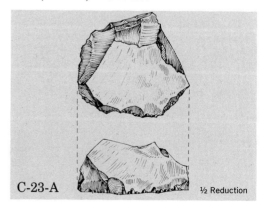

C-23-A ½ Reduction

Malcolm Rogers felt such implements should be called "pulping planes," and, he noted:

Because of their conformation they were employed with a to-and-fro motion, similar to that of a carpenter's plane. Kumeyai women informants (in the early 1930's) related that such tools were used to pulp agave leaves as a preliminary state in procuring fibre for cordage.

Convex End Scrapers

Four of the seven type specimens are made from blade-like flakes, with a portion of the striking platform remaining and a bulb of percussion at one end. At the opposite end, the convex working edge is retouched by percussion and/or pressure flaking. The other end scrapers are made from thick, irregular flakes, but their general shape (irregular outline and plano-convex cross-section) are like the rest. There is some size range, but they average 1½ inches in diameter by ½ inch thick. The specimens come from C-4, C-40-A, C-43-A (illustrated), C-43-B, C-80-P, C-166, and N-13.

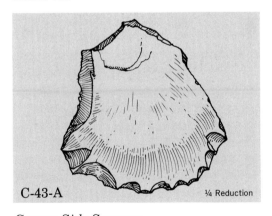

C-43-A   ¼ Reduction

Convex Side Scrapers

These tools are very irregular in both size and shape. Two specimens, from C-122 and M-56 are flakes struck from prepared cores. Most are amorphous shapes, but tend to be plano-convex in cross-section. A specimen from LC-61 (illustrated) is an exception to this. It is a large, triangular flake, with a straight, rather than truly convex edge. The edge is retouched by percussion. Other type specimens are from C-4, C-43-A, C-63, C-70-A, C-70-C, and

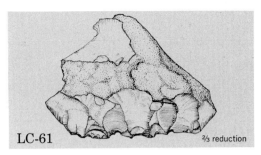

LC-61   ⅔ reduction

the M-40 trail. Their size ranges from 2 inches long by 1 inch wide to 5½ inches long by 3½ inches wide.

Concave Scrapers

The tremendous range in size, shape, and manufacture of these tools indicate they may not all have had the same function. Ten of the type specimens are made from irregular flakes showing neither bulbs of percussion or striking platforms. They are all plano-convex in cross-section and average 2 inches long by ½ inch thick. The concave scraping edge may be on the end

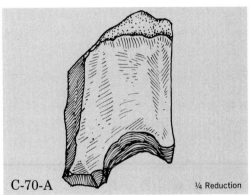

C-70-A   ¼ Reduction

or side, or both. They were found at C-4, C-43-A, C-43-B, C-70-A (illustrated), C-70-C, LC-61, M-40-A, and N-56.

Two specimens made from amorphous

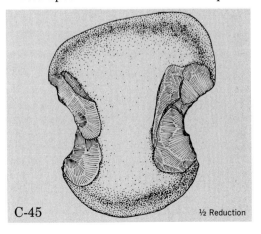

C-45   ½ Reduction

cores about 4 inches long are from C-70-A and C-70-C. One unusual tool from C-45 is a binotched quartzite cobble (illustrated). Malcolm Rogers felt this implement was a maul, notched for hafting. There is a faint bruise on one end of the cobble, but the notches exhibit considerable abrasive wear.

Rectangular Scrapers

These scrapers have a fairly uniform, rectangular shape, with a tabular cross-section. They average 3 inches long by 2 inches wide and are just under 1 inch thick. All are made from thick flakes, and one exhibits a bulb of percussion and a vestige of the platform. Functionally, these tools are end-and-side scrapers, since both sides and both ends are percussion-retouched and used. The type specimens come from C-43-A, C-45 (illustrated), and N-13.

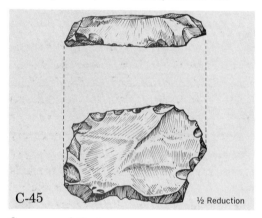

C-45 ½ Reduction

Compound Tools

Tools having more than one function are found throughout the San Dieguito collections, and variations will be described in subsequent sections. In the Phase I type collection, however, the only implements clearly demonstrating two functions are

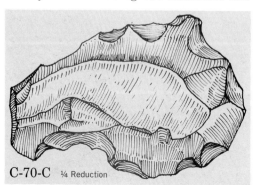

C-70-C ¼ Reduction

three combination convex-concave side scrapers. They are made like other side scrapers and are about 3 inches long, but they have one concave scraping edge opposite the convex scraping edge. Examples are from C-40-A, C-70-C (illustrated), and M-40-A.

ARTIFACTS, PHASES II AND III

Cores

Amorphous cores predominate in Central Aspect sites, and just as in the first phase, the specimens look as though flakes were removed in a haphazard, patternless fashion. Basalt, jasper, chalcedony, and various felsite porphyries were all used in the manufacture of San Dieguito II and III tools. Quartzite was also put to use, but not as commonly as in the first phase. Amorphous cores in the Type Collection are from C-43-A, C-80-S, C-185-A, M-75-A, and M-115-B.

Prepared-platform cores do occur in Central Aspect sites, and they are well made. However, such specimens account for less than one percent of the total San Dieguito collection, while approximately ten percent of the total collection (which consists of more than 5,000 artifacts) are amorphous cores.

There are two prepared cores in the Type Collection. One of them, from M-115-C (illustrated) almost falls into the "tortoise"

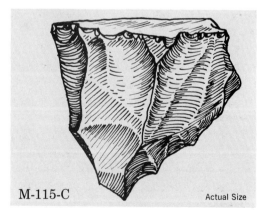

M-115-C Actual Size

core class. The other core, from M-100, is flaked on opposite sides so that it resembles a wedge. Neither specimen could produce a very long blade, since they are both less than 3 inches high.

Hammers

Definite hammerstones occur, although they are rare. The one specimen (illustrated) in the Type Collection, from M-17, is

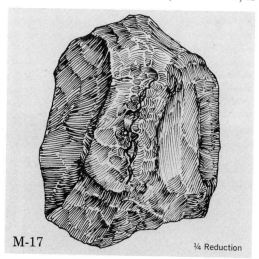

M-17   ¼ Reduction

made of a basalt porphyry. Its shape suggests use as a core or chopping tool prior to its use as a hammer. The margins of the tool are battered and rounded. It has a diameter of approximately 3 inches. The so-called "fabricators" of the first phase seem to be absent in the second and third phase.

Flakes

Trimming flakes are found in great quantities on most of the San Dieguito II and III sites, especially at locales which might be defined as quarry-workshops. No effort has been made to determine what quantity of primary flakes and trimming flakes were put to use as tools.

Malcolm Rogers indicates, in his manuscript, the presence of teshoa flakes on San Dieguito II and III sites, but no examples could be found in the collections of the Museum of Man.

Blades from the San Dieguito II and III pattern show considerable improvement in their manufacturing technique over their counterparts in the first phase. They are struck from prepared cores, and the flakes average about 3 inches long, are quite thin, more or less parallel-sided, and prismatic. Like prepared cores, however, they account for less than one percent of the total collection. They lack the

length and the quality of manufacture that is usually found in European or eastern North American specimens. Blades in the Type Collection are from C-128-A, M-42, M-67, M-110, M-115-B, and M-115-C (illustrated). All specimens show signs of having been used.

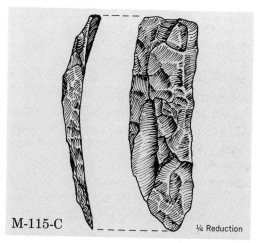

M-115-C   ¼ Reduction

Biface Preforms

First phase bifaces are so crude and relatively scarce, that it is more expedient to describe both preform and finished product under one heading. In the second and third phase pattern, however, bifaces take on many variations and, presumably, functions. Even specimens classed as preforms, which are the roughed-out stage of a biface implement, show greater control and skill on the part of the knapper. It is

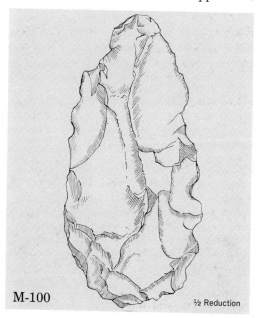

M-100   ½ Reduction

161

not possible to tell, with any surety, what sort of tool was being made, but most of the blanks could easily be transformed into ovate bifaces or large, leaf-shaped knives. All specimens are bifacially percussion-flaked into an essentially ovoid form, lenticular in cross-section. Examples come from sites M-42, M-57, M-75-A, and M-100 (illustrated).

Ovate Bifaces

The ovate biface class is a rather arbitrary one, since the specimens were selected because they are too large to be points and too thick to be knives, but not bulky enough to be chopping tools. Yet, they share attributes with each of the other categories. Generally, ovate bifaces are more or less ovate to elliptical in outline, lenticular in cross-section, and tend to be pointed more on one end than at the other. They usually have a thick cross-section (about one-half of their width), and all but one are percussion-flaked over their entire perimeters. Specimens come from C-128-A, M-38, M-57, M-110, M-110-B, M-115, M-115-B, and M-130-C (illustrated).

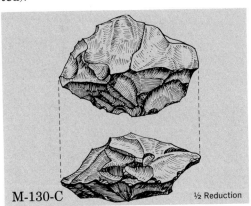

M-130-C   ½ Reduction

Chopping Tools

No unifacial choppers exist in the San Dieguito II and III collections at the Museum of Man, although a few of the large side-scrapers might fall into this category.

The bifacially flaked "chopping tool" does exist, however, and tools in this class were made in the same manner as the chopping tools of Phase I. They are percussion-flaked around their entire perimeter, thick and lenticular in cross-sect-

ion, and more or less ovoid in outline. Chopping tools are thicker than ovate bifaces, but are otherwise about the same size (approximately 3 inches in diameter). Type specimens are from C-40, C-43-B, C-128-A, M-17, M-57, M-75-A (illustrated), M-115, and M-115-B.

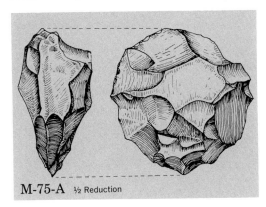

M-75-A ½ Reduction

Gravers

There are four specimens in the Type Collection showing apparent use as engraving tools. All are pressure-flaked from small, amorphous flakes, are plano-convex in cross-section, and are sharply pointed on one end. Two could have been used for scraping as well as engraving, but are not heavy enough to be classed as chisel gravers. They are from sites M-115-C, M-115-G (illustrated), M-130, and M-130-C.

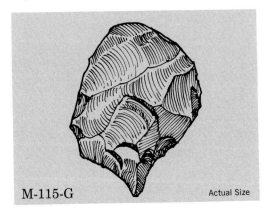

M-115-G   Actual Size

Chisel Gravers

Similar to gravers are "chisel gravers" having a bulk and shape which possibly implies a different function. They are pressure-flaked from plano-convex flakes, rather thick (about one-half of their width), average about 2 inches long, and come to a curving point at one end. The opposite end is rounded into an end scraper, and the sides are pressure-retouched for scraping, as is the pointed end. The tool would make an excellent chisel. Type specimens come from sites M-110, M-115-C (illustrated), M-115-E, and M-115-G.

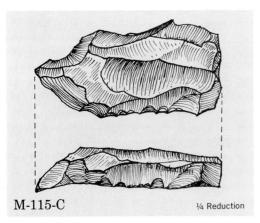

M-115-C   ¼ Reduction

Planes

The same criteria set up for planes in the first phase holds true for those of the Phase II and III pattern. They are all percussion-flaked core tools. Some may actually be cores which were put to secondary use as planes. They all have a rake-angle of greater than 45° on their working edges (usually about 90°), are more or less plano-convex, and tend to have rather irregular ovoid shapes. Large planes, averaging 3 inches in diameter by 2 inches high, come from M-17, M-100, and M-135 (illustrated).

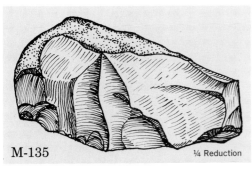

M-135   ¼ Reduction

Small planes, averaging 2 inches in diameter by 1½ inches high, seem to be more plentiful in the collections. Type specimens come from C-127-A, C-128-A, M-57, M-67, M-75-A, M-115, M-115-B (illustrated), M-115-G, M-115-H, and M-135.

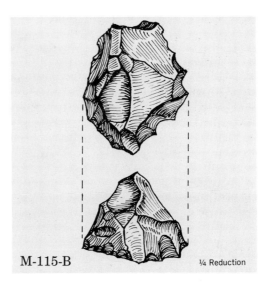

M-115-B   ¼ Reduction

Convex End Scrapers

End scrapers are one of the most uniform tools in the assemblage. They have a rectangular shape, are plano-convex in cross-section, and all are long, thick flakes, struck from prepared-platform cores. Each exhibits a bulb of percussion and shows a vestige of the platform. The sides and one end are pressure-retouched. The specimens average 3 inches long by 1½ inches wide by ½ inch thick, and they were found on sites C-1-N, C-43-A, M-57, M-67, M-115, M-115-B, M-115-C, and M-115-D (illustrated). Although most are

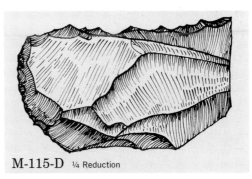

M-115-D ¼ Reduction

parallel-sided, three specimens, from C-185-A, M-67 and M-115, are trimmed to a triangular shape. The tapering does not appear to have been made for hafting.

Convex Side Scrapers

The side scrapers are less regular in form than the end scrapers. One specimen in the type collection (from M-42) is a large percussion-flaked triangular flake 5 inches long, with a triangular cross-section, which might almost be classed as a flake plane. Six others are made from thin amorphous flakes having pressure-flaked working margins. They are from C-43, M-115-A, M-115-B, and M-115-C (illustrated).

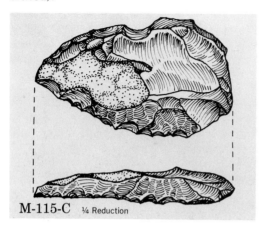

M-115-C ¼ Reduction

Another variation is made from thick flakes split off of large pebbles or amorphous cores. All are plano-convex in cross-section. Two, from M-35-L and M-110, are biconvex, having pressure-flaked working margins on two sides. The remainder have one retouched working edge and often have a portion of the corticle surface of the rock left opposite the working edge. Type specimens are from M-57, M-67, M-115-B, M-130 (illustrated), M-130-A, and M-134-A.

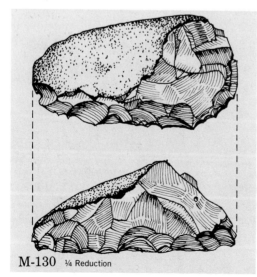

M-130 ¼ Reduction

Concave Scrapers
Four concave scrapers in the Type Collection are made on amorphous flakes, are more or less plano-convex in cross-section, and have one concave working margin that was pressure retouched. They are from C-128, M-115-C, and M-115-G.

The remaining three were made on blade-like flakes and are pressure-flaked into an "hour-glass" shape, with concave scraping edges on opposite sides of the flake. Specimens are from C-43-B, M-115-B, and M-115-C (illustrated).

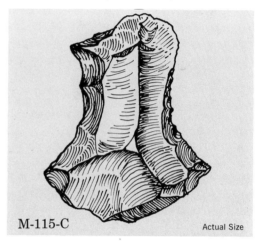

M-115-C   Actual Size

Rectangular Scrapers
These specimens differ from the Phase I type and from those found in the Southwestern Aspect, both of which have tabular cross-sections. These have plano-convex cross-sections, which may not be a critical difference. In other respects, the three examples are like other scrapers having a rectangular shape: they were made from a large (probably side-struck) flake, and are retouched on both ends and both sides. They average 3 inches long by 2 inches wide by 1 inch thick. Three speci-

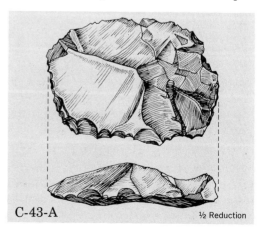

C-43-A   ½ Reduction

mens are from C-43-A (illustrated) and M-110.

Compound Tools

Just as in Phase I, San Dieguito II and III tools from the type collection which demonstrate a dual purpose manufacture are limited to concave-convex scrapers. Four of the specimens are small, average 2 inches long by 3/4 inch wide by 1/2 inch thick, are plano-convex in cross-section, and made on flakes. They are pressure-retouched and come from M-115-B, and M-110.

One large example from M-100 is biconvex in cross-section and is percussion-flaked from an amorphous core. It measures 5 inches long, 2 inches wide, is 1½ inches thick, and shows heavy wear on both the convex and concave margins.

Two specimens are beaked. One, with multiple beaking comes from C-127-A.

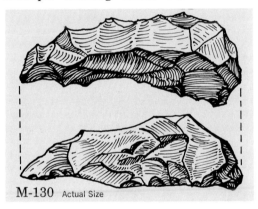

M-130 Actual Size

The other, from M-130 (illustrated) has only one beak. Both are plano-convex in cross-section and are pressure-retouched around their scraping margins.

Beaked Scrapers

Beaking occurs on several classes of scrapers, and consequently was probably intended to serve for more than one function. One specimen, from M-57 is simply a thin amorphous flake scraper with one beak on it. Two examples from C-81 and C-128-A are small planes, each with one beak on the working margin. End scrapers with a beaked working end were found at C-127 (illustrated) and M-115. Convex side scrapers with beaks occurred at M-67, M-115-G, M-115-J, and M-130-A. Two

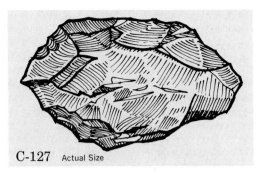

C-127 Actual Size

of the type specimens had multiple beaking; one from M-130, and the other from M-130-C (illustrated).

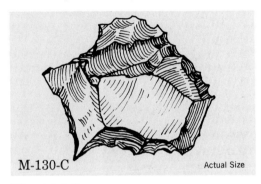

M-130-C Actual Size

Discoidal Scrapers

In terms of its manufacture, the discoidal scraper is the most refined tool in the scraper class. Ovoid in outline, tabular in cross-section, such tools are made on fairly thin side-struck flakes (average about 1/2 inch thick and 2 inches in diameter). Bottom surfaces in six type specimens show only one bulb of percussion. The remaining five have bottom surfaces that are reduced by multiple flaking. All examples

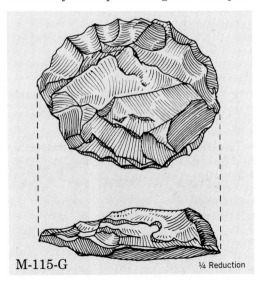

M-115-G ¼ Reduction

165

have their top surfaces trimmed off by percussion flaking, and all are retouched around their entire perimeter by percussion and/or pressure flaking. Type specimens are from C-43, C-127, M-38, M-67, M-110, M-115-B, and M-115-G (illustrated).

Domed Discoidal Scrapers

Often given the name "turtle-back" scrapers, these tools are oval in outline, plano-convex in cross-section, and are made on large, thick flakes. They are steeply percussion-flaked around their periphery and convex surface, forming a flake-scarred dome. Like planes, domed discoidal scrapers are made in both large and small forms, but large specimens are rare in the Museum of Man collections. The only type

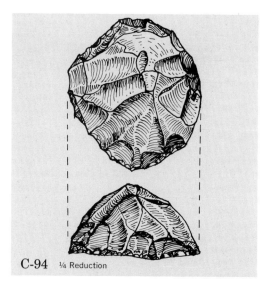

C-94　¼ Reduction

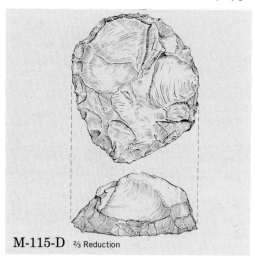

M-115-D　⅔ Reduction

specimen is from M-115-D (illustrated). It measures 4 inches in diameter by 2 inches thick.

Small domed discoidal scrapers, which average 1¾ inches in diameter by 1 inch thick are more common Central Aspect collections. Type examples are from C-94 (illustrated), M-17, M-115, M-115-B, and M-118.

Rogers offered a possible explanation for the scarcity of whole tools and for the large number of broken tools, when he suggested the sacrifice of personal property of the San Dieguitoans:

Breakage through use is an unsatisfactory explanation because even heavy-duty tools are involved. The large (domed-

discoidal scrapers) seem to have been placed on a rock and struck on the crown with a heavy cobble, as they are found in halves and thirds.

Referring to small domed scrapers, Rogers noted:

Even in historic time a similar artifact was used by the Australian Aborigines as a mounted adze blade.

Knives

Three basic knife forms occur in the Central Aspect, a lanceolate blunt-point, a leaf-shaped, and a leaf-shaped bipoint. Of the three the bipoint is the most common, while only two broken specimens of the lanceolate blunt-point form are in the Museum of Man collections from the Central Aspect. (This type occurs frequently in the Southwestern Aspect, however).

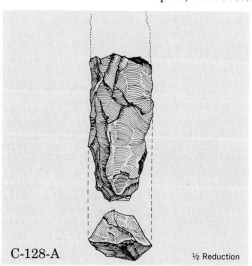

C-128-A　½ Reduction

Lanceolate blunt-point: These are percussion-flaked with a well-controlled technique. They are relatively blunt at both ends (whole specimens occur in the Southwestern Aspect), have roughly parallel edges, and have a thick, lenticular cross-section. Examples are from C-128-A (illustrated) and M-135.

Leaf-shaped: Once again, the technique is well-controlled percussion flaking. The specimens are relatively thin, leaf-shaped,

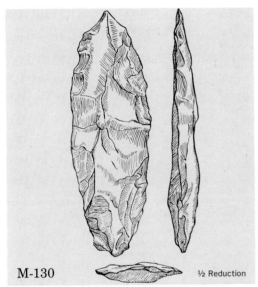

M-130   ½ Reduction

with one pointed and one rounded end. Examples come from sites M-110, M-115-B, M-115-F, and M-130 (illustrated).

Leaf-shaped bipoint: This form is made in the same manner as the single-pointed

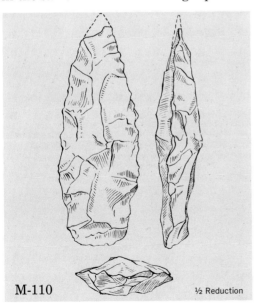

M-110   ½ Reduction

leaf-shaped knife, except that it has a point at both ends. Type specimens are from M-110 (illustrated), M-120-A, M-115-E, M-115-F, M-115-I, and M-130-A.

In his comments on the possibility of property sacrifice, Rogers stated:

A count was made of the artifacts from a remote site in the center of the Mojave Desert (M-110), which at the time, in 1932, gave no evidence of ever having been visited by relic hunters. Out of a total of 154 knives, only three were found intact. Another peculiar situation was that of all of the broken halves, no two parts could be fitted together.

Points

Malcolm Rogers' notes contained an explanation of his application of the phrase "projectile point:"

The term "projectile point" is applied in a broad sense to any artifact with the slenderness or basal or marginal treatment requisite for attachment to a shaft. "Projectile" does not imply how the object was propelled once it was mounted. It could have become a thrust spear, a spear thrown with the hand and arm, or a dart propelled with the aid of an atlatl.

There are five point types that fit solidly into the San Dieguito pattern in the Central Aspect. These are the ovoid point, the leaf-shaped point, the leaf-shaped bipoint, the Lake Mojave point, and the Silver Lake point. Three more point types have been found on the sites, but they occur in such rare instances that their cultural association is still in question. These are the lanceolate point, the lozengic point, and the channelled (or fluted) point.

Ovoid: Basically, all of the first five point types are variations on the ovoid shape, but there is enough consistency in the variations to set up classifications. Ovoid points are ovoid in outline, fairly thin (average ¼ inch thick), and lenticular in cross-section. There is a considerable size range, which is true for all of the San Dieguito point types (ovoid points range from 1½ inches long to 2½ inches long). All were made with a well-controlled percussion technique, with very little apparent pressure retouch. Type specimens are from M-110, M-110-B, (illustrated), M-115, M-115-A (illustrated), M-115 B, M-115-F, and M-130-C.

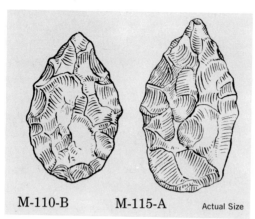

M-110-B   M-115-A   Actual Size

Leaf-shaped: These points are a small version of the leaf-shaped knife, with one pointed and one rounded end. They are lenticular in cross-section, and all are made by controlled percussion flaking, with a minimum of pressure retouch. Type specimens are from sites M-60-A, M-110-

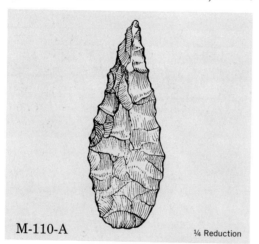

M-110-A   ¼ Reduction

A (illustrated), M-115-B, M-115-C, and M-115-G.

Leaf-shaped bipoint: Similar to the leaf-shaped bipoint knife, only smaller, these points (and the regular leaf-shaped ones) average less than 3 inches long. They are lenticular in cross-section, and are made by a controlled percussion flaking technique, with a minimum of pressure retouch around the edges. Types come from M-110-A, M-115-A, M-115-B (illustrated), M-115-E, and M-115-1.

M-115-B   Actual Size

Lake Mojave: One of the two artifact-types in the total San Dieguito pattern that have a formal name is the Lake Mojave point (Amsden, 1937). All the specimens in the Museum of Man type collections were found on terrace sites around ancient Lake Mojave. The points are characterized by long, slender stems, produced by very slight shouldering. The tip ends are somewhat shorter than the stem ends, and the maximum breadth is generally slightly above the midsection. The bases are rounded, and the points are lenticular in cross-section. They are made by a well-controlled percussion flaking, but some specimens exhibit pressure retouch. Their size ranges from $1\frac{3}{4}$ inches to 4 inches long. Type specimens are from M-115 (illustrated), M-115-B (illustrated), and M-115-C.

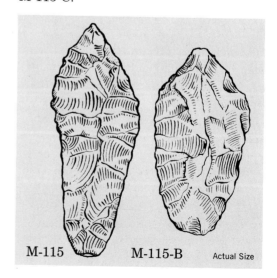

M-115   M-115-B   Actual Size

168

Silver Lake: This type has also been given a formal name (Amsden, 1937). If the type collection is any indication, this form has greater range, frequency, and variation than any of the other types of San Dieguito points. They are related in form to the Lake Mojave points, but Silver Lake points have less basal taper and more clearly defined shoulders. Four specimens are illustrated to demonstrate the

M-110-A   ¼ Reduction

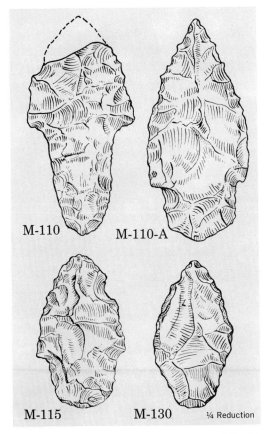

M-110   M-110-A

M-115   M-130   ¼ Reduction

range of variation (examples from M-110, M-110-A, M-115, and M-130). Other type specimens, not illustrated are from sites M-110, M-110-A, M-115, M-115-B, M-115-E, M-115-F, M-115-G, M-120, and M-130-A.

Lanceolate: Only two examples of this point are in the type collection. One is from M-110-A (illustrated); the other is from C-127. These points bear a resemblance to Angostura points (Wormington, 1957). They have symmetrical sides which incurve to the tip. On one point the base is slightly concave, and straight on the other. The technique is well-controlled

percussion with some pressure retouch. The bases on both specimens are thinned, but neither the bases nor the lateral edges are ground smooth.

Lozengic: Once again, there are only two examples of this form in the type collections from the Central Aspect. However, these points may be just one more variation of the basic Ovoid-Lake Mojave-Silver Lake point class, and would have been included as such, except that lozengic points also occur in the Southwestern Aspect without the Lake Mojave and Silver Lake shapes. They are essentially diamond-shaped, lenticular in cross-section, and are made by percussion

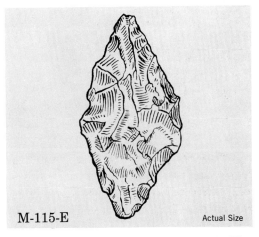

M-115-E   Actual Size

flaking followed by pressure retouch. The specimens are from M-115-B and M-115-E (illustrated).

Channeled: The association of fluted points with Far Western Paleo-Indian sites has been under discussion and scrutiny for several years, still with no satisfactory conclusions. In the Museum of Man collections there are three channeled points from Central Aspect sites. All were surface finds and are broken. Two, made from obsidian, closely resemble the large channeled Clovis points (Wormington, 1957). They come from M-130-A (illustra-

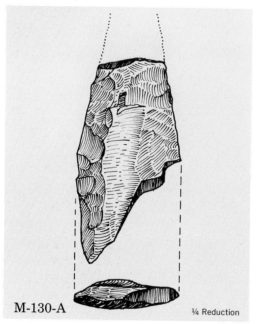

M-130-A   ¼ Reduction

ted), a mixed San Dieguito and Amargosa site, and N-34, a dry lake terrace site in Nevada which yielded material classified by M. J. Rogers as "early Amargosa."

The third point, of chalcedony, also recalls the Clovis form, with a concave base and the lower lateral edges smoothed by

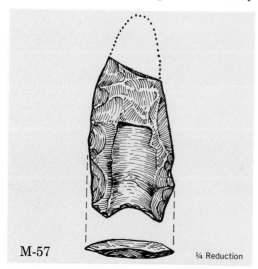

M-57   ¼ Reduction

grinding. One flute extends about halfway from the base to the tip, while the opposite flute extends only one-third of the way. It, too, is illustrated and comes from M-57, a site that Rogers concluded was utilized by both San Dieguito and Amargosa people. All three of these points appear to be somewhat "out of place" when compared to the other artifacts, flaking techniques, and lithic types employed at the three sites.

A related point type, which does not have channeling or fluting, but has basal thinning, occurs in great numbers in the Central Aspect. Such points are associated almost exclusively with sites classified as "early Amargosa" by M. J. Rogers, and the collections from these sites usually contain several Pinto Points (Amsden, 1935). Four such specimens were found on

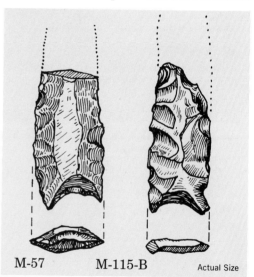

M-57   M-115-B   Actual Size

San Dieguito sites M-57 (illustrated), M-110-A, M-115-B (illustrated), and M-130-A.

Crescentic Stones

Regarding crescentic stones, Rogers stated:

In attempting to explain its purpose (Rogers, 1929), I followed earlier speculations that they were part of the paraphernalia of shamans, who used them either for scarifying patients or for exhibition. After devoting some time to the study of their distribution and cultural affiliations in North America, I became convinced that speci-

mens found in the San Dieguito domain were hunting amulets. It is true that in certain Middle American cultures similar items were found under circumstances leading one to believe they were cult accessories. This is not true of those found in the Arctic regions. The Middle American examples, which exhibit the most elaborate eccentricities of all, were found in groups either within cinerary urns or cached within temple precincts (Gann and Thompson, 1931). The Arctic ones (Murdoch, 1892) were found singly, in camp middens, as were the San Dieguito specimens. Among Arctic peoples, amulets were made until historic time, and some are identical with certain San Dieguito forms.

Two types of crescentic stones are found in the Central Aspect, the simple lunate and the biconcave lunate. All examples are lenticular in cross-section and all except one, from M-115 are pressure-flaked. A few are thinned in the median section. Chalcedony, basalt, and felsite phorphyry are the main materials used.

Simple lunate: Just as the name implies, this form resembles a simple crescent in its most common shape. In some specimens, the tips are pointed, but in others, the tips are rounded. Type specimens are

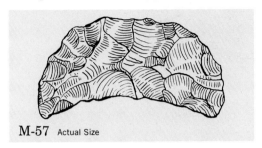

M-57 Actual Size

from M-57 (illustrated), M-115-B, M-115-C, and N-13-A.

Biconcave lunate: Closely resembling the simple lunate, this form has a shallow concavity on the outer or convex side of the crescent. Specimens are from M-35-I, M-115, M-115-B (illustrated), and M-115-C.

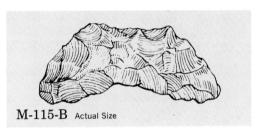

M-115-B Actual Size

THE SOUTHEASTERN ASPECT

SITE SUMMARIES

A-1
Location: Secret Pass, west central Mojave County, Arizona. *Cultures:* Amargosa II, Yuman. *Type:* Mountain pass; trails; scattered camps in open areas; small caves and rock shelters. *Architecture;* Cobble shrine; trails. *Pictographs:* Four of the caves have pictographs in them; there are petroglyphs on a volcanic dyke at the east entrance to the pass.

A-2
Location: Sitgreaves Pass, central western Mojave County, Arizona. *Cultures:* San Dieguito II, Amargosa II, and Yuman. *Type:* Tuffa caves; petroglyph sites; and a few open camps and a large quarry. *Architecture:* None.

The Southeastern Aspect of the San Dieguito Complex, consisting of western Arizona and northwestern Sonora, appears to be a marginal zone. Artifacts from the region resemble both early San Dieguito and Sulphur Springs Cochise material.

Malcolm Rogers divided the aspect into Phases I and II, and he considered the bottom level, or volcanic debris layer, of Ventana Cave as related to Phase I. A radiocarbon date of 9350 B.C. has been obtained for that level.

The assignment of Southeastern Aspect artifacts to Phase I or II was done very tentatively by Rogers, and he indicated considerable overlapping.

In view of the tentative position of this material, only a few examples are shown here. These are representative of several hundred specimens collected from surface sites in the area. (Scale in inches).

The specimens in this photograph were assigned to Phase I. The artifacts at the top, left to right, are a chopper from A-125 and an ovate biface from A-135-A. The lower specimens are a large plane from A-109 and a concave scraper from A-134.

A-12
Location: Signal Wash, McCracken Basin; Mojave County, Arizona. One mile long and one-half mile wide. *Cultures:* San Dieguito I, Amargosa II and Walapai. *Type:* Quarry site. *Architecture:* None.

A-17
Location: Rawhide Canyon, southeast margin of Mojave County, Arizona. *Cultures:* San Dieguito I and II, Amargosa II and Walapai. *Type:* Cave dwelling and open camp site on valley floor. *Architecture:* None.

A-25-A
Location: Northwest side of Castle Dome Mountains, south central Yuma County, Arizona. *Cultures:* San Dieguito I. *Type:* Rocky mesas with scattered thin camping areas. *Architecture:* San Dieguito I circles are common and many have boulder-rimmed perimeters. This type is quite large, some having a maximum diameter of 15 feet.

A-29-A
Location: West central margin of Yuma County, Arizona. Trail runs into Colorado River opposite Palo Verde. *Cultures:* San Dieguito I; Amargosa II; Yuman. *Type:* Trail site. *Architecture:* Trail shrine.

A-30-A
Location: Dry Tank, west central Yuma County, Arizona in the northern end of the Trigo Mountains. *Cultures:* San Dieguito I, Amargosa II and Yuman. *Type:* Stony bench in canyon forks. *Architecture:* None; a few early Yuman petroglyphs.

A-31-A
Location: Mojave Tank, west central Yuma County, Arizona. *Cultures:* San Dieguito I, Amargosa II and Yuman. *Type:* Stony mesa land, with scattered camps. *Architecture:* A few San Dieguito cleared

circles present. One San Dieguito I trail shrine on a trail coming in from the east.

A-35-A
Location: Alamo Spring, central Yuma County, Arizona. *Cultures:* San Dieguito I and II, Amargosa II and Yuman. *Type:* Petroglyphs; open camping on stony benches; trail. *Architecture:* San Dieguito I circles.

A-42-A
Location: New Water Springs, west central Yuma County, Arizona. Site covers approximately 20 acres. *Cultures:* San Dieguito I, Amargosa II and Yuman. *Type:* San Dieguito I and Amargosa II are on gravel banks in mesquite, near two springs. *Architecture:* San Dieguito I stone circles; Amargosa II house sites have cobble groups on margin suggesting pole supports. Yumans left some cobble hearths, and a few rectangular cobble house rims; Yuman and pre-Yuman petroglyphs.

A-44-B
Location: Horse Tank, central Yuma County, Arizona. Site covers five acres of discontinuous occupation. *Cultures:* San Dieguito I and traces of Amargosa II. *Type:* Desert pavement in a mountain pass. *Ar-*

Precise functions of Early Man tools probably will always be something of a mystery.

However, the uses of many artifact types are suggested by their size, shape, working edges, and by comparison with tools made by historic aboriginal groups.

Shown here are six implements Malcolm Rogers tentatively assigned to Phase II of the San Dieguito Complex in the Southeastern Aspect.

The three artifacts at the top, left to right, are a discoidal scraper from A-135-A, a small plane from A-111-A, and a chopper from A-111-A. (Scale in inches).

In the bottom row are a leaf-shaped knife, with the tip missing, from A-111-B, an ovate biface from A-111-B, and a lanceolate knife fragment from A-135-A.

chitecture: San Dieguito I cleared circles, with some boulder-rimmed ones present. Several caves have boulder wind breaks. Some petroglyphs in caves. There is one San Dieguito I boulder "ceremonial," partly obliterated.

A-47-A
Location: Black Tank, northwest end of Castle Dome Mountains, central western Yuma County, Arizona. One acre of intensive occupation plus several square miles of San Dieguito I debris. *Cultures:* San Dieguito I, Amargosa II and Yuman. *Type:* Mountain canyon with rocky benches, and a few caves with stony mesa land in front. *Architecture:* San Dieguito I circles are common in this area, and most have cobble rims.

A-53-A
Location: On the northern bank of the Gila River, southwestern Yuma County, Arizona. *Cultures:* San Dieguito I. *Type:* Gravel terrace. *Architecture:* a few scattered San Dieguito I cleared circles on the south side of the river, as well as on the north side.

A-59
Location: Antelope Hill, south central Yuma County, Arizona. *Cultures:* Pre-Yuman and Yuman. *Type:* Petroglyph site on talus boulders. *Architecture:* None. *Petroglyphs:* Approximately 100 were counted in 1926; age range probably spreads from pre-Yuman to modern American.

A-66
Location: South central Maricopa County, Arizona. *Cultures:* San Dieguito I, Hohokam and Yuman. *Type:* Petroglyph sites on vertical lava cliffs and talus boulders. Some small camps on gravel terrace in front of cliffs. *Architecture:* Some San Dieguito I cleared circles without boulder rims, scattered throughout the area; pre-Hohokam, Hohokam and Yuman petroglyphs.

175

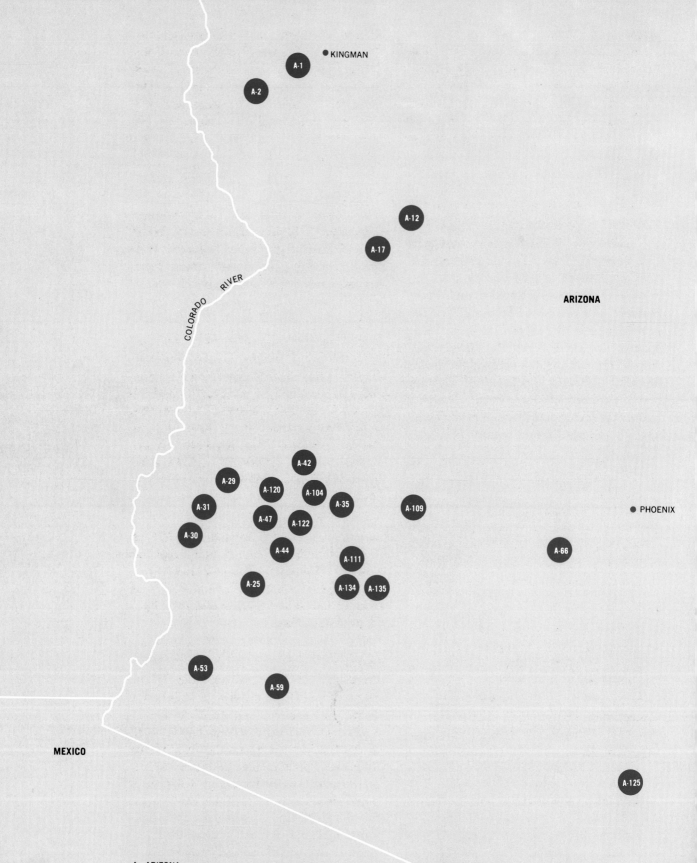

MAJOR SITE LOCATIONS OF THE SOUTHEASTERN ASPECT

A—ARIZONA

A-104

Location: Owl Tank, Alamo Wash, east central Yuma County, Arizona. *Cultures:* San Dieguito I and II and Amargosa II. *Type:* Quarry and camps on an old terrace above a recent channel. *Architecture:* None except for a few cobble hearths of Amargosa II.

A-109

Location: Black Rock Mesa, east central Yuma County, Arizona. *Cultures:* San Dieguito I and II and Amargosa II. *Type:* Rocky mesa land surrounding a coarse sand basin. *Architecture:* San Dieguito I cleared circles, some boulder-rimmed, are scattered over the surrounding mesa lands. Three black lava boulder alignments of great length run east from the bottom of the basin (are parallel and about 50 feet apart) up a fairly steep bank to the top of the mesa.

A-111

Location: White Tanks, southeast central Yuma County, Arizona. *Cultures:* San Dieguito I and II; some Amargosa II. *Type:* Mountain camps on stony mesas and in caves. Petroglyphs and quarries are present. *Architecture:* San Dieguito I boulder-rimmed circles are present, and there is a San Dieguito I boulder shrine on the A-112-A trail near this area.

A-113

Location: Texas Hill, southern Yuma County, Arizona. *Cultures:* San Dieguito I and Yuman. *Type:* Fine sandy gravel ridges for San Dieguito I with scattered camps; sand dune and silt for Yuman. *Architecture:* No San Dieguito I circles, some Yuman cobble hearths. Many Yuman petroglyphs present.

A-120-A

Location: Jasper Spring, central Yuma County, Arizona. *Cultures:* San Dieguito I, Amargosa III, and Yuman. *Type:* Open sites on inner and upper terraces of a foothill drainage system. *Architecture:* San Dieguito I cleared circles all around the site, but those on the site have been destroyed by miners and ranchers. Some cobble hearths are still left.

A-122

Location: Four Peaks, central Yuma County, Arizona. *Cultures:* San Dieguito I or II, and Yuman. *Type:* Mountain tank with no flat land; some cave occupation. *Architecture:* None.

A-125

Location: Ventana Cave, north central Pima County, Arizona. The surrounding area is four square miles. *Cultures:* San Dieguito I, Amargosa, Hohokam and Papago. *Type:* Rock shelters, mesa camps, and wash terrace camps. *Architecture:* None in the cave except cobble hearths. On the terrace of Ventana Wash there are a few San Dieguito I circles.

A-134

Location: White Tanks Basin, White Tanks Mountains, Yuma County, Arizona. *Cultures:* Amargosa II and Yuman. *Type:* Six large caves plus a few small rock shelters. *Architecture:* Some evidence of boulder-outlined "beds."

A-135-A

Location: Ajo Wash, White Tanks Mountains, Yuma County, Arizona. This basin forms the upper drainage to White Tanks. *Cultures:* San Dieguito I and Amargosa II. *Type:* Basin mesa open sites, and many small caves; quarries present. *Architecture:* A few disturbed San Dieguito I stone circles.

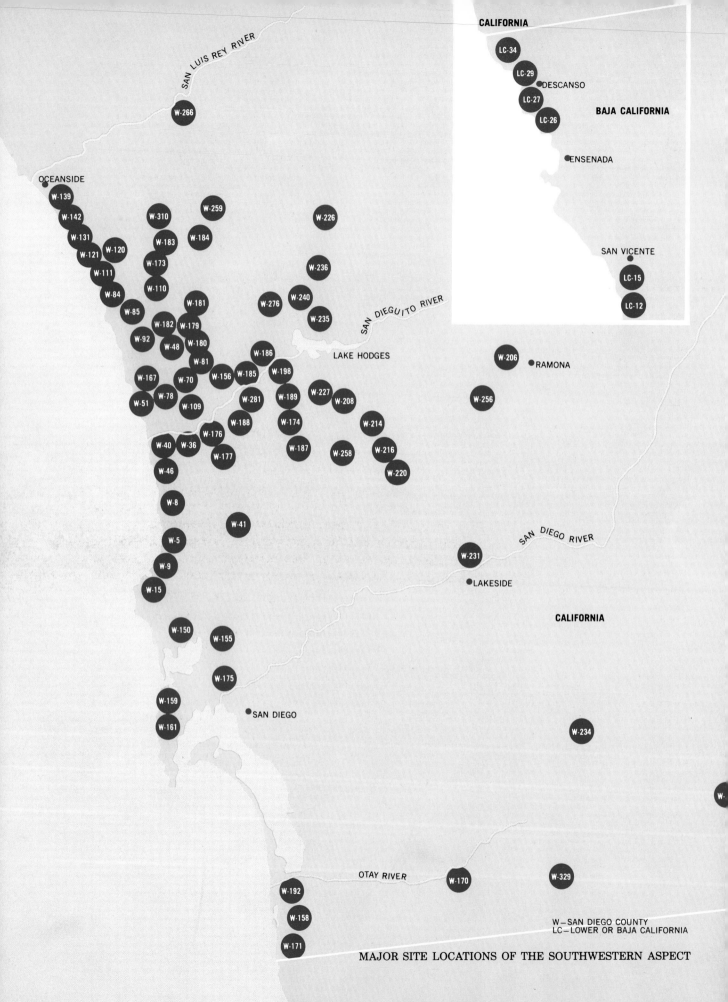

MAJOR SITE LOCATIONS OF THE SOUTHWESTERN ASPECT

W—SAN DIEGO COUNTY
LC—LOWER OR BAJA CALIFORNIA

SOUTHWESTERN ASPECT

SITE SUMMARIES
Western San Diego County, California
W-5-A
Location: Scripps Plateau; elevation 350 feet above sea level. *Cultures:* San Dieguito III and La Jolla II. *Type:* Highland shell midden resting on marine sandstone. *Architecture:* La Jolla II horizon has many cobble hearths. The site has not been trenched enough to disclose La Jolla I architecture.

W-8
Location: Sorrento Slough; elevation 400 feet above sea level. *Cultures:* San Dieguito III and La Jolla II. *Type:* Highland midden resting on a thin gray sand over a red marine sandstone. *Architecture:* Cobble hearths.

W-9
Location: Scripps Plateau; elevation 375 feet above sea level. *Cultures:* San Dieguito III, La Jolla I and II, and Diegueño. *Architecture:* The land has been ploughed; undisturbed La Jolla II hearths below plough level.

W-15
Location: Torrey Pines Park; elevation about 300 feet above sea level; area is about ¼ acre, nearly destroyed by erosion. *Cultures:* San Dieguito III, La Jolla II and Diegueño. *Type:* Highland site with scattered hearths. *Arthitecture:* La Jolla II hearths.

W-36
Location: San Dieguito River Slough, 50 feet above sea level, ½ mile from the ocean, San Diego County, California. *Cultures:* San Dieguito II and La Jolla II. *Type:* The San Dieguito material is scattered over the terrace; the La Jolla material is concentrated in a shell midden, approximately 18 inches deep. *Architecture:* Several La Jolla II cobble hearths are present.

W-40
Location: San Dieguito River; elevation 150 feet above sea level. *Cultures:* San Dieguito II and La Jolla II. *Type:* Highland camps in a scattered condition without any shell concentration. *Architecture:* Many cobble hearths, scattered by ploughing.

W-41
Location: Osuna Ranch; elevation 75 feet above sea level. *Cultures:* San Dieguito II and La Jolla II. *Type:* Slough terrace, of unusually heavy soil for San Dieguito people. *Architecture:* Slight amount of fire-cracked rock for La Jolla II.

W-46
Location: Del Mar area; on the 300 foot contour. *Cultures:* San Dieguito II and La Jolla II. *Type:* Highland midden resting on "red crag" formation. *Architecture:* None.

W-48
Location: Encinitas Creek on lowest terrace of the 125-foot level, above sea level. *Cultures:* San Dieguito II, La Jolla II and Diegueño. *Type:* Creek margin terrace camp. *Architecture:* La Jolla hearths.

W-51
Location: San Elijo Slough; elevation 25 to 30 feet above sea level. *Cultures:* San Dieguito II, La Jolla I (?) and La Jolla II. *Type:* Slough terrace midden; high shell content; permanent camp for La Jolla II people. *Architecture:* Large number of hearths (La Jolla II).

W-70
Location: West central (coastal) edge of County on the 250-foot contour. *Cultures:* San Dieguito II, La Jolla II (trace) and Diegueño. *Type:* Highland middens of a permanent village; rests on gray sandstone. *Architecture:* La Jolla cobble hearths.

W-78

Location:

San Elijo Slough; elevation is 25 to 75 feet above sea level. *Cultures:* San Dieguito II and La Jolla II. *Type:* Slough margin midden built on a steep gradient of yellow outwash sand. *Architecture:* Cobble hearths near the base, upper level ploughed.

W-81

Location: Rancho Santa Fe; elevation 325 feet above sea level. *Cultures:* This is a "pure" San Dieguito II site. *Type:* Highland camp on sandy loam. *Architecture:* None.

W-84

Location: Batiquitos Lagoon on the 25-foot terrace. *Cultures:* San Dieguito II and III, and La Jolla II. *Type:* Slough terrace midden, rests on gray estuary sands and gravel. *Architecture:* San Dieguito level has a few cobble hearths.

W-85

Location: Batiquitos Slough on the 50 to 80-foot level; farming and erosion have scattered midden. *Cultures:* Slough terrace midden of the concentrated type. *Architecture:* La Jolla II hearths.

W-92

Location: West central (coastal) San Diego County; elevation 300 feet above sea level. *Cultures:* San Dieguito II and III, La Jolla and Diegueño. *Type:* Highland village of either long intermittent camping or permanent settlement; rests on gray sandstone. *Architecture:* San Dieguito and La Jolla hearths. *Burials:* One La Jolla II burial.

W-109-A

Location: La Costa area; elevation 320 feet above sea level. *Cultures:* San Dieguito II, La Jolla II and Diegueño. *Type:* Highland winter camp. *Architecture:* La Jolla and Diegueño hearths.

W-110

Location: La Costa area; elevation 250 feet

above sea level. *Cultures:* San Dieguito II and III, and La Jolla II. *Type:* Highland permanent village; rests on gray decomposed sandstone. *Architecture:* La Jolla II hearths.

W-111

Location: Encino Slough; elevation 50 feet above sea level. *Cultures:* San Dieguito II and III, and La Jolla II. *Type:* Marine terrace midden. *Architecture:* None.

W-120

Location: Hedionda Slough on the 200-foot contour. *Cultures:* San Dieguito III, La Jolla II and Diegueño. *Type:* Highland permanent camp; rests on gray sandstone. *Architecture:* Cobble hearths.

W-121

Location: Hedionda Slough; elevation 50 to 100 feet above sea level. *Cultures:* San Dieguito II, La Jolla I (?), La Jolla II and Diegueño. *Type:* Slough terrace midden of a permanent type. *Architecture:* Cobble hearths weak for so large a site.

W-131

Location: Hedionda Slough; elevation 50 feet above sea level. *Cultures:* San Dieguito II and III and La Jolla II. *Type:* Slough terrace midden of rather constant occupation. *Architecture:* La Jolla II hearths.

W-139

Location: South Oceanside, elevation 250 feet above sea level. *Cultures:* San Dieguito II, La Jolla II and Luiseño. *Type:* Highland midden with extensive occupation. *Architecture:* La Jolla hearths (disturbed).

W-142

Location: Carlsbad Slough; elevation 50 feet above sea level. *Cultures:* San Dieguito II and III, La Jolla II and Luiseño. *Type:* Slough terrace midden. *Architecture:* La Jolla II hearths.

W-150

Location: At mouth of Rose Canyon in Pacific Beach; elevation 15 to 40 feet above sea level. *Cultures:* San Dieguito II and III, La Jolla II, and Diegueño. *Type:* Slough margin terrace. *Architecture:* Cobble hearths, and four Diegueño house pits with cobbles and fire-broken rock ruins.

W-155
Location: Kearny Mesa; elevation 300 feet to 400 feet above sea level. *Cultures:* San Dieguito II, La Jolla II and Diegueño. *Type:* Highland camps. *Architecture:* Cobble hearths.

W-156
Location: Rancho Santa Fe; elevation 275 feet above sea level. *Cultures:* San Dieguito II and III. *Type:* Highland camp. *Architecture:* None.

W-158
Location: South side of Tijuana River; elevation 50 to 75 feet above sea level. *Cultures:* San Dieguito II and III, La Jolla II and Diegueño. *Type:* River terrace camp. *Architecture:* La Jolla II hearths.

W-159
Location: Point Loma area; elevation 174 feet above sea level. *Cultures:* San Dieguito II and La Jolla II. *Type:* Highland camps on sandy loam soil. *Architecture:* None.

W-161
Location: Point Loma area; elevation 300 feet to 375 feet above sea level. *Cultures:* San Dieguito II, La Jolla II and Diegueño. *Type:* Highland temporary camps. *Architecture:* La Jolla II cobble hearths, scattered all over the area.

W-167
Location: Cardiff; elevation 250 feet above sea level. *Cultures:* San Dieguito II and III, and La Jolla II. *Type:* Highland temporary camp. *Architecture:* La Jolla hearths; La Jolla II "sweat house."

W-170
Location: Otay Canyon; elevation 400 feet above sea level. *Cultures:* San Dieguito II and III, La Jolla II and Diegueño. *Type:*

River bend permanent village. *Architecture:* None evident.

W-171
Location: San Ysidro Mountains; elevation 700 feet above sea level. *Cultures:* San Dieguito II. *Type:* Ledge rock quarry and camp. *Architecture:* None.

W-173
Location: Las Encinas Canyon; elevation 325 feet above sea level. *Cultures:* San Dieguito II and III. *Type:* Highland camp. *Architecture:* Some San Dieguito II cobble hearths found *in situ* here.

W-174
Location: Lusardi Plateau; elevation 550 feet above sea level. *Cultures:* San Dieguito II and III, and La Jolla II. *Type:* Highland sandy terrace camp. *Architecture:* Hearths appear to be present; much disturbance.

W-175
Location: Mission Valley; elevation 25 to 35 feet above sea level. *Cultures:* San Dieguito II and III, La Jolla II, and Diegueño. *Type:* River terrace of sandy gravels. Probably never a permanent camp until the Diegueño period. *Architecture:* La Jolla II cobble hearths present.

W-176
Location: Del Mar Plateau; elevation 300 feet above sea level. *Cultures:* San Dieguito II and trace of La Jolla II and Diegueño. *Type:* Highland temporary camp on sandy soil. *Architecture:* A few large La Jolla II hearths and one San Dieguito hearth.

W-177
Location: Del Mar Plateau; elevation 325 feet above sea level. *Cultures:* San Dieguito II and La Jolla II. *Type:* Highland temporary camp site. *Architecture:* None.

W-179
Location: Encinitas Creek; elevation 275 feet above sea level. *Cultures:* San Die-

guito II and La Jolla II. *Type:* Highland camping site. *Architecture:* La Jolla II hearths present.

W-180
Location: Encinitas Creek; elevation 275 feet above sea level. *Cultures:* San Dieguito II and III, and La Jolla II. *Type:* Highland scattered camps; very extensive site. *Architecture:* Some San Dieguito II cobble hearths and a larger number of La Jolla II hearths.

W-181
Location: Encinitas Creek; elevation 325 feet above sea level. *Cultures:* San Dieguito II and III, and La Jolla II. *Type:* Highland camp with adjacent scattered camps. *Architecture:* La Jolla II possible roasting platforms and/or sweat house.

W-182
Location: Encinitas Creek; elevation 250 to 275 feet above sea level. *Cultures:* San Dieguito II and III, La Jolla II, and Diegueño. *Type:* Highland camping site. *Architecture:* Some La Jolla cobble hearths.

W-183
Location: Agua Hedionda Creek; elevation 475 feet above sea level. *Cultures:* San Dieguito II and La Jolla II. *Type:* Highland camp. *Architecture:* None.

W-184
Location: Agua Hedionda Creek; elevation 650 feet above sea level. *Cultures:* San Dieguito II and La Jolla II. *Type:* Highland camp; lies in gray sandy loam. *Architecture:* La Jolla II cobble hearths.

W-185
Location: San Dieguito River Canyon; elevation 250 feet above sea level. *Cultures:* San Dieguito II, and La Jolla II. *Type:* Highland camps on rolling mesa land. *Architecture:* None.

W-186
Location: An island in the San Dieguito River bottom; elevation 150 feet above sea level. *Cultures:* San Dieguito II and III seem to be present with a capping of Diegueño. *Type:* An unusual river bottom camp; probably was a work shop. *Burials:* One Diegueño cremation found.

W-187
Location: Lusardi Valley; elevation 550 feet above sea level. *Cultures:* San Dieguito II and III, and La Jolla II. *Type:* Highland camp. *Architecture:* A few La Jolla II cobble hearths.

W-188
Location: North rim of La Zanja Canyon; elevation 375 feet above sea level. *Cultures:* San Dieguito II and III, trace of La Jolla II and Diegueño. *Type:* Highland camp. *Architecture:* Some La Jolla II hearths present.

W-189
Location: Lusardi Mesa; elevation 500 feet above sea level. *Cultures:* San Dieguito II and III, and a trace of La Jolla II. *Type:* Highland camp in sandy loam. *Architecture:* None.

W-192
Location: South San Diego Bay on the 25-foot terrace. *Cultures:* San Dieguito II and III, and La Jolla II. *Type:* Slough terrace camping. *Architecture:* Some La Jolla II cobble hearths.

W-198
Location: San Dieguito River Valley (C. W. Harris Site). *Cultures:* San Dieguito II and III, La Jolla II and Diegueño. *Type:* Camps and workshops in ancient stream channel with terrace camps above. *Architecture:* La Jolla II and Diegueño cobble hearths. *Burials:* One La Jolla II burial in upper strata, disturbed.

W-205
Location: Cottonwood Valley; elevation unknown. *Cultures:* San Dieguito II and Diegueño. *Type:* Mountain village grouped around granite outcrops. *Architecture:* Seven stone houses with common

walls of which the highest standing section is 4½ feet high. They are grouped around one very large room which has an entrance; one other room opens off from this one; four have no entrances; all are Diegueño.

W-206-A

Location: Ramona area; elevation 1450 feet above sea level. *Cultures:* San Dieguito II and Diegueño. *Type:* Mountain camp. *Architecture:* Six stone houses, probably Diegueño.

W-208

Location: Green Valley, Rancho Bernardo; elevation 500 feet above sea level. *Cultures:* San Dieguito II and III, and Diegueño. *Type:* Open camps on rolling hills; one group of granite boulder shelters; complex site area. *Architecture:* Some Diegueño cobble hearths. At W-208-A there are a few windbreaks (boulder) between the shelters. *Burials:* Cremation reported from W-208-B. *Pictographs:* Greatest concentration in the Western area.

W-214

Location: North Poway Valley; elevation 750 feet above sea level. *Cultures:* San Dieguito II and Diegueño. *Type:* Inland plateau; open camps on reddish sandy loam. *Architecture:* None.

W-216

Location: In extreme east end of Poway Valley. *Cultures:* San Dieguito II and Diegueño. *Type:* Ridge above a canyon; thin-bedded camp. *Architecture:* None.

W-220

Location: East side of Poway Valley; elevation 850 to 900 feet above sea level. *Cultures:* San Dieguito II. *Type:* Mountain terrace camp. *Architecture:* None.

W-226-A

Location: Burnt Mountain; elevation 800 feet above sea level. *Cultures:* W-226 Luiseño and Diegueño; W-226-A San Dieguito III. *Type:* Open sites, rock shelters and

pictographs. *Architecture:* Luiseño pit houses evident.

W-227

Location: Bernardo Grant; elevation 450 feet above sea level. *Cultures:* San Dieguito II and III, and Diegueño. *Type:* San Dieguito site is on a sandy loam hog-back, and Diegueño site is on a sandy hillside pitching east. *Architecture:* The Diegueño site has a number of house pits.

W-231

Location: On San Diego River above Lakeside; elevation 500 feet above sea level. *Cultures:* San Dieguito III and Diegueño. *Type:* River valley permanent village on the bank and in boulders of a talus slope. *Architecture:* Three rough boulder-walled rooms, very irregular in shape; walls three feet high (Diegueño).

W-234-A

Location: Lee Valley in east Jamul. *Cultures:* San Dieguito II and III, and Diegueño. *Type:* Mountain valley permanent camp for Diegueño on creek bench. Sandy knolls for San Dieguito III. *Architecture:* None.

W-235

Location: Bernardo Grant; elevation 500 to 800 feet above sea level. *Cultures:* San Dieguito II and Diegueño. *Type:* Boulder-strewn oak canyon for Diegueño, and red loam benches above canyon for San Dieguito. *Architecture:* None.

W-236

Location: Escondido Valley; elevation 700 feet above sea level. *Cultures:* San Dieguito II and Luiseño. *Type:* Valley bottom for Luiseño; round-top loamy hills above water hole for San Dieguito. *Architecture:* None.

W-240

Location: Escondido area; elevation 800 feet above sea level; covers about 20 square acres, with two concentrations. *Cultures:* San Dieguito II and III; this is the original discovery site of the San Die-guito culture made in 1919, and included at a later time in the site numbering system. *Type:* Reddish, sandy-loam rolling hills on the Escondido plain. *Architecture:* None.

W-256-A
Location: Valley on east flank of Woodson Mountain; elevation 1600 feet above sea level. *Cultures:* San Dieguito III. *Type:* Mountain valley with scattered camps. *Architecture:* None.

W-258
Location: Poway; elevation 500 to 550 feet above sea level. *Cultures:* San Dieguito II and La Jolla II. *Type:* Sandy loam knolls for San Dieguito, and adobe benches for La Jolla II. *Architecture:* None.

W-259
Location: Agua Hedionda Creek. *Cultures:* San Dieguito II. *Type:* Sandy, loam-topped hill in a rolling terrain; surface campsite. *Architecture:* None.

W-266
Location: Bonsall; elevation 200 feet above sea level. *Cultures:* San Dieguito II and III. *Type:* River valley marginal highlands of sandy loam; surface campsite. *Architecture:* None.

W-276
Location: Cerro de las Posas; elevation 700 feet above sea level. *Cultures:* San Dieguito III and Diegueño. *Type:* Coast range canyon rim camp on red loam spur. *Architecture:* None.

W-281
Location: La Zanja Plateau; elevation 325 feet above sea level. *Cultures:* San Dieguito II and La Jolla II. *Type:* Plateau "hog-backs" of sandy loam with adobe underlying it; some river gravel in patches; scattered camps. *Architecture:* None.

W-310
Location: Agua Hedionda Creek; elevation

125 to 150 feet above sea level. *Cultures:* La Jolla II, Luiseño, and a trace of San Dieguito II on hill back of site. *Type:* Coastal valley creek terrace of sandy adobe. *Architecture:* La Jolla II hearths.

W-329
Location: Otay Mountain area. *Cultures:* San Dieguito II and III. *Type:* Quarry and camp workshop. *Architecture:* None.

Northwestern Coastal Baja California
LC-12
Location: South of Johnson Ranch; elevation 300 feet above sea level. *Cultures:* La Jolla II principally, with a trace of Diegueño and San Dieguito III. *Type:* Midden on mesa, inland from sea three miles; soil is sandy. *Architecture:* Some La Jolla cobble hearths present.

LC-15
Location: San Vicente, on a marl ridge overlooking the valley. *Cultures:* San Dieguito II and III. *Type:* Residual ridge with shallow midden. *Architecture:* None.

LC-26
Location: Descanso River on the ocean front; elevation 25 feet above sea level. *Cultures:* San Dieguito III, La Jolla II, and Diegueño. *Type:* Coastal site near river mouth; permanent camp for all cultures except Diegueño. *Architecture:* La Jolla II cobble hearths and many large cairns of sacrificed metates.

LC-27
Location: Directly back of LC-26 on a raised marine terrace. Elevation is 100 to 130 feet above sea level. *Cultures:* San Dieguito III and La Jolla II and Diegueño. *Type:* High slough margin midden of permanent occupation for La Jolla II; rests on a soft sandstone. *Architecture:* La Jolla cobble hearths.

LC-29
Location: Occupies a long strip of the coast between the Descanso and Medano Rivers. *Cultures:* San Dieguito III, La Jolla II and

Diegueño. *Type:* San Dieguito camps rest on raised estuary sands. Scattered La Jolla II hearths occur on same level due to erosion. Small Diegueño camps on one end in late dunes. *Architecture:* Some La Jolla II cobble hearths.

LC-34-A
Location: Rosario River; elevation unknown. *Cultures:* San Dieguito III, La Jolla I and II, and Diegueño. *Type:* Permanent midden; rests on adobe. *Architecture:* Cobble hearths for La Jolla II.

ARTIFACTS, PHASES II AND III

Several sites in the Southwestern Aspect have yielded large quantities of artifacts, often numbering hundreds of specimens. These collections were analyzed to be certain the Type Collection represented typical San Dieguito forms and the common variations. One-of-a-kind artifacts from surface collections were avoided. The "general pattern" is the one being presented, and the questionable cultural association of certain unusual specimens makes them undesirable as pattern indicators. However, the reader should keep in mind that the artifacts described are a sampling taken from the total mass of data. No effort is made to present an attribute study or percentage analysis.

Many artifact types from the Southwestern Aspect are essentially the same as types from the Central Aspect. When such duplications occur, the descriptions are not repeated. Variations are noted, however, and specimens are illustrated.

Cores
As with all Aspects of the San Dieguito Complex, amorphous cores predominate in the Southwestern Aspect. No examples are in the Type Collection, but nearly every site assemblage contains at least one, and it was decided not to enumerate or illustrate them.

An unofficial tally disclosed that prepared-platform cores appear more frequently in the Southwestern Aspect than they do in the Central Aspect. Three examples are from W-36, W-156-A, and W-167.

A few of the prepared-platform cores are sophisticated enough to be classed as "tortoise" cores, which means their flake-scarred sides and bottom (opposite the platform) form a sort of crude hemisphere. The illustrated specimen is from W-234-A.

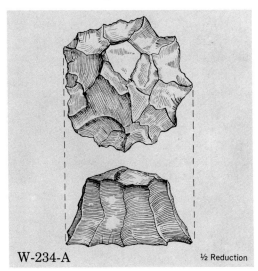

W-234-A   ½ Reduction

Hammers
There is a definite increase in the number of tabular core hammers in the Southwestern Aspect. One example of a cobble "chopping-tool" type hammer comes from W-198-O, but all the rest of the type specimens are uniform in their manufacture. They are percussion-flaked on all surfaces and resemble tabular cores that were used as hammers. Examples are from W-180, W-182 (illustrated), and W-208-E.

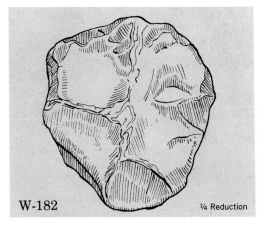

W-182   ¼ Reduction

Flakes
The quantity of unmodified flakes at nearly all sites, and the presence of "macro-

flakes" (some of which measure 8 to 10 inches across) at other than quarry workshops, suggests the need for a closer study of such specimens. Did the San Dieguito people make extensive use of large flakes, and if so, for what?

Teshoa flakes make a reappearance in the Southwestern Aspect, but there seem to be only a few of them, and it is difficult to determine if they were used. Specimens are from W-40 and W-266.

Since prepared-platform cores occur in greater numbers, one would expect to find more blades on the same sites. Blades do occur more frequently, but they still seem to play a very minor role in the total San Dieguito pattern. All of the specimens in the type sample show pressure retouch. They come from W-70, W-173 (illustrated). W-174, W-180-A, and W-181.

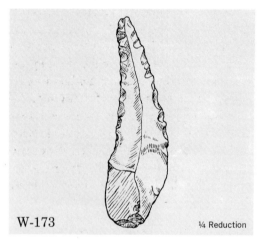

W-173   ¼ Reduction

Biface Preforms
These preforms match the description of those from the Central Aspect, except for the choice of stone, felsite porphyry being preferred in the Southwestern Aspect. Most of the specimens resemble the roughed-out stage of knives. Examples are from W-81-B, W-110, W-139, W-156, W-174, W-177-A, W-179, W-181-A, and W-186.

Ovate Bifaces
The ovate bifaces of the Southwestern Aspect differ from those previously described. These specimens are more or less discoidal to slightly rectangular in outline, lenticular in cross-section, and are care-

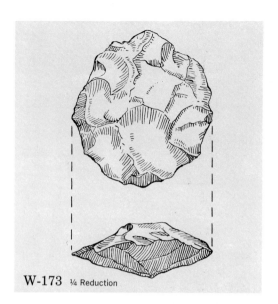

W-173 ¼ Reduction

fully made by well-controlled percussion flaking. The margins of most specimens look as though they were used for scraping rather than knife-like cutting. They are from sites W-156, W-173 (illustrated), W-183-A, W-186, and W-227.

Choppers and Chopping Tools
Unifacial choppers reappear in the San Dieguito II and III pattern of the Southwestern Aspect, and they closely resemble the same type of implement from Phase I of the Central Aspect. They are percussion-flaked on small cobbles or on macro-flakes. Examples are from W-167, W-174 (illustrated), W-180-A, W-187, and W-189-A.

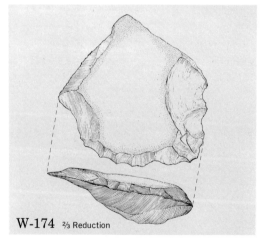

W-174 ⅔ Reduction

The bifacial chopping tool assemblage continues, resembling such tools from other aspects. One specimen from W-188 (illustrated) is sharply pointed like a

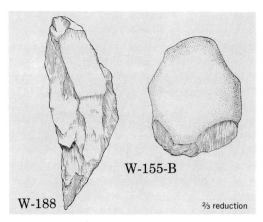

W-155-B

W-188   ⅔ reduction

"pick." Other examples are from W-155-B (illustrated), W-208-A and W-234-A.

Gravers

These tools are quite similar to the gravers of the Central Aspect. They are percussion-flaked with pressure retouch, and the use of felsitic material instead of basalt, as in the Central Aspect, allowed for improved control of the flaking. Examples are from W-167 and W-234-A (illustrated).

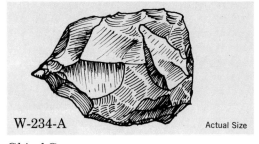

W-234-A   Actual Size

Chisel Gravers

One of the chisel gravers in the Type Collection, from W-167, is pointed at both ends. Another example, from W-180, is fabricated from the broken butt of a knife. The remaining specimens resemble those

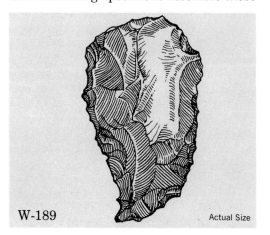

W-189   Actual Size

from the Central Aspect and are from sites W-187, W-189 (illustrated), W-208-U, and W-226.

Planes

The majority of Southwestern Aspect planes are made of felsite porphyry. Examples of large planes are from sites W-176-B, W-180-A (illustrated), W-189-B, and W-198.

W-180-A   ½ Reduction

The number of small planes is so great that a preliminary estimate indicates approximately 1,000 specimens (or about 20 percent of the total collection) have been found in San Diego County sites. They seem to be equaled in their frequency only by the small domed discoidal scrapers, which differ from planes by having a lower rake-angle on their working edges and by being flaked with greater care. Every San Dieguito site in the Southwestern Aspect has yielded at least one small plane. The illustrated specimen is from W-173.

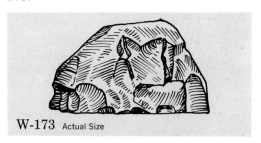

W-173 Actual Size

Convex End Scrapers

There are three forms of end scrapers: a) the regular, rectangular, and plano-convex type with samples from W-167, W-173 (illustrated), W-180, and W-227; b) the triangular shape, demonstrated by samples from W-92, W-176, W-183, W-208-A (illustrated), and W-329; and c) a form which is crudely percussion-flaked on an amorphous flake. This third type is quite

187

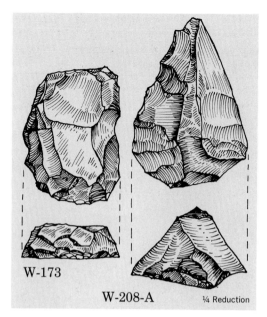

W-173

W-208-A ¼ Reduction

irregular, and is included in this class only because they demonstrate use on one end. They come from W-48, W-173, W-329, and W-240.

Convex Side Scrapers

What has been said about this rather irregular class of artifacts for the Central Aspect could be repeated for the Southwestern Aspect. All manner of flakes, including blades, are used in the manufacture of convex side scrapers. It is likely that this class actually represents several different functional forms, but suggesting functions would be pure guess work. Every San Dieguito site in San Diego County has produced at least one convex side scraper. Most of the specimens, including the two illustrated, were used as side-and-end scrapers. The rectangular example which is made on a blade is from W-180-A.

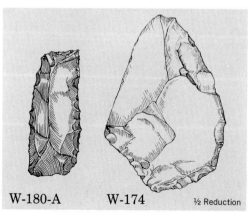

W-180-A W-174 ½ Reduction

The other example is made on a side-struck flake and comes from W-174.

Concave Scrapers

Five concave scrapers in the Type Collection are made on blade-like flakes and are pressure-flaked into an "hour-glass" shape with concave scraping edges on opposite sides of the flake. They come from W-51, W-182, W-186, W-188, and W-234-A.

The remainder of the sampling are all made on amorphous flakes. Examples are from sites W-70 (illustrated), W-156, W-121, W-226-A (illustrated), and W-266.

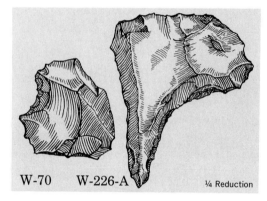

W-70 W-226-A ¼ Reduction

Rectangular Scrapers

Two examples are in the Type Collection. They have tabular cross-sections, are rectangular in outline, and are made on fairly thick flakes. The type plays a very minor role in the pattern and may only be a variation of the discoidal scraper, which it resembles. Specimens are from W-167 (illustrated) and W-198.

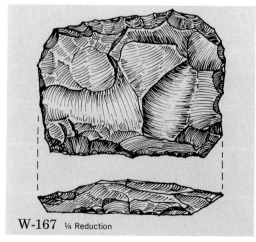

W-167 ¼ Reduction

Compound Tools

Concave-convex scrapers constitute all of

the clearly recognizable tools exhibiting a dual-purpose manufacture in the Southwestern Aspect. True, some of the beaked scrapers (see below) could be called "compound," but it is not possible to determine if such items were actually made to serve more than a single function.

All of the implements are made on flakes. Some are thin and amorphous, while others are actually small domed discoidal scrapers with a concave scraping edge on one side. Examples are from W-40, W-48, W-81 (illustrated), W-92, W-109-A, W-167 (illustrated), W-171, W-173, W-174, W-181, W-182, W-235, and W-329.

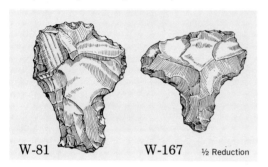

W-81 W-167 ½ Reduction

Beaked Scrapers

A great many artifacts in the Southwestern Aspect have one or two little projections on them which might be called "beaks," but it is not always possible to determine if the spur is fortuitous or intentional. Probably, the majority of sharp little projections on San Dieguito artifacts were purposely left, since it would not be difficult to remove them.

The most common artifacts to occur with beaking are planes, discoidal scra-

pers, and convex scrapers. Samples of planes with beaks come from W-156, W-167, W-174, W-180, W-181, W-183, W-188, and W-189. A convex scraper type comes from W-240, and discoidal samples are from sites W-173, W-109-A, W-167, and W-208-F (illustrated).

Keeled Scrapers

The term encompasses a class of planes that are rectangular to elliptical in outline, triangular in cross-section, and percussion-flaked from thick flakes or re-

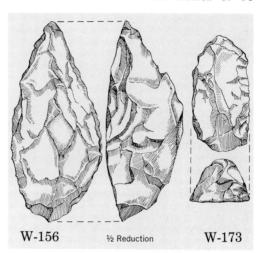

W-156 ½ Reduction W-173

duced from platform cores (it is hard to tell which, and the result is the same). The working edge is on either or both sides, but a few show use on a broad end. Examples are from W-85, W-156 (illustrated), W-173 (illustrated), W-180, W-198, and W-227.

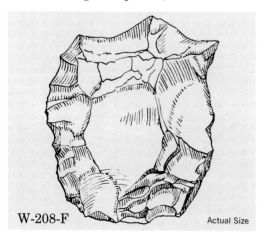

W-208-F Actual Size

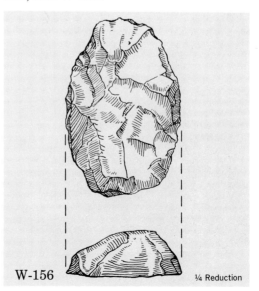

W-156 ¼ Reduction

Discoidal Scrapers

This is the most refined tool in the scraper class, and the percussion flaking on all the examples demonstrates a well-controlled technique. Type specimens are from W-70, W-92, W-156 (illustrated), W-173, W-174, W-180, W-182, W-183, W-240, W-259, and W-310.

Domed Discoidal Scrapers

The type is identical in its manufacture to specimens from the Central Aspect, but such implements occur in much greater frequency in the Southwestern Aspect collections. Examples of large domed discoidal scrapers are from W-167, W-174, W-180 (illustrated), W-180-A, W-181, W-234-A, and W-281.

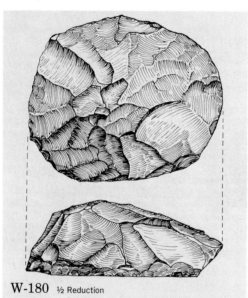

W-180 ½ Reduction

Small domed discoidal scrapers in the Type Collection are from sites W-48, W-109-A, W-155-A (illustrated), W-156, W-173, W-181-A, W-184, W-189, W-208, W-227, W-234-A, and W-258-A.

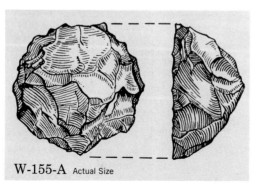

W-155-A Actual Size

Knives

Four knife forms have been found in the Southwestern Aspect, a lanceolate, a lanceolate blunt-point, a leaf-shaped, and a leaf-shaped bipoint. The reader should keep in mind that the generic term "knife" is a somewhat arbitrary one. Specimens are classed as knives when their length, width, and thickness make them unwieldy for use as projectile points. However, nearly every knife specimen could double as a spear-point, All knives appear to be percussion-flaked.

Lanceolate: This type is not found in the Central Aspect. It has roughly parallel edges, a straight base, and the tip is essentially sharp-pointed. The specimens are thick and lenticular in cross-section. Examples are from W-156, W-173 (illustrated), and W-180.

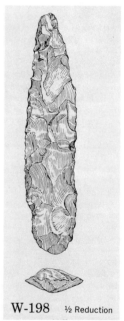

W-173 ½ Reduction   W-198 ½ Reduction

Lanceolate blunt-point: This type is basically the same as those described for the Central Aspect. They occur more commonly in the Southwestern Aspect, but most specimens found are broken, with one portion missing from the site. Examples are from W-176, W-187, and W-198 (illustrated).

Leaf-shaped: This type is the most common form of knife in the Museum of Man collections. Actually, it could be divided into two variations, a thick version and a thin variety. The thick specimens have a cross-section that is greater than half the width of the knife, and they usually show one extra-thick "knot" on one surface. This thickness, and the presence of the "knot" may be caused by problems in manufacture rather than by any desire to make a different form. The specimen illustrated is an example from W-183. Other

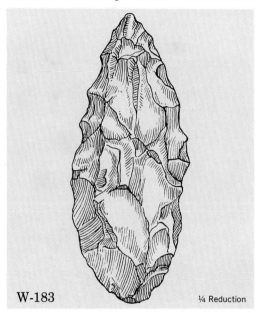

W-183   ¼ Reduction

samples are from W-156, W-110, W-187, W-188-A, W-189, W-214, and W-256-A.

Leaf-shaped bipoint: These are similar to the same type from the Central Aspect, except that the "points" at each end are rounded, rather than pointed. Examples

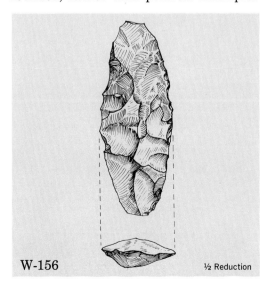

W-156   ½ Reduction

are from sites W-109-A, W-156 (illustrated), W-167, W-173, W-189, and W-256-A.

Points

Once again, the term "projectile point" is somewhat arbitrary. Nearly all of the so-called points, with the exception of the triangular one, would make excellent small knives. There are five point types in the Southwestern Aspect that can be associated with some surety to the San Dieguito Complex. These are the ovoid (which has a blunt-base variation), the leaf-shaped, the leaf-shaped bipoint, the lozengic, and the triangular.

Ovoid: This is a very common form, and if its "blunted base" variation is included, it accounts for more than half of the points

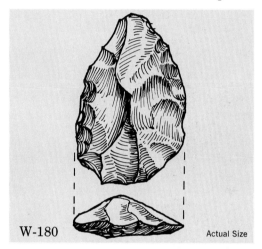

W-180   Actual Size

in the Type Collection. The "blunt-base" form differs only by having a portion of the base straightened by pressure flaking. Both percussion and pressure flaking are employed in the manufacture of all the points. Ovoid point samples are from W-

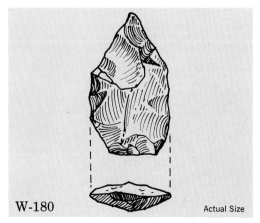

W-180   Actual Size

191

142, W-173 (which was made on a blade), W-174, W-180 (illustrated), W-189 (also made on a blade), and W-329.

Specimens having a blunted base are from sites W-5-A, W-9, W-180 (illustrated), and W-189.

Leaf-shaped: The description of these points duplicates what has been said for leaf-shaped points in the Central Aspect,

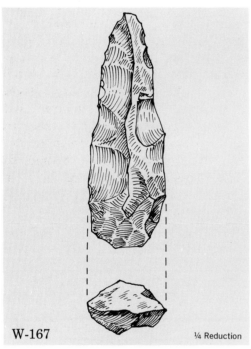

W-167   ¼ Reduction

except that the San Diego County variety tend to be a little thicker. Specimens come from W-9, W-167 (illustrated), W-173, W-180, W-181, W-214, and W-256-A.

W-182   Actual Size

Leaf-shaped bipoint: Specimens in the Type Collection are from sites W-110, W-

173, W-180, W-182 (illustrated), W-208, and W-240.

Lozengic: This still seems to be a rare type, and its cultural association should be held in question pending discovery of a

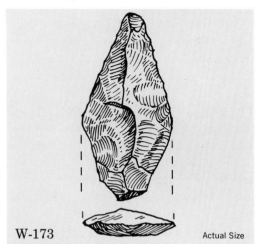

W-173   Actual Size

specimen in stratified deposits. The form is essentially identical to Central Aspect examples. Types are from W-173 (illustrated), W-186, and W-256-A.

Triangular: Another type that is rare, the triangular forms may transcend several culture patterns, because they are found in association with later La Jolla and Yuman (Diegueño) material. However, the type is found in both the Locus I and Locus 2 deposits at the Harris Site, so its association with the San Dieguito Complex is fairly certain. These points have a triangular outline, a concave, slightly thinned base, and a thin, lenticular cross-section. They are percussion-

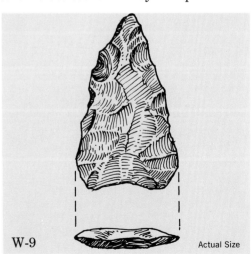

W-9   Actual Size

flaked, but show some pressure retouch. Examples are from W-9 (illustrated) and W-198.

Crescentic Stones

A greater number of crescentic stones have been found in sites of the Southwestern Aspect, but of twenty-seven specimens in the Museum of Man Type Collection, only two were found in subsurface positions. One specimen (illustrated) from Locus I at the Harris Site, is a simple lunate form with an additional projection in the middle of the concave side. The other example was excavated at W-181, at a depth of six inches in a twelve-inch deep San Dieguito III stratum. This specimen is more complex, resembling a biconcave lunate with double spurs on each end.

Two other forms occur in addition to the simple lunate, the biconcave lunate,

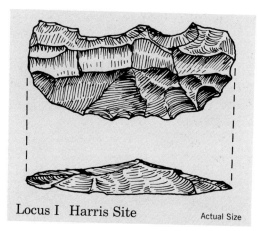

Locus I   Harris Site   Actual Size

and the biconcave lunate with double spurs. These are a lunate with "ventral" projections, and a biconcave lunate with single projections. Actually, the names of these artifacts are not important, since the variations even within a small collection preclude any sort of taxonomy.

BIBLIOGRAPHY

Agogino, George and W. D. Frankforter
1960a THE BREWSTER SITE: AN AGATE BASIN FOL-
SOM MULTIPLE COMPONENT SITE IN EASTERN WYO-
MING. *The Masterkey, vol. 34, no. 3.*

1960b A PALEO-INDIAN BISON KILL IN NORTHWEST-
ERN IOWA. *American Antiquity, vol. 25, no. 3, pp.
414-415.*

Allison, Ira S.
1952 DATING OF PLUVIAL LAKES IN THE GREAT BA-
SIN. *American Journal of Science, vol. 250, no. 12,
pp. 907-909.*

Amsden, Charles Avery
1935 THE PINTO BASIN ARTIFACTS in THE PINTO
BASIN SITE. *Southwest Museum Papers, no. 9, pp.
33-50.*

1937 THE LAKE MOHAVE ARTIFACTS in THE AR-
CHAEOLOGY OF PLEISTOCENE LAKE MOHAVE: A SYM-
POSIUM. *Southwest Museum Papers, no. 11, pp.
51-97.*

Anderson, Duane C.
1966 THE GORDON CREEK BURIAL. *Southwestern
Lore, vol. 32, no. 1.*

Antevs, Ernst
1936 PLUVIAL AND POSTPLUVIAL FLUCTUATIONS OF
CLIMATE IN THE SOUTHWEST. *Carnegie Institution
of Washington Yearbook, no. 35, pp. 322-323.*

1938 POSTPLUVIAL CLIMATIC VARIATIONS IN THE
SOUTHWEST. *American Meteorological Society. Bulletin, vol. 19, no. 5, pp. 190-193.*

1941 AGE OF THE COCHISE CULTURE STAGES in THE
COCHISE CULTURE. *Medallion Papers, no. 29, pp.
31-55.*

1948 CLIMATIC CHANGES AND PRE-WHITE MAN in
THE GREAT BASIN WITH EMPHASIS ON GLACIAL AND
POSTGLACIAL TIMES. *University of Utah. Bulletin,
vol. 38, no. 20, pp. 168-191.*

1952a CLIMATIC HISTORY AND ANTIQUITY OF MAN
IN CALIFORNIA. *University of California Archaeological Survey. Report, no. 16, pp. 23-29.*

1952b CENZOIC CLIMATES OF THE GREAT BASIN.
Geologische Rundschau, Bd. 40, Heft 2, pp. 94-108.

1953 GEOCHRONOLOGY OF THE DEGLACIAL AND NEO-
THERMAL AGES. *Journal of Geology, vol. 61, no. 3,
pp. 195-230.*

Arnold, Brigham A.
1957 LATE PLEISTOCENE AND RECENT CHANGES IN
LAND FORMS, CLIMATE AND ARCHAEOLOGY IN CEN-
TRAL BAJA CALIFORNIA. *University of California
Publications in Geography, vol. 10, no. 4, pp. 201-318.*

Arnold, J. R. and W. F. Libby
1951 RADIOCARBON DATES. *Science, vol. 113, no.
2927, pp. 111-120.*

Aschmann, Homer
1952 A FLUTED POINT FROM CENTRAL BAJA CALI-
FORNIA. *American Antiquity, vol. 17, no. 3, pp.
262-263.*

1959 THE CENTRAL DESERT OF BAJA CALIFORNIA:
DEMOGRAPHY AND ECOLOGY. *Ibero-Americana, no.
42.*

Ashby, G. E., and J. W. Winterbourne
1939 A STUDY OF PRIMITIVE MAN IN ORANGE
COUNTY AND SOME OF ITS COASTAL AREAS. *Typescript, Santa Ana, Calif.*

Baegert, Jacob
1772 AN ACCOUNT OF THE ABORIGINAL INHABIT-
ANTS OF THE CALIFORNIA PENINSULA. *Smithsonian
Institution Annual Report, 1863. Washington 1872,
pp. 360-361.*

Baldwin, Gordon C.
1944 MESCAL KNIVES FROM SOUTHERN NEVADA.
American Antiquity, vol. 9, no. 3, pp. 330-332.

Bancroft, Griffing
1932 LOWER CALIFORNIA, A CRUISE: THE FLIGHT
OF THE LEAST PETREL. *Putnam, New York.*

Barbieri, Joseph A.
1937 TECHNIQUE OF THE IMPLEMENTS FROM LAKE
MOHAVE in THE ARCHAEOLOGY OF PLEISTOCENE
LAKE MOHAVE. *Southwest Museum Papers, no. 11,
pp. 99-108.*

Belding, L.
1885 THE PERICUE INDIANS. *West American Scientist, vol. 1, no. 4, pp. 20-21.*

Bennett, J. W.
1943 RECENT DEVELOPMENTS IN THE FUNCTIONAL
INTERPRETATION OF ARCHAEOLOGICAL DATA. *American Antiquity, vol. 9, no. 2, pp. 208-219.*

Berger, Rainer and W. F. Libby
1965 UCLA RADIOCARBON DATES V. *University of
California at Los Angeles. Institute of Geophysics
and Planetary Physics. Publication, no. 480.*

Birdsell, Joseph B.
1951 THE PROBLEMS OF THE EARLY PEOPLING OF
THE AMERICAS AS VIEWED FROM ASIA in PAPERS ON
THE PHYSICAL ANTHROPOLOGY OF THE AMERICAN
INDIAN. *Viking Fund, New York, pp. 1-68.*

Botelho, Eugene
1955 PINTO BASIN POINTS IN UTAH. *American Antiquity, vol. 21, no. 2, pp. 185-186.*

Brainerd, George W.
1952 THE STUDY OF EARLY MAN IN SOUTHERN CAL-
IFORNIA in SYMPOSIUM OF THE ANTIQUITY OF MAN
IN CALIFORNIA. *University of California Archaeological Survey Report, no. 16, pp. 18-22.*

1953 A RE-EXAMINATION OF THE DATING EVIDENCE
FOR THE LAKE MOHAVE ARTIFACT ASSEMBLAGE.
American Antiquity, vol. 18, no. 3, pp. 270-271.

Breternitz, David A.
1957 A BRIEF ARCHAEOLOGICAL SURVEY OF THE
LOWER GILA RIVER. *Kiva, vol. 22, nos. 2 and 3.*

Bright, Marcia
1965 CALIFORNIA RADIOCARBON DATES. *University*

of California at Los Angeles. *Archaeological Survey Annual Report, pp. 363-375.*

Broecker, Wallace
1966 ABSOLUTE DATING AND THE ASTRONOMICAL THEORY OF GLACIATION. *Science, vol. 151, no. 3708, pp. 299-304.*

Broecker, Wallace, and Aaron Kaufman
1965 RADIOCARBON CHRONOLOGY OF LAKE LAHONTAN AND LAKE BONNEVILLE II, GREAT BASIN. *Geological Society of America. Bulletin, vol. 76, pp. 537-566.*

Bryan, Kirk
1939 STONE CULTURES NEAR CERRO PEDERNAL AND THEIR GEOLOGICAL ANTIQUITY. *Texas Archaeological and Paleontological Society. Bulletin, vol. 11, pp. 9-46.*

1950 GEOLOGICAL INTERPRETATION OF THE DEPOSITS in THE STRATIGRAPHY AND ARCHAEOLOGY OF VENTANA CAVE, ARIZONA. *University of New Mexico Press, Albuquerque, pp. 75-125.*

Butler, B. Robert
1961 THE OLD CORDILLERAN CULTURE IN THE PACIFIC NORTHWEST. *Idaho State College Museum. Occasional Papers, no. 5, Pocatello.*

Butzer, Karl W.
1964 ENVIRONMENT AND ARCHAEOLOGY: AN INTRODUCTION TO PLEISTOCENE GEOGRAPHY. *Aldine, Chicago.*

Byers, Douglas S.
1954 BULL BROOK—A FLUTED POINT SITE IN IPSWICH, MASSACHUSETTS. *American Antiquity, vol. 19, no. 4, pp. 343-351.*

1959 RADIOCARBON DATES FOR THE BULL BROOK SITE, MASSACHUSETTS. *American Antiquity, vol. 24, pp. 427-429.*

Campbell, Elizabeth W. Crozer
1949 TWO ANCIENT ARCHAEOLOGICAL SITES IN THE GREAT BASIN. *Science, vol. 109, no. 2831, p. 340.*

Campbell, Elizabeth W. Crozer, and William H. Campbell
1935 THE PINTO BASIN SITE: AN ANCIENT ABORIGINAL CAMPING GROUND IN THE CALIFORNIA DESERT. *Southwest Museum Papers, no. 9.*

1937 THE LAKE MOHAVE SITE in THE ARCHAEOLOGY OF PLEISTOCENE LAKE MOHAVE: A SYMPOSIUM. *Southwest Museum Papers, no. 11, pp. 9-43.*

1940 A FOLSOM COMPLEX IN THE GREAT BASIN. *Masterkey, vol. 14, no. 1, pp. 7-11.*

Campbell, John M.
1961 THE KOBRUK COMPLEX OF ANAKTUVUK PASS, ALASKA, *Anthropologica, n. s. 3, pp. 3-20.*

Carter, George F.
1949 EVIDENCE FOR PLEISTOCENE MAN AT LA JOLLA, CALIFORNIA. *New York Academy of Sciences. Transactions, Series II, vol. 11, no. 7, pp. 254-257.*

1950a ECOLOGY—GEOGRAPHY—ETHNOBOTANY. *Scientific Monthly, vol. 70, pp. 73-80.*

1950b EVIDENCE FOR PLEISTOCENE MAN IN SOUTHERN CALIFORNIA. *Geographical Review, vol. 40, no. 1, pp. 84-102.*

1952 INTERGLACIAL ARTIFACTS FROM THE SAN DIEGO AREA. *Southwestern Journal of Anthropology, vol. 8, no. 4, pp. 444-456.*

1954 AN INTERGLACIAL SITE AT SAN DIEGO, CALIFORNIA. *Masterkey, vol. 28, no. 5, pp. 165-174.*

1957 PLEISTOCENE MAN AT SAN DIEGO. *Johns Hopkins Press, Baltimore.*

Carter, George F., and Robert L. Pendleton
1956 THE HUMID SOIL: PROCESS AND TIME. *Geographical Review, vol. 46, no. 4, pp. 488-507.*

Clark, Donovan
1964 ARCHAEOLOGICAL CHRONOLOGY IN CALIFORNIA AND THE OBSIDIAN HYDRATION METHOD: PART I. *University of California at Los Angeles. Archaeological Survey Annual Report, pp. 139-228.*

Clavijero, Francisco Xavier
1787 THE HISTORY OF MEXICO. *Translated from the Italian by Charles Cullen. G. G. J. and J. Robinson, London, 2 vols.*

1937 THE HISTORY OF (LOWER) CALIFORNIA. *Translated from the Italian and edited by Sara E. Lake and A. A. Gray. Stanford University Press, Stanford.*

Clements, Lydia
1954 A PRELIMINARY STUDY OF SOME PLEISTOCENE CULTURES OF THE CALIFORNIA DESERT. *Masterkey, vol. 28, no. 5, pp. 177-185.*

Clements, Thomas
1952 LAKE ROGERS, A PLEISTOCENE LAKE IN THE NORTH END OF DEATH VALLEY, CALIFORNIA. *Geological Society of America. Bulletin, vol. 63, p. 1324 (abstract).*

Clements, Thomas and Lydia Clements
1953 EVIDENCE OF PLEISTOCENE MAN IN DEATH VALLEY, CALIFORNIA. *Geological Society of America. Bulletin, vol. 64, no. 10, pp. 1189-1204.*

Coe, Joffre Lanning
1964 THE FORMATIVE CULTURES OF THE CAROLINA PIEDMONT. *American Philosophical Society. Transactions n.s., vol. 54, p. 5.*

Collins, Henry B.
1964 THE ARCTIC AND SUBARCTIC in PREHISTORIC MAN IN THE NEW WORLD. *University of Chicago Press, Chicago, pp. 85-116.*

Cook, S. F.
1946 A RECONSIDERATION OF SHELLMOUNDS WITH RESPECT TO POPULATION AND NUTRITION. *American Antiquity, vol. 12, no. 1, pp. 50-53.*

Cotter, John Lambert
1937 THE OCCURRENCE OF FLINTS AND EXTINCT ANIMALS IN PLUVIAL DEPOSITS NEAR CLOVIS, NEW MEXICO: PART IV, REPORT ON THE EXCAVATIONS AT THE GRAVEL PIT IN 1936. *Philadelphia Academy of Natural Sciences. Proceedings, vol. 89, pp. 2-16.*

1938 THE OCCURRENCE OF FLINTS AND EXTINCT ANIMALS IN PLUVIAL DEPOSITS NEAR CLOVIS, NEW MEXICO: PART VI, REPORT ON FIELD SEASON OF

1937. *Philadelphia Academy of Natural Sciences. Proceedings, vol. 90, pp. 113-117.*

Count, Earl W.
1941 The Australoid Problem and the Peopling of America. *Universidad Nacional, Instituto de Antropología, Tucumán. Revista, vol. 2, no. 7, pp. 121-176.*

1950 This is Race: An Anthology. *Schuman, New York.*

Cressman, Luther S.
1939 Early Man and Culture in the Northern Great Basin Region of South-Central Oregon. *Carnegie Institution of Washington. Yearbook, no. 38, pp. 314-317.*

1940 Studies on Early Man in South Oregon. *Carnegie Institution of Washington. Yearbook, no. 39, pp. 300-306.*

1942 Archaeological Researches in the Northern Great Basin. *Carnegie Institution of Washington. Publication 538.*

1943 Results of Recent Archaeological Research in the Northern Great Basin Region of South Central Oregon. *American Philosophical Society. Proceedings, vol. 86, no. 2, pp. 236-237.*

1951 Western Prehistory in the Light of Carbon 14 Dating. *Southwestern Journal of Anthropology, vol. 7, no. 3, pp. 289-313.*

1956a Klamath Prehistory. *Appendices by William G. Haag and William S. Laughlin. American Philosophical Society. Transactions, n.s., vol. 46, pt. 4.*

1956b Additional Radiocarbon Dates, Lovelock Cave, Nevada. *American Antiquity, vol. 21, no. 3, pp. 311-312.*

1960 Cultural Sequence at the Dalles, Oregon. *American Philosophical Society. Transactions, M.S., vol. 50, pt. 10.*

Cressman, L. S., Howel Williams, and Alex D. Krieger
1940 Early Man in Oregon: Archaeological Studies in the Northern Great Basin. *University of Oregon Monographs. Studies in Anthropology, no. 3.*

Crook, Wilson W., Jr., and R. K. Harris
1958 A Pleistocene Campsite near Lewisville, Texas. *American Antiquity, vol. 23, no. 3, pp. 233-246.*

Daugherty, Richard D.
1956 Archaeology of the Lind Coulee Site, Washington. *American Philosophical Society. Proceedings, vol. 100, no. 3, pp. 223-278.*

1962 The Intermontane Western Tradition. *American Antiquity, vol. 28, no. 2, pp. 144-150.*

Davidson, D. S.
1938 Stone Axes of Western Australia. *American Anthropologist, vol. 40, no. 1, pp. 38-48.*

Davis, E. L.
1965 An Ethnography of the Kuzedika Paiute of Mono Lake, Mono County, California. *University of Utah, Department of Anthropology. Miscellaneous Paper, no. 8.*

Davis, E. L., et al.
1966 The Archaeology and Environment of Panamint Valley. *Typescript, University of California, Los Angeles.*

Deevey, Edward S., L. J. Gralenski, and Väinö Hoffren
1959 Yale Natural Radiocarbon Measurements, IV. *American Journal of Science. Radiocarbon Supplement, no. 1, pp. 144-172.*

De Geer, G.
1912 A Geochronology of the Last 12,000 Years. *International Geological Congress, 11th, Stockholm. Proceedings, pp. 241-258.*

De Jarnette, David L., Edward B. Kurjack and James W. Cambron
1962 Stanfield-Worley Bluff Shelter Excavations. *Journal of Alabama Archaeology, vol. 8, nos. 1 and 2.*

De Terra, Helmut, Javier Romero, and T. D. Stewart
1949 Tepexpan Man. *Viking Fund. Publications in Anthropology, no. 11.*

Dibble, David S.
1965 Bonfire Shelter: A Stratified Bison Kill Site in the Amistad Reservoir Area, Val Verde County, Texas. *Texas Archaeological Salvage Project, Austin. Miscellaneous Papers, no. 5.*

Diguet, Léon
1905 Anciennes sépultures indigènes de la Basse-Californie méridionale. *Société des Américanistes de Paris. Journal, n.s., vol. 1, pp. 329-333.*

Dixon, Roland B.
1923 The Racial History of Man. *Scribners, New York.*

Eaton, J. E.
1928 Divisions and Duration of the Pleistocene in Southern California. *American Association of Petroleum Geologists. Bulletin, vol. 12, no. 2, pp. 111-141.*

Eiseley, Loren C.
1955 The Paleo-Indians: Their Survival and Diffusion in New Interpretations of Aboriginal American Culture History. *Anthropological Society of Washington, 75th Anniversary Volume, pp. 1-11.*

Emery, K. O.
1950 Ironstone Concretions and Beach Ridges of San Diego County, California. *California Journal of Mines and Geology, vol. 46, no. 2, pp. 213-221.*

Engel, Celeste G., and Robert P. Sharp
1958 Chemical Data on Desert Varnish. *Geological Society of America. Bulletin, vol. 69, pp. 487-518.*

Engerrand, G.
1913 Estado actual de la cuestión de los eoli-

TOS. *Mexico, Museo Nacional de Arqueología, Historia y Etnología. Boletín, vol. 2, no. 8, pp. 150-160.*

Evernden, J. F. and G. H. Curtis
1965 POTASSIUM-ARGON DATING OF LATE CENOZOIC ROCKS IN EAST AFRICA AND ITALY. *Current Anthropology, vol. 6, no. 4, pp. 343-385.*

Fay, George E.
1956 THE PERALTA COMPLEX—A SONORAN VARIANT OF THE COCHISE CULTURE. *International Congress of Americanists, 32nd, Copenhagen. Proceedings, pp. 491-493.*

1957 A PRE-POTTERY LITHIC COMPLEX FROM SONORA, MEXICO. *Man, vol. 57, pp. 98-99.*

Fergusson, G. J.
1964 DATING BY RADIOACTIVE ISOTOPES in BIOLOGY TEACHER'S HANDBOOK. *John Wiley, New York, pp. 331-352.*

Fleischer, R. L., et al.
FISSION-TRACK DATING OF BED I, OLDUVAI GORGE. *Science, vol. 148, no. 3666, pp. 72-74.*

Fowler, Melvin
1959 SUMMARY REPORT OF MODOC ROCK SHELTER. *Illinois State Museum. Investigations, Report no. 8.*

Fryxell, Roald and Richard D. Daugherty
1963 LATE GLACIAL AND POST GLACIAL GEOLOGICAL AND ARCHAEOLOGICAL CHRONOLOGY AT THE COLUMBIA PLATEAU, WASHINGTON. *Washington State University, Pullman Report of Investigations, no. 23.*

Gale, Hoyt S.
1915 SALINES IN THE OWENS, SEARLES AND PANAMINT BASINS, SOUTHEASTERN CALIFORNIA. *U.S. Geological Survey. Bulletin, no. 580, pp. 251-323.*

Gann, Thomas and J. Eric Thompson
1931 THE HISTORY OF THE MAYA. *Scribners, New York, pl. XIX.*

Giddings, J. L.
1961 CULTURAL CONTINUITIES OF ESKIMOS. *American Antiquity, vol. 27, no. 2, pp. 155-173.*

1963 SOME ARCTIC SPEAR POINTS AND THEIR COUNTERPARTS in EARLY MAN IN THE WESTERN AMERICAN ARCTIC. *University of Alaska. Anthropological Papers, vol. 10, no. 2, pp. 1-12.*

1966 CROSS-DATING THE ARCHAEOLOGY OF NORTHWESTERN ALASKA. *Science, vol. 153, no. 3732, pp. 127-135.*

Green, F. E.
1963 THE CLOVIS BLADES: AN IMPORTANT ADDITION TO THE LLANO COMPLEX. *American Antiquity, vol. 29, no. 2, pp. 145-165.*

Greengo, Robert E.
1951 MOLLUSCAN SPECIES IN CALIFORNIA SHELL MIDDENS. *University of California Archaeological Survey. Report, no. 13.*

Griffin, James B.
1964 THE NORTHEAST WOODLANDS AREA in PREHISTORIC MAN IN THE NEW WORLD. *University of Chicago Press, Chicago.*

1965 LATE QUATERNARY PREHISTORY IN THE NORTHEASTERN WOODLANDS in THE QUATERNARY OF THE UNITED STATES. *Princeton University Press, Princeton.*

Grosscup, Gordon L.
1956 THE ARCHAEOLOGY OF THE CARSON SINK AREA. *University of California Archaeological Survey. Report, no. 33, pp. 58-64.*

Gruhn, Ruth
1961 THE ARCHAEOLOGY OF WILSON BUTTE CAVE, SOUTH CENTRAL IDAHO. *Idaho State College Museum, Pocatello. Occasional Papers, no. 6.*

Haag, William G.
1962 THE BERING STRAIT LAND BRIDGE. *Scientific American, vol. 206, no. 1, pp. 112-123.*

Hansen, Henry P.
1947 POSTGLACIAL FOREST SUCCESSION, CLIMATE AND CHRONOLOGY IN THE PACIFIC NORTHWEST. *American Philosophical Society. Transactions, n.s., vol. 37, pt. 1, pp. 1-130.*

Harding, Mabel
1951 LA JOLLAN CULTURE. *El Museo, n.s., vol. 1, no. 1, pp. 10-11, 31-38.*

Harrington, Mark R.
1933 GYPSUM CAVE, NEVADA. *Southwest Museum Papers, no. 8.*

1934 A CAMEL HUNTER'S CAMP IN NEVADA. *Masterkey, vol. 8, no. 1, pp. 22-24.*

1937 A STRATIFIED CAMP-SITE near BOULDER DAM. *Masterkey, vol. 11, no. 3, pp. 86-89.*

1938 FOLSOM MAN IN CALIFORNIA. *Masterkey, vol. 12, no. 4, pp. 133-137.*

1942 A RARE MESCAL KNIFE. *Masterkey, vol. 16, no. 2, pp. 67-68.*

1948a A NEW PINTO SITE. *Masterkey, vol. 22, no. 4, pp. 116-118.*

1948b AMERICA'S OLDEST DWELLING? *Masterkey, vol. 22, no. 5, pp. 148-152.*

1948c AN ANCIENT SITE AT BORAX LAKE, CALIFORNIA. *Southwest Museum Papers, no. 16.*

1949 A NEW OLD HOUSE AT LITTLE LAKE. *Masterkey, vol. 23, no. 5, pp. 135-136.*

1951 LATEST FROM LITTLE LAKE. *Masterkey, vol. 25, no. 6, pp. 188-191.*

1954 THE OLDEST CAMPFIRES. *Masterkey, vol. 28, no. 6, p. 233.*

1955 A NEW TULE SPRINGS EXPEDITION. *Masterkey, vol. 29, no. 4, pp. 112-114.*

1957 A PINTO SITE AT LITTLE LAKE, CALIFORNIA. *Southwest Museum Papers, no. 17.*

Harrington, Mark Raymond and Ruth D. Simpson
1961 TULE SPRINGS, NEVADA, WITH OTHER EVIDENCE OF PLEISTOCENE MAN IN NORTH AMERICA. *Southwest Museum Papers, no. 18.*

Haury, Emil W.
1943 THE STRATIGRAPHY OF VENTANA CAVE, ARIZONA. *American Antiquity, vol. 8, no. 3, pp. 218-223.*

1956 THE LEHNER MAMMOTH SITE. *Kiva, vol. 21, nos. 3 and 4, pp. 23-24.*

1958 TWO FOSSIL ELEPHANT KILL SITES IN THE AMERICAN SOUTHWEST. *International Congress of Americanists, 32nd, Copenhagen, 1956. Proceedings, pp. 433-440.*

Haury, Emil W., et al.
1950 THE STRATIGRAPHY AND ARCHAEOLOGY OF VENTANA CAVE, ARIZONA. *University of New Mexico Press, Albuquerque.*

Hay, Oliver P.
1927 THE PLEISTOCENE OF THE WESTERN REGION OF NORTH AMERICA AND ITS VERTEBRATED ANIMALS. *Carnegie Institution of Washington. Publication 322B.*

Haynes, C. Vance
1964 GEOCHRONOLOGY OF CLOVIS AND FOLSOM PROJECTILE POINTS AND THE PROBLEM OF DISPERSION. *Science, vol. 145, no. 3639, pp. 1408-1413.*

n.d. CARBON 14 DATES AND EARLY MAN IN THE NEW WORLD.

Haynes, C. Vance, and George Agogino
1960 GEOLOGIC SIGNIFICANCE OF A NEW RADIOCARBON DATE FROM THE LINDENMEIER SITE. *Denver Museum of Natural History. Proceedings, no. 9.*

Heizer, Robert F.
1938 A COMPLETE ATLATL DART FROM PERSHING COUNTY, NEVADA. *New Mexican Anthropologist, vol. 2, no. 4, pp. 68, 70-71.*

1941 REVIEW OF PREHISTORIC MAN OF THE SANTA BARBARA COAST BY DAVID BANKS ROGERS. *American Antiquity, vol. 6, no. 9, pp. 372-375.*

1948 A BIBLIOGRAPHY OF ANCIENT MAN IN CALIFORNIA. *University of California Archaeological Survey. Report, no. 2.*

1949 THE ARCHAEOLOGY OF CENTRAL CALIFORNIA, I: THE EARLY HORIZON. *University of California. Anthropological Records, vol. 12, no. 1.*

1951 PRELIMINARY REPORT ON THE LEONARD ROCKSHELTER SITE, PERSHING COUNTY, NEVADA. *American Antiquity, vol. 17, no. 2, pp. 89-98.*

1952 A REVIEW OF PROBLEMS IN THE ANTIQUITY OF MAN IN CALIFORNIA. *University of California Archaeological Survey. Report, no. 16, pp. 3-17.*

1953 SITES ATTRIBUTED TO EARLY MAN IN CALIFORNIA. *University of California Archaeological Survey. Report, no. 22, pp. 1-4.*

1964 THE WESTERN COAST OF NORTH AMERICA in PREHISTORIC MAN IN THE NEW WORLD. *University of Chicago Press, Chicago, pp. 117-148.*

Heizer, Robert F., and Sherburne F. Cook
1952 FLUORINE AND OTHER CHEMICAL TESTS OF SOME NORTH AMERICAN HUMAN FOSSIL BONES. *American Journal of Physical Anthropology, n.s., vol. 10, no. 3, pp. 289-303.*

1960 THE APPLICATION OF QUANTITATIVE METHODS IN ARCHAEOLOGY. *Viking Fund. Publications in Anthropology, no. 28.*

Heizer, Robert F., Edwin M. Lemert,

and Adan E. Treganza
1947 OBSERVATIONS ON ARCHAEOLOGICAL SITES IN TOPANGA CANYON. *University of California. Publications in American Archaeology and Ethnology, vol. 44, no. 2, pp. 237-258.*

Heizer, Robert F., and Adan E. Treganza
1944 MINES AND QUARRIES OF THE INDIANS OF CALIFORNIA. *California Journal of Mines and Geology, vol. 40, no. 3, pp. 291-360.*

Hester, Jim J.
1960 LATE PLEISTOCENE EXTINCTION AND RADIOCARBON DATES. *American Antiquity, vol. 26, no. 1, pp. 58-77.*

Hewes, Gordon W.
1943 CAMEL, HORSE AND BISON ASSOCIATED WITH HUMAN BURIALS AND ARTIFACTS NEAR FRESNO, CALIFORNIA. *Science, vol. 97, no. 2519, pp. 328-329.*

1946 EARLY MAN IN CALIFORNIA AND THE TRANQUILLITY SITE. *American Antiquity, vol. 11, no. 4, pp. 209-215.*

Hewett, D. F.
1955 STRUCTURAL FEATURES OF THE MOJAVE DESERT REGION. *Geological Society of America. Special Paper, no. 62, pp. 377-390.*

Hibbard, C. W., et al.
1965 QUATERNARY MAMMALS OF NORTH AMERICA in THE QUATERNARY OF THE UNITED STATES. *Princeton University Press, Princeton, pp. 509-525.*

Hibben, Frank C.
1941 EVIDENCES OF EARLY OCCUPATION OF SANDIA CAVE, NEW MEXICO, AND OTHER SITES IN THE SANDIA-MANZANO REGION. *Smithsonian Miscellaneous Collections, vol. 99, no. 23.*

Howard, Edgar B.
1935 OCCURRENCE OF FLINTS AND EXTINCT ANIMALS IN PLUVIAL DEPOSITS NEAR CLOVIS, NEW MEXICO. *Philadelphia Academy of Natural Sciences. Proceedings, vol. 87, pp. 299-303.*

Hubbs, Carl L., George S. Bien, and Hans E. Suess
1960 LA JOLLA NATURAL RADIOCARBON MEASUREMENTS. *American Journal of Science. Radiocarbon Supplement, vol. 2, pp. 197-223.*

Hubbs, Carl L., and Robert R. Miller
1948 THE GREAT BASIN WITH EMPHASIS ON GLACIAL AND POST-GLACIAL TIMES: THE ZOOLOGICAL EVIDENCE: CORRELATION BETWEEN FISH DISTRIBUTION AND HYDROGRAPHIC HISTORY IN THE DESERT BASINS OF THE WESTERN UNITED STATES. *University of Utah. Bulletin, vol. 38, no. 20, pp. 17-166.*

Hunt, Charles B.
1954 DESERT VARNISH. *Science, vol. 120, no. 3109, pp. 183-184.*

1956 A SCEPTIC'S VIEW OF RADIOCARBON DATES in PAPERS OF THE THIRD GREAT BASIN ARCHAEOLOGICAL CONFERENCE. *University of Utah, Department of Anthropology. Anthropological Papers, no. 26, pp. 35-46*

Hunt, Wesley R., Jr.
1953 A Comparative Study of the Preceramic Occupations of North America. *American Antiquity, vol. 18, no. 3, pp. 204-222.*

Idress, Ion L.
1931 Lasseter's Last Ride: An Epic of Central Australian Gold Discovery. *Angus and Robertson, Sydney.*

Imbelloni, José
1943 The Peopling of America. *Acta Americana, vol. 1, no. 3, pp. 309-330.*

Irwin, Henry V., Cynthia Irwin-Williams, and George Agogino
1961 Ice Age Man versus Mammoth. *National Geographic Magazine, June.*

1966 Resume of Cultural Complexes at the Hell Gap Site, Guernsey, Wyoming. *The Wyoming Archaeologist, vol. 9, no. 2, pp. 11-13.*

Jenks, Albert E.
1936 Pleistocene Man in Minnesota: A Fossil Homo Sapiens. *The University of Minnesota Press, Minneapolis.*

Jennings, Jesse D.
1957 Danger Cave. *University of Utah. Anthropological Papers, no. 27.*

Jepsen, Glenn L.
1953 Ancient Buffalo Hunters of Northwestern Wyoming. *Southwestern Lore, vol. 19, no. 2, pp. 19-25.*

Johnson, Frederick (ed.)
1951 Radiocarbon Dating: A Report on the Program to Aid in the Development of the Method of Dating. *Society for American Archaeology. Memoirs, no. 8.*

Kate, H. F. C. ten
1884 Matériaux pour servir a l'anthropologie de la presqu'île californienne. *Société d'anthropologie de Paris. Bulletin, series 3, vol. 7, pp. 551-569.*

Kelly, Isabel T.
1932 Ethnography of the Surprise Valley Paiute. *University of California Publications in American Archaeology and Ethnology, vol. 31, no. 3, pp. 67-210.*

1964 Southern Paiute Ethnography. *University of Utah. Anthropological Papers, no. 69, Glen Canyon Series, no. 21.*

Krieger, Alex D.
1950 A Suggested General Sequence in North American Projectile Points. *University of Utah. Anthropological Papers, no. 11, pp. 117-124.*

1951 Review of "Prehistoria de Mexico" by Luis Aveleyra Arroyo de Anda. *American Antiquity, vol. 16, no. 4, pp. 357-359.*

Laudermilk, J. D.
1931 On the Origin of Desert Varnish. *American Journal of Science, 5th series, vol. 21, pp. 51-66.*

Laughlin, William S., and Gordon H. Marsh

1954 The Lamellar Flake Manufacturing Site on Anagula Island in the Aleutians. *American Antiquity, vol. 20, no. 1, pp. 27-39.*

Leidy, Joseph
1873 On Remains of Primitive Art in the Bridger Basin of Southern Wyoming. *United States Geological and Geographical Survey of the Territories. 6th Annual Report, pp. 651-653.*

Libby, Willard F.
1951 Radiocarbon Dates, II. *Science, vol. 114, no. 2960, pp. 291-296.*

1961 Radiocarbon Dating. *Science, vol. 133, no. 3453, pp. 621-629.*

Logan, Wilfred D.
1952 Graham Cave, an Archaic Site in Montgomery County, Missouri. *Missouri Archaeological Society. Memoirs, no. 2.*

Lopatin, Ivan A.
1940 Fossil Man in the Vicinity of Los Angeles, California. *Pacific Science Congress, 6th, Berkeley, 1939. Proceedings vol. 4, pp. 177-181.*

Loud, Llewllyn L., and M. R. Harrington
1929 Lovelock Cave. *University of California Publications in Archaeology and Ethnology, vol. 25, no. 1, pp. 1-183.*

McCary, Ben C.
1951 A Workshop Site of Early Man in Dinwiddie County, Virginia. *American Antiquity, vol. 17, no. 1, pt. 1, pp. 9-17.*

McCown, Theodore D.
1950 The Antiquity of Man in South America in Handbook of South American Indians. *Vol. 6, pp. 1-9.*

MacNeish, Richard
1956 The Engigstciak Site on the Yukon Arctic Coast. *University of Alaska. Anthropological Papers, vol. 4, no. 2, pp. 91-111.*

Martin, Paul S., and Peter Mehringer, Jr.
1965 Pleistocene Pollen Analysis and Biogeography of the Southwest in The Quaternary of the United States. *Princeton University Press, Princeton, pp. 433-451.*

Mason, Ronald J.
1962 The Paleo-Indian Tradition in Eastern North America. *Current Anthropology, vol. 3, no. 3, pp. 227-278.*

Mason, Ronald J., and Carol Irwin
1960 An Eden-Scottsbluff Burial in Northeastern Wisconsin. *American Antiquity, vol. 26, no. 1, pp. 43-57.*

Massey, William C.
1947 Brief Report on Archaeological Investigations in Baja California. *Southwestern Journal of Anthropology, vol. 3, no. 4, pp. 344-359.*

Mathiassen, Therkel
1930 Notes on Knud Rasmussen's Archaeological Collections from the Western Eskimo. *In-*

ternational Congress of Americanists, 23rd, New York, 1928, pp. 395-399.

Meighan, Clement W.

1965 PACIFIC COAST ARCHAEOLOGY in THE QUATERNARY OF THE UNITED STATES. *Princeton University Press, Princeton.*

1966 PREHISTORIC ROCK PAINTINGS IN BAJA CALIFORNIA, PART I. *American Antiquity, vol. 31, no. 3, pp. 372-392.*

Michels, Joseph W.

1965 A PROGRESS REPORT ON THE UCLA OBSIDIAN HYDRATION DATING LABORATORY. *University of California at Los Angeles. Archaeological Survey Annual Report, pp. 377-388.*

Moriarty, J. R., G. Shumway, and C. H. Warren

1959 SCRIPPS ESTATES SITE 1 (S.D. I.-525): A PRELIMINARY REPORT ON AN EARLY SITE ON THE SAN DIEGO COAST. *University of California at Los Angeles. Archaeological Survey Annual Report, pp. 185-217.*

Murdoch, John

1892 ETHNOLOGICAL RESULTS OF THE POINT BARROW EXPEDITION. *United States Bureau of American Ethnology. 9th Annual Report, 1887-1888, pp. 19-434.*

Noetling, Fritz

1907 NOTES ON THE TASMANIAN AMORPHOLITHES. *Royal Society of Tasmania. Proceedings, pp. 1-37.*

Oakley, Kenneth P.

1964 FRAMEWORKS FOR DATING FOSSIL MAN. *Aldine, Chicago.*

Oakley, Kenneth P., and J. S. Weiner

1955 PILTDOWN MAN. *American Scientist, vol. 43, pp. 573-583.*

Olson, Ronald L.

1930 CHUMASH PREHISTORY. *University of California Publications in American Archaeology and Ethnology, vol. 28, pp. 1-21.*

Orr, P. C.

1956a RADIOCARBON DATES FROM SANTA ROSA ISLAND I. *Santa Barbara Museum of Natural History. Anthropological Bulletin, no. 2.*

1956b PLEISTOCENE MAN IN FISHBONE CAVE, PERSHING COUNTY, NEVADA. *Nevada State Museum, Department of Archaeology. Bulletin no. 2, pp. 1-20.*

1960 RADIOCARBON DATES FROM SANTA ROSA ISLAND II. *Santa Barbara Museum of Natural History. Anthropological Bulletin, no. 3.*

Prufer, Olaf H.

1960 SURVEY OF OHIO FLUTED POINTS, No. 1. *Cleveland Museum of Natural History, Cleveland.*

Prufer, Olaf H., and Raymond S. Baby

1963 PALEO-INDIANS OF OHIO. *The Ohio Historical Society, Columbia.*

Ritchie, William A.

1953 A PROBABLE PALEO-INDIAN SITE IN VERMONT.

American Antiquity, vol. 18, no. 3, pp. 249-258.

Roberts, Frank H. H., Jr.

1935 A FOLSOM COMPLEX: PRELIMINARY REPORT ON INVESTIGATIONS AT THE LINDENMEIER SITE IN NORTHERN COLORADO. *Smithsonian Miscellaneous Collections, vol. 94.*

1936 ADDITIONAL INFORMATION ON THE FOLSOM COMPLEX: REPORT ON THE SECOND SEASON'S INVESTIGATIONS AT THE LINDENMEIER SITE IN NORTHERN COLORADO. *Smithsonian Miscellaneous Collections, vol. 95, no. 10.*

1940 DEVELOPMENTS IN THE PROBLEM OF THE NORTH AMERICAN PALEO-INDIAN in ESSAYS IN HISTORICAL ANTHROPOLOGY OF NORTH AMERICA. *Smithsonian Miscellaneous Collections, vol. 100, pp. 51-116.*

1943a EVIDENCE FOR A PALEO-INDIAN IN THE NEW WORLD. *Acta Americana, vol. 1, no. 2, pp. 171-201.*

1943b "A NEW SITE" in NOTES AND NEWS. *American Antiquity, vol. 8, no. 3, p. 300.*

1961 THE AGATE BASIN COMPLEX in HOMENAJE A PABLO MARTINEZ DEL RIO. *Instituto Nacional de Antropologia e Historia, Mexico, D. F.*

Rogers, David Banks

1929 PREHISTORIC MAN OF THE SANTA BARBARA COAST. *Santa Barbara Museum of Natural History, Santa Barbara.*

Rogers, Malcolm J.

1929a REPORT OF AN ARCHAEOLOGICAL RECONNAISSANCE IN THE MOHAVE SINK REGION. *San Diego Museum Papers, no. 1.*

1929b THE STONE ART OF THE SAN DIEGUITO PLATEAU. *American Anthropologist, vol. 31, no. 3, pp. 454-467.*

1932 PILED CEREMONIAL STONES FOUND ON WATERLESS MESA. *Science Newsletter, vol. 21, p. 244.*

1938 ARCHAEOLOGICAL AND GEOLOGICAL INVESTIGATIONS OF THE CULTURAL LEVELS IN AN OLD CHANNEL OF SAN DIEGUITO VALLEY. *Carnegie Institution of Washington. Yearbook, no. 37, pp. 344-345.*

1939 EARLY LITHIC INDUSTRIES OF THE LOWER BASIN OF THE COLORADO RIVER AND ADJACENT DESERT AREAS. *San Diego Museum Papers, no. 3.*

1945 AN OUTLINE OF YUMAN PREHISTORY. *Southwestern Journal of Anthropology, vol. 1, no. 2, p 167.*

1948 THE ABORIGINES OF THE DESERT in THE CALIFORNIA DESERTS: A VISITOR'S HANDBOOK. *Stanford University Press, Stanford.*

1950 TABLE 12 in THE STRATIGRAPHY AND ARCHAEOLOGY OF VENTANA CAVE, ARIZONA. *University of Arizona Press, Tucson.*

1958 SAN DIEGUITO IMPLEMENTS FROM THE TERRACES OF THE RINCON-PANTANO AND RILLITO DRAINAGE SYSTEM. *Kiva, vol. 24, no. 1, pp. 1-23.*

1960 THE CHRONOLOGICAL PROBLEMS OF THE SOUTHWESTERN ASPECT AND ITS RELATIONSHIP TO OTHER ASPECTS. *Typescript.*

Rudy, Jack R., and Robert D. Stirland
1950 An Archeological Reconnaissance in Washington County, Utah. *University of Utah. Anthropological Papers, no. 9.*

Rudy, Jack R., and Earl Stoddard
1954 Site on Fremont Island in Great Salt Lake. *American Antiquity, vol. 19, no. 3, pp. 285-290.*

Sample, L. L.
1950 Trade and Trails in Aboriginal California. *University of California Archaeological Survey Report, no. 8.*

Sayles, E. B.
1941 Archaeology of the Cochise Culture in The Cochise Culture. *Medallion Papers, no. 29, pp. 1-27.*

Schroeder, Albert H.
1957 The Hakataya Cultural Tradition. *American Antiquity, vol. 23, no. 2, pp. 176-178.*

Schwab, Joseph J.
1964 Biology Teacher's Handbook. *Wiley, New York.*

Sellards, Elias Howard
1952 Early Man in America. *University of Texas Press, Austin.*

Sellards, Elias Howard, Glen L. Evans, and Grayson E. Meade
1947 Fossil Bison and Associated Artifacts from Plainview, Texas, with Description of Artifacts by Alex D. Krieger. *Geological Society of America. Bulletin, vol. 58, pp. 927-954.*

Service, Elman
1941 Lithic Patina as an Age Criterion. *Michigan Academy of Science, Arts, and Letters. Papers, vol. 27, pp. 553-558.*

Shepard, F. P., and H. E. Suess
1956 Rate of Postglacial Rise of Sea Level. *Science, vol. 123. no. 3207, pp. 1082-1083.*

Simpson, George Gaylord
1933 A Nevada Fauna of Pleistocene Type and Its Probable Association with Man. *American Museum of Natural History. Novitates, no. 667.*

Simpson, Ruth DeEtte
1949 The Plot Thickens at Little Lake. *Masterkey, vol. 23, no. 1, p. 19.*

1955 Hunting Elephants in Nevada. *Masterkey, vol. 29, no. 4, pp. 114-116.*

1958 The Manix Lake Archaeological Survey. *Masterkey, vol. 32, no. 1, pp. 4-10.*

Smith, Gerald A., et al.
1957 The Archaeology of Newberry Cave, San Bernardino County, Newberry, California. *San Bernardino County Museum. Scientific Series, no. 1.*

Soday, Frank J.
1954 The Quad Site: A Paleo-Indian Village in Northern Alabama. *The Tennessee Archaeologist, vol. 10, no. 1, pp. 1-20.*

Steward, Julian H.
1933 Ethnography of the Owens Valley Paiute. *University of California Publications in American Archaeology and Ethnology, vol. 34, no. 5.*

1937 Ancient Caves of the Great Salt Lake Region. *U.S. Bureau of American Ethnology. Bulletin 116.*

1938 Basin-Plateau Aboriginal Sociopolitical Groups. *U.S. Bureau of American Ethnology. Bulletin 120.*

Stewart, T. D.
1940 Some Historical Implications of Physical Anthropology in North America. *Smithsonian Miscellaneous Collections, vol. 100, pp. 15-50.*

Stock, Chester
1924 A Recent Discovery of Ancient Human Remains in Los Angeles, California. *Science, vol. 60, no. 1540, pp. 2-5.*

1931 Problems of Antiquity Presented in Gypsum Cave, Nevada. *Scientific Monthly, vol. 32, pp. 22-32.*

1942 Rancho La Brea: A Record of Pleistocene Life in California. *Los Angeles County Museum. Science Series: Paleontology, no. 4.*

Swanson, Earl H.
1962 Early Cultures in Northwestern America. *American Antiquity, vol. 28, pp. 151-158.*

Taylor, Dee Calderwood
1954 The Garrison Site. *University of Utah. Anthropological Papers, no. 16.*

Thompson, David G.
1921 Pleistocene Lakes Along Mohave River, California. *Washington Academy of Science. Journal, vol. 11, pp. 423-425.*

Treganza, A. E.
1947 Notes on the San Dieguito Lithic Industry of Southern California and Northern Baja California in Observations on Archaeological Sites in Topanga Canyon, California. *University of California Publications in American Archaeology and Ethnology, vol. 44, no. 2, pp. 253-255.*

Treganza, A. E., and A. Bierman
1958 The Topanga Culture: Final Report on Excavations, 1948. *University of California. Anthropological Records, vol. 20, no. 2.*

Treganza, A. E., and C. G. Malamud
1950 The Topanga Culture: First Season's Excavation of the Tank Site, 1947. *University of California. Anthropological Records, vol. 12, no. 4, pp. 129-157.*

True, D. L.
1958 An Early Complex in San Diego County, California. *American Antiquity, vol. 23, no. 3, pp. 255-263.*

Van der Post, Laurens
1958 The Lost World of the Kalahari. *William Morrow, New York.*

Venegas, Miguel
1759 A NATURAL AND CIVIL HISTORY OF CALIFORNIA. *J. Rivington and J. Fletcher, London.*

Vogelin, C. F.
1945 RELATIVE CHRONOLOGY OF NORTH AMERICAN LINGUISTIC TYPES. *American Anthropologist, vol. 47, no. 2, pp. 232-234.*

Walker, Edwin Francis
1937 SEQUENCE OF PREHISTORIC MATERIAL CULTURE AT MALAGA CAVE, CALIFORNIA. *Masterkey, vol. 11, no. 6, pp. 210-214.*

1952 FIVE PREHISTORIC ARCHAEOLOGICAL SITES IN LOS ANGELES COUNTY, CALIFORNIA. *Southwest Museum, Frederick Webb Hodge Anniversary Fund. Publication, no. 6.*

Wallace, W. J.
1954 THE LITTLE SYCAMORE SITE AND THE EARLY MILLING STONE CULTURES OF SOUTHERN CALIFORNIA. *American Antiquity, vol. 20, pp. 112-123.*

Wallace, W. J., and Edith S. Taylor
1960 THE INDIAN HILL ROCK SHELTER: PRELIMINARY EXCAVATIONS. *Masterkey, vol. 34, no. 2, pp. 66-82.*

Warnica, James M.
1966 NEW DISCOVERIES AT THE CLOVIS SITE. *American Antiquity, vol. 31, no. 3. pt. 1.*

Warren, Claude N. (ed.)
1966 A STRATIFIED SAN DIEGUITO SITE: MALCOLM ROGERS' 1938 EXCAVATION IN THE SAN DIEGUITO RIVER VALLEY. *San Diego Museum Papers, no. 5.*

Warren, Claude N., and D. L. True
1960 THE SAN DIEGUITO COMPLEX AND ITS PLACE IN CALIFORNIA PREHISTORY. *University of California at Los Angeles. Archaeological Survey Annual Report, pp. 246-348.*

Wedel, Waldo R.
1941 ARCHAEOLOGICAL INVESTIGATIONS AT BUENA VISTA LAKE, KERN COUNTY, CALIFORNIA. *U.S. Bureau of American Ethnology. Bulletin 130.*

Wendorf, Fred, Alex D. Krieger,
Claude C. Albritton, and T. D. Stewart
1955 THE MIDLAND DISCOVERY. *University of Texas Press, Austin.*

Wendorf, Fred, and Tully H. Thomas
1951 EARLY MAN SITES NEAR CONCHO, ARIZONA. *American Antiquity, vol. 17, no. 2, pp. 107-114.*

Williams, Stephan, and James B. Stoltman
1965 AN OUTLINE OF A SOUTHEASTERN UNITED STATES PREHISTORY WITH PARTICULAR EMPHASIS ON THE PALEO-INDIAN PERIOD in THE QUATERNARY OF THE UNITED STATES. *Princeton University Press, Princeton, pp. 669-683.*

Wise, Edward N., and Dick Shutler, Jr.
1958 UNIVERSITY OF ARIZONA RADIOCARBON DATES. *Science, vol. 127, no. 3289, pp. 72-74.*

Witthoft, John
1952 A PALEO-INDIAN SITE IN EASTERN PENNSYLVANIA: AN EARLY HUNTING CULTURE. *American Philosophical Society. Proceedings, vol. 96, no. 4, pp. 464-495.*

Wordward, Arthur
1937 ATLATL DART FORESHAFTS FROM THE LA BREA PITS. *Southern California Academy of Sciences. Bulletin, vol. 36, pt. 2, pp. 41-60.*

Wormington, H. M.
1957 ANCIENT MAN IN NORTH AMERICA. *Denver Museum of Natural History. Popular Series, no. 4.*

Wormington, H. M., and Richard G. Forbis
1965 AN INTRODUCTION TO THE ARCHAEOLOGY OF ALBERTA, CANADA. *Denver Museum of Natural History. Proceedings, no. 11.*

Wright, H. E., Jr., and David G. Frey (eds.)
1965 THE QUATERNARY OF THE UNITED STATES: REVIEW VOLUME OF THE 7TH INQUA CONGRESS. *Princeton University Press, Princeton.*

Zeuner, F. E.
1960 ADVANCES IN CHRONOLOGICAL RESEARCH in THE APPLICATION OF QUANTITATIVE METHODS IN ARCHAEOLOGY. *Viking Fund. Publications in Anthropology, no. 28.*

1962 DATING THE PAST: AN INTRODUCTION TO GEOCHRONOLOGY. *Methuen, London.*

LIST OF ILLUSTRATIONS

Special photography for this book, in color and black and white, by Harry Crosby (C), Ed Neil (N), and the U.S. Navy (USN). Other pictorial materials from the collections of the Arizona State Museum (A), Homer Dana (D), Denver Museum of Natural History (DM), Henry Huntington Museum and Art Gallery (H), Los Angeles County Museum (L), San Diego Museum of Man (M), and Southwest Museum (S). The identifying letter is used in the list of illustrations to indicate contributors.

INDEX

Ancient Hunters of the Far West was designed by Jim Millard, Art Director for Image, the Art Division of Frye & Smith, Ltd. Lithography by Frye & Smith, Ltd., on Kimberly-Clark's 80 pound suede finish Lithofect Book. Typography by Linotron, the Typesetting Division of Frye & Smith, Ltd., using Mergenthaler's Linofilm system. The type face used in this book is Century Schoolbook. Binding is by Cardoza Bookbinding Co.